DEAR ME

Peter Ustinov was born in London in 1921, of Russian, French and Ethiopian descent. During the war he served with the Royal Sussex Regiment and the RAOC, and he wrote his first play, *House of Regrets*, which was produced in 1942. His other plays include *Romanoff and Juliet*, *Photo Finish* and *The Love of Four Colonels*. He directed and acted in the award-winning *Billy Budd* and was the author and co-director of *School for Secrets*. His acting roles have ranged from Nero to Hercule Poirot. He has produced operas and his books include novels, short stories and *My Russia* (1983). He was the Rector of Dundee University for six years and is a member of the Académie des Beaux-Arts. For many years he has worked on behalf of UNICEF and in 1974 he was awarded the Order of the Smile for dedication to the idea of international assistance to children. He was awarded the CBE in 1975 and he was knighted in 1990. He lives in Switzerland.

PETER USTINOV

− *Dear Me* −

ARROW

Reprinted in Arrow Books, 1998

27 29 30 28

First published in the United Kingdom in 1977 by William Heinemann

This edition first published in 1992 by Mandarin Paperbacks
and reprinted 24 times

Arrow Books
The Random House Group Limited
20 Vauxhall Bridge Road, London SW1V 2SA

Random House Australia (Pty) Limited
20 Alfred Street, Milsons Point, Sydney,
New South Wales 2061, Australia

Random House New Zealand Limited
18 Poland Road, Glenfield
Auckland 10, New Zealand

Random House South Africa (Pty) Limited
Endulini, 5a Jubilee Road, Parktown 2193, South Africa

The Random House Group Limited Reg. No. 954009
www.randomhouse.co.uk

A CIP catalogue record for this book
is available from the British Library

Papers used by Random House
are natural, recyclable products made from wood grown in
sustainable forests. The manufacturing processes conform to
the environmental regulations of the country of origin

Printed and bound in Great Britain by
Cox & Wyman Ltd, Reading, Berkshire

To all those who,
by accident or design,
have not been included
in this book

ILLUSTRATIONS

ACKNOWLEDGEMENTS

The author is indebted to the following for permission to reproduce illustrations: Keystone Press Agency Ltd for photographs nos. 15 and 21; London News Agency Photos Ltd for photograph no. 18; Tom Hustler Ltd for photograph no. 33; Rayner Fichel for photograph no. 48; Commercial Photography Department of United Press International for photograph no. 50; D.P.A. for photograph no. 52.

The majority of the photographs which appear in this autobiography are from the author's own private collection. Certain of the photographs used as illustrations are of unknown provenance and are believed not to be the subject of claimed copyright. If copyright is claimed in any of them the publishers will be pleased to correspond with the claimant and to make any arrangements which may prove to be appropriate.

Dear Me,

I have always thought – and stop me if I have wearied you with this reflection too often in the past – that most of the anomalies which afflict mankind are merely figments of nature blown up out of recognizable proportion. In other words, split personality, schizophrenia, is an exaggeration of a natural state at a point where the whole of a person's character is coloured by its overweening contradictions. And yet, the personality of any normally constituted person must be capable of at least a certain flexibility, otherwise the machinery for doubt would be absent, and what is a more irrefutable proof of madness than an inability to have a doubt?

No, no, to ensure sanity, there must be at least the elements of an internal disagreement ever present in a personality, and it is for that reason, in the dearest hope that you exist, that I address this attempt at an autobiography to you, dear me.

We were born in the normal manner in a London nursing-home, and here I must already give up the collective pronoun in case it be mistaken for *folie-de-grandeur* on my part, speaking for both of us. Grandeur there always has been, in a purely physical sense, although I hope not folie. I weighed nearly twelve pounds as a consequence of a reluctant and tardy birth. I have always been loath to acknowledge the applause of an audience unless its volume more than justified such an initiative and I must have started the habit very early on, at my first public appearance in fact.

Of the actual events surrounding my birth I remember very little, and must therefore base my report on data from other sources. What I do know for certain is that, whereas I was born in London (in a section ominously called Swiss Cottage), I was in fact conceived in Leningrad, in a tall, draughty and shell-pocked house to which I made a pilgrimage of thanksgiving relatively late in life. It stands to reason that I travelled a great deal during the more than nine months which separated my conception in the shadow of revolution and political slogan to my birth in the cold embrace of industrial smog and respectability, but once again, my memory of the great social upheavals through which I passed disguised as a piece of overweight luggage can only be described as hazy, and therefore unreliable.

My mother, whose recollection of these events was curiously enough more acute than mine, in spite of her advanced age, wrote a book called *Klop* about her married life – a book I found charming and fascinating when it dealt with the period before my birth, and intensely embarrassing thereafter, which, I suppose, is human. 'Klop', as I discovered later, was the name by which my father was known, a name denoting 'Bed-bug', somewhat unflattering perhaps, but preferred by him to his only Christian name of Jona. There is no accounting for taste, as those who believe they are blessed with it never cease to say.

At the time of my birth, 'Klop' was the London representative of the German News Agency, at that time called the Wolff Büro. He was selected for this job not only because of his natural talent, which was considerable, but because Ustinov is a name which sounded, and was, un-German. Only a little while ago many minds had been eased in their wartime tasks by the pleasant prospect of hanging the Kaiser, and it stood to reason that after four years of exhaustion, deprivation and tragedy, the Germans had exacerbated British phlegm. This the Germans themselves shrewdly guessed, and so my father with his Russian surname, his Russian wife, and his urbane manner were sent in as pioneers to pave the way for a later normalization of relations.

It was, I gather, no easy task, although I must say that in the nursing-home any hint of prejudice was in my favour. Once I had actually been cajoled to enter this world, I apparently behaved as though I had never hesitated, and held up my head to look around, even when suspended by my feet like a bat. In case of general incredulity, I must say that I have always benefited from an unusually powerful neck, which an Italian singing professor discovered to his cost many years later when he tried to strangle me. I recovered almost immediately, whereas he has been prone to depressions ever since, which is understandable since he is only five feet seven inches high. He was foolhardy to give in to temptation.

My initiative in the nursing-home provoked cries of admiration from the matron, who said to my mother, 'He's a very strong little chap, aren't you, precious? Yes, you are, my little Blessing.'

It was as well to know. My mother's reaction to me was of a less factual nature. In spite of my exploit she found me helpless and vulnerable, which is of course the prerogative of all mothers, at the same time curiously wise and reminiscent of certain rotund statuettes of Buddha. However, she told me at a time when her opinion was less prone to the exigencies of literary style, that in reality I was spherical in form, and that everyone heaved a sigh of relief whenever I performed the exploit with my neck, since at those moments it was possible to see whether I was the right way up or not.

I gather that I was not very talkative, which is rather understandable under the circumstances; that I very rarely cried, and that I smiled almost constantly, from which I deduce that my indigestion was usually bad enough to produce the kind of writhing grin which mothers confound with contentment, but that it rarely became unbearable enough to reduce me to tears.

So much for me and my limited means of expression at the time. It might be well to pause at this early juncture to try and make some order out of the arbitrary events which led me to my appointment with the gynaecologist in Swiss Cottage at eleven

3

o'clock on April 16th, 1921. I was, of course, accompanied by my mother, since I was too young to go alone.

I remember with pleasure and a shudder a reflection of that great advocate Clarence Darrow in his memoirs. He always regarded the chapter of accidents which led back from his birth into prehistory as utterly extraordinary, and therefore had the same feelings about his presence in the world as though he had won a lottery against staggering odds, and moreover added, not without an element of self-pity, that if any one of thousands of people had been late for an appointment with destiny, he would not have been born at all. I have at least as much cause as Clarence Darrow to entertain such a thought, without having had the originality to conceive of such a terrifying speculation.

Consider the facts. One great-great-grandfather born in 1730, living the life of a pious county squire in Saratov on the lower reaches of the Volga; another great-great-grandfather born in 1775 in Venice, winning the competition for the post of organist at St Mark's, a third great-great-grandfather a village schoolmaster a hundred kilometres south-east of Paris; a fourth, no doubt a strict Protestant, living in Rheinfelden, near Basel, while a fifth survived the endless struggle for power in Addis Ababa. One does not need to know the activities of the other eleven to understand that the likelihood of all these gentlemen joining forces to produce me was extremely slim. By the time the situation had whittled itself down to the level of grandfathers, the odds against my birth had hardly improved. Admittedly my paternal grandfather had been exiled to the West, but meanwhile my mother's family had emigrated to the East, a lack of co-ordination remarkable to the point of perversity. My father's father had acquired German nationality; and after a period of living in Italy – a singular choice for a Protestant convert – he settled in Jaffa of all places, and married, *en seconde noce*, the daughter of a Swiss missionary and an Ethiopian lady. They had nothing but miscarriages for seven years, my father, their firstborn, making his appearance when his father was fifty-seven years of age. Imbued with none of my reticence, Klop displayed an

4

extraordinary eagerness to be born, and rushed into life, allowing his mother a pregnancy of something under seven months, and weighing only just over two pounds. He was kept alive by the extraordinary patience and application of my grandfather, who fed him his milk, drop by drop, from the container of a Waterman fountain-pen. This is no place for commercials, but I do wish to take this opportunity of publicly thanking a company to whom I feel I owe so much.

My mother, on the other hand, was the youngest of the large family of Louis Benois, architect, in St Petersburg. She skated on the frozen Neva while my father galloped his Arab steed alongside trains in Palestine, frightening the passengers by racing them to the level-crossings. It needed the precipitate action of a Serbian student in Sarajevo, the sabre-rattling of the Austro-Hungarian war party, the limitless ambitions of the Kaiser, the French desire for revenge, the immense speed of the Russian mobilization, the war at sea, in the air, on land; gas, revolution, humiliation and conquest to bring them together. I can never hope to repay the immense war-debt which I personally owe to millions of people, whose concerted egotism, self-sacrifice, stupidity, wisdom, bravery, cowardice, honour and dishonour made it possible for my parents to meet under the least likely of circumstances and with the most far-fetched of pretexts. There is no alternative but humility for me.

It is not without reason that Russia and the United States have drifted into a sort of collusion after their years of bitter opposition to one another, for the fact of the matter is that they have a great deal in common, and not the least of these shared characteristics is size. Britain, France and others have hacked Empires out of the available corners of the earth, and the sun set over seascapes while rising over other seascapes, but neither Britain nor France has ever had to come to terms with the endless horizon, mile after mile in all directions, leading to an infinity of miles, and then a few more for good measure. In America the wild men, the lawless, those with a golden glimmer in the drink-sodden eye, opened up the West just as before them the shaggy cowboys called Cossacks, fugitives from justice all, opened up the East in Siberia, hotly pursued by the soldiers of the Central Government. There it was not yet the Gold Rush, merely the Fur Rush. As long ago as 1689 the Cossacks reached the Pacific, founding the town of Okhotsk, and were rewarded with freedom from pursuit for their pains. At first tentatively the Russian antennae, so far from their head in St Petersburg, felt their cautious way over to the American mainland, and Alaska became the eastern outpost of the Russian Empire, enabling her merchants to trade with China, exchanging silks and tea for pelts, European glass, and strangest of all exports, dogs.

Whereas the younger sons of socially accepted families in the West went to the Colonies to make good; to India or Canada in the case of England, to Africa or Indo-China in the case of France; to Sumatra, or Angola, or the Congo, for the others, wherever Europe had cast an avid eye and a possessive net. It was quite in order for young Russians to scour Siberia in search of possibilities. This huge land was not merely a system of penal colonies as it appears in the Western imagination, but a place of untold wealth, a place where fortunes could be made. The rigours of its climate have given it the kind of reputation which even as rapidly evolving a country as Australia has only recently shaken off. In a sense, Siberia was Russia's Australia, at once a punishment and a new life, an arena for worldly redemption.

As long ago as the last year or two of the seventeenth century, Adrian Mikhailovich Ustinov returned from his stint in Siberia a wealthy man. He had made his money in salt.

Russia had acquired all the trappings of conventional European heraldry late in her history, and consequently took them with the seriousness accorded by American tourists to researches into the origin of coronet and kilt. Already, in order to guarantee the Pharisaic isolation of the nobility from the low practices of the merchants, an Imperial decree had compelled those of high birth to relinquish their titles should they stoop to commercial activity. Later this somewhat draconian measure was amended, but made even more humiliating for those who take such symbols seriously, by insisting that the nature of a family's business be placed on the crest for all to see. As always, such decrees change their character with the passage of the years. What constituted a humiliation then is by now a proof of relative antiquity, to be displayed with pride. In the case of the Ustinovs, it is a primitive salt-press which occupies its quartering alongside an eagle's wing, a star, and a bee buzzing away over two crossed blades of wheat.

Adrian Mikhailovich's son, Mikhail Adrianovich, was the great-great-grandfather born in 1730, and he benefited from a law decreeing that two and a half hectares of land (just over six acres) at any one time could be sold at a price reduced in proportion to every lamb raised on it. He settled in Saratov, where he must have raised an inordinate number of lambs, because at his death in 1838, at the age of 108, he left his children 240,000 hectares of land, spread over various districts, and 6,000 serfs to work it, as well as sixteen brand-new churches for prayer and contemplation. The biography of the Chevalier Guards Regiment states specifically that estimations of the old man's age at death range between 108 and 113, and that 108 must be taken as a conservative estimate. So here again we have, if not a cattle-baron, at least a baron of lamb in the fine young tradition of the Wild West. Even the name of his country mansion, Almazovo, is redolent of the New World rather than the Old, Almaz meaning diamond, the name of a ranch rather than that of a country seat.

The portrait of this exceptional man suggests that he was stout, his bald head the shape of a rugby football set on his body so that the ears would be near the pointed ends, and garnished with wisps of white hair. His mouth was small and puckered in mischief, while his eyes display a healthy playfulness. That he was overweight is certain, but evidently he owed his unusual longevity to the fact that in those days there were no doctors

7

competent to warn him of the dangers of obesity. He married twice, at first to Varvara Guerassimovna Ossorgina, who died when he was seventy-eight, and then to a Marfa Andreievna Vechniakova for the remaining thirty years of his life. Among the other acquisitions of his fruitful life were five sons, who settled in their various country houses with the exception of the third one, Mikhail Mikhailovich, who became Russian ambassador to Constantinople, and who was to be of enormous help to my grandfather later on. The youngest of the five boys, Grigori Mikhailovich, was evidently a poor specimen of mankind, living only fifty-four years of rare dissipation and libertinage.

Owning two lavish town houses in St Petersburg as well as inheriting Almazovo, Grigori Mikhailovich married a woman of exceptional beauty, Maria Ivanovna Panshina, who brought the village of Troitskoïe, near Moscow, as part of her dowry. By all accounts he behaved disgracefully, setting her up in one of the town houses while he caroused in the other with teenage peasant girls from his estate, only emerging occasionally from his bedroom to pick at a table covered with 'zakouski', pickled herrings, salted cucumbers, and the like, in order to renew his failing powers for further onslaughts on his victims, whom he preferred to enjoy two or three at a time. It was small wonder that his three sons grew up with a deep feeling of revulsion for their father, and in the case of my grandfather it inspired an introspection about the state of Russia and the corruptibility of the Orthodox Church.

As a young subaltern in the Chevalier Guards Regiment, he fell off his horse during manœuvres, damaging his back. As a consequence of this accident, he was bedridden for more than a year, which caused him to read a great deal, and to think even more. Over the Volga was the settlement of German Protestants, and before long my grandfather made the acquaintance of a pastor eager to add to his score of conversions, and of his pretty daughter. As all too often in this life, the affairs of the heart and the affairs of the mind were soon hopelessly entangled, and he embraced both the Lutheran faith and Fräulein Metzler.

At this time, the Imperial Army compelled all officers to take an oath of allegiance once a year to both the Czar and the true faith, which meant, of course, the Russian Orthodox Church. You could evidently be a Protestant if you were a Balt, or be a Catholic if you were Polish, or be a Moslem if you came from Azerbaidjan, but you couldn't become anything as exotic if you had the misfortune to be Russian. That year, in the so-called House of the Nobility at Saratov, my grandfather took his yearly oath to the Little Father of all the Russias, but refused to take it to the God of the Eastern rite. A scandal ensued, which resulted in my grandfather's exile to Siberia. His uncle, the aforementioned ambassador, heard about this family disgrace, and, galloping north from the Golden Horn, engaged the Czar in a game of cards interspersed with bouts of drinking, the outcome of which was a commutation of the sentence to an exile of forty years abroad, a penalty which bears a strange similarity to a more recent example of enforced estrangement under the Communists, that between Solzhenitsyn and the source of his inspiration.

This exile was a severe punishment, and yet, from the point of view of my grandfather's personal safety it was probably just as well, for he was defiant enough and courageous enough to have decided to liberate his serfs, and this only eight months before their ultimate liberation by decree. And here once again we encounter a similarity between the histories of Russia and America. The liberation of the serfs was almost coeval with the American Civil War and the freeing of the slaves. Emancipation of a sort was in the air.

My grandfather was allowed to sell his vast estates for a handsome sum, and left for the West a rich man, a condition which suited his life-style but ran counter to his convictions. The logical place for a Russian exile to head for in those days was the Kingdom of Württemberg. Bismarck had not yet decreed the Union of Germany – that was to come ten years later in the

Palace of Versailles, and Stuttgart was the pleasant capital of a small and civilized monarchy. More important still, its queen was a daughter of the Czar, contaminated by liberal practice, and she extended a hand both welcoming and generous to any victim of her father's severity. My grandfather's titles of nobility were restored, a fact which seems to have had considerable value in those days, and so, in his Germanized form, he became the Baron Plato Von Ustinow. His repayment of all this hospitality was hardly exemplary, however, since he decided to settle down in Italy, and built himself a villa at Nervi, near Genoa.

Altogether, he must have been an extremely difficult man to live with, especially for the pretty Fräulein Metzler, who had meanwhile become his wife. According to legend, or perhaps his own account, which is worse, he discovered on their wedding-night that she was no longer a virgin, and consequently declined to have anything more to do with her. It is hard to conceive of a more monstrous excuse for a withdrawal of marriage vows, and yet to the austere Protestant convert of a century ago it seemed reason enough. He had other peculiarities beside his irrevocable decision about his wife. Money was a thing almost unbearably vulgar to him, a scourge, and a carrier of disease. As a result of his abhorrence, he never invested any of it in a bank, but carried his fortune around with him in satchels, trunks and suitcases, spilling coins into a sink in order to wash them in carbolic before going shopping, and, as an added precaution, never handling the degrading stuff without gloves. Christ's scourging of the moneylenders in the temple probably supplied the mental block for this extraordinarily convenient view of money as a source of physical and moral contagion, without any reference whatever to its undoubted value as a means for survival.

Whatever the quirks of his character, it was hardly they which rapidly drove his wife to other sources of comfort, a fact which he seemed to ignore, as well he might, for he regarded divorce as even more unthinkable than adultery. His wife did not share his prejudices, and eventually ran away with a sea-captain, which was about the best solution for all concerned. After the Second World War I received a charming letter from an Australian aviator who turned out to be her grandson, and who supplied the proof that her escapade was not merely another deception, and also gave a pretty clear indication of the direction in which her ship had sailed. Before this happy ending she had apparently been involved in an attempt to dispose of my grandfather with the aid of a gardener with whom she was carrying on, à la Chatterley. The conspirators knew my grandfather to be a man of powerful temper, and so plugged the muzzle of his pistol with lead, and then attempted to incite him to use it on them, the idea being that he would blow himself up in the process. Unfortunately for them, my grandfather was meticulous as well as emotional, and noticed that someone had been tampering with his fire-arm. I believe he dismissed the gardener.

Divorce turned Platon Grigorievich's thoughts to introspection, and eventually he gave up Italy for the Holy Land, building a large house in Jaffa which became the Park Hotel, and is, at the time of writing, the residence of an English vicar and his small family. It was here that my father, his three brothers, and his sister were born, to a mother whose origins have remained stubbornly mysterious to this day.

As I have said before, her father was a Swiss pastor from Rheinfelden near Basel, who was also (and here the evidence is an ancient photograph) a missionary in Ethiopia. Being Swiss, he was apparently something of an engineer, and among his other religious duties, he built a cannon for the mad Emperor Theodore, who had him chained to his own invention so that he couldn't get away and build a cannon for anyone else, a strategy which confirms the Emperor's lunacy to many, whereas to me it seems primitive perhaps, yet certainly effective. The result was that my grandmother, whose Christian name was Magdalena, was born in a tent during the battle of Magdala, which opposed Ethiopian forces to British ones under Lord Napier, while the expectant father was being shaken to pieces by his own invention on another part of the battlefield.

There was also some connection with Portugal through my grandmother's mother, who had lived for a time in Goa, and my grandmother's youngest sister was still, until recently, a lady-in-waiting at the Court of Haile Selassie, when she was granted quarters in the Governor's Palace in Asmara, where the altitude was less detrimental to her aged heart. This suggests that, whatever their origins, they were *personae gratae* with the Lion of Judah.

I remember my grandmother quite well as one of the simplest and most sentimental of souls, and with the readiest of tears. The story of the Crucifixion was enough to set her off, as though it were not so much a monumental tragedy as a personal misfortune. When it came to the two robbers, the sobbing began. It was her habit to capture me and place me on her knee for the evening recital, pressing me to her ample bosom, and I still remember my striped flannel pyjama-tops dampened by tears which soon grew chill against the skin. At times I asked for some more conventional story at bedtime, but even if it began with wolves and piglets and fairies, gingerbread street quickly changed to Calvary, and I was left with the mystery of the passion to fret over in my sleep.

No doubt my father was subject to the same treatment, perhaps to an even more passionate degree, for his mother was younger then, with a more objective and even colder tear, which may explain the fact that he was the most irreligious man I ever knew, not in the sense of blasphemy or of agnosticism; he merely completely ignored the whole business and never seemed to feel the need to accept it or reject it, or even fear it as a superstition. It didn't exist.

By his own admission, he was extremely spoiled, which is the normal outcome for a heavenly gift after seven years of fruitless attempts to have issue. There were to be four subsequent children, but all the fervour of thanksgiving was invested in my father. He could do no wrong. And yet all was not perfect.

My grandfather was frequently a source of embarrassment to those close to him. He was anti-social to the extent of retiring to his room if his guests bored him, and yet he frequently appeared on the beach naked, since it never occurred to him that there was a difference between being dressed and undressed, an ideal absence of complex perhaps, and yet hardly considerate towards those less endowed with indifference. He also found it impossible to understand why eating in public should have social connotations, and thought that if people defaecated together, the hated social contacts might be that much briefer. In other words, he was what is known as an eccentric, and eccentrics have the gift of making their children ill at ease.

The world was changing rapidly around the quiet, inefficient, and on the whole curiously benevolent Turkish Palestine, which knew an unparalleled epoch of religious tolerance at the time. The Kingdom of Württemberg existed only as a junior partner in the German Federation. The Kaiser visited Jerusalem, and his statue, in the absurd guise of a Siegfried, still stands within the enclave of the Lutheran Hospital, staring disease unflinchingly in the eye. Without really realizing it, my grandfather was now German, and 1914 was rapidly approaching.

At the outbreak of hostilities, my father and his brother Peter found themselves in Düsseldorf, and entered the German Army as a matter of course. In a regiment of Grenadiers, my father's company commander was the future General Speidel, of Wehrmacht and ultimately NATO fame, and his orderly was Erwin Piscator, the celebrated theatre director of the pre-Hitler Communist avant-garde. As the war dragged on, both brothers transferred to the Air Force, and Peter, after whom I am named, was shot down and killed on Friday, July 13th, 1917, near Ypres. He had white streamers on his wing-tips, and was delivering mail from British prisoners-of-war over the allied lines. Blinded by the sun, the British anti-aircraft batteries failed to see the streamers, and shot the aircraft down over no-man's-land. They apologized for their mistake.

Meanwhile, in Jerusalem, Platon Grigorievich, now eighty years old, his exile up nearly fifteen years previously, suddenly remembered that, Martin Luther or no Martin Luther, he was a reserve officer of the Chevalier Guards Regiment. He had spent his fortune, and there was precious little left, so that the prospect of negotiating the eye of the needle was no longer as formidable as it had seemed when he was younger. But now his country was in danger, and there had to be a riderless horse just waiting to convey his valour to within striking distance of the enemy. He presented himself to the Russian Consul-General in Jerusalem, standing rigidly to attention so that his five foot four would look at its impressive best in the white alpaca he always wore, even during winter visits to the North, and placed his sword at the disposal of the authorities. He was told very gently that his services were not urgently required, an allegation he refused to accept. Selling his properties (the one in Jerusalem to Haile Selassie), he packed his belongings, including his enviable collection of Greek, Roman and Egyptian antiquities and the last remaining suitcases full of money, and set off with his family on the long sea road to Russia. He paused in London long enough to put his two younger sons into a school at Denmark Hill, where they suffered like martyrs under the stinging tongue of a sadistic headmaster, who goaded them about the German prefix 'von', and never ceased mentioning their nationality in class, blaming them for every local success of Hindenburg and Ludendorff, and rejoicing with indecent glee at every counter-blow of Foch or Haig.

The penultimate step on my grandfather's odyssey was Oslo, where he sold his collection for a derisory price to a Norwegian shipping magnate, and then sailed on with his wife and his daughter Tabitha to be swallowed by darkness and confusion.

The war ended with revolution, not only in Russia, as everyone knows, but also in Germany, which most people have forgotten. My father's epaulettes were ripped off his shoulders in a Hamburg tram. People took their pleasures where and how they could. He realized it was time to return to civilian life, and he managed to become the representative of the German press agency in Amsterdam. From here he took some leave almost before he had begun his work, and set off in the direction of the Soviet Union in order to trace the whereabouts of his parents and his sister. Since it was difficult to travel to Russia at a time when so many people were bent on getting out of it, he managed to integrate himself into a large group of prisoners-of-war being repatriated. They knew about the Revolution, of course, and they also knew that it was they who were the starvelings so recently awakened from their slumbers, to which 'The Internationale' alludes. Their enthusiasm overflowed into song and simple rapture as the day of their return to the paradise of the workers approached. Many of them had bicycles which they had acquired at the end of their captivity, and these undreamed-of vehicles became the status symbols of the new dawn, grasped possessively by those about to cross the threshold of Utopia. As soon as the ship steamed into Narva harbour, at the frontier between the Soviet Union and Estonia, the bicycles were confiscated for the urgent needs of the war against the Poles, and the returned prisoners, including my father, were locked into cattle trucks to be shunted to recruiting centres further in the hinterland for induction into the Red Army.

As the train crept through the night with its embittered complement of silent men, cringing amid the dung and straw, my father planned his escape. Stops were frequent, and at one of them, he forced open the door. The first traces of dawn were visible, flecks in the icy sky, and in the distance, the unseen evidence of a city, a glint, a certain unmistakable heaviness about the horizon, the roar of silence, as in a sea-shell. He dropped off the train with his suitcase, full of chocolate, rashers of bacon, lumps of sugar, the backlash of troubled times. An hour or two later, he was in the heart of Leningrad. He spoke very little Russian, which did not seem much of a hindrance when the Herculean nature of his labour is taken

15

into consideration; which was quite simply to find an old man and his wife and daughter in a country which covers one-sixth of the earth's surface. He began by meeting my mother socially, and that seemed to be a step in the right direction. At least I think so.

How my mother kept her rendezvous with my father is a story
no less dramatic or curious. Denis Benois, or Bénois, was a
labourer in the village of St Denis-les-Sezanne, which seems to
have disappeared off the map. His wife came from the town of
Coulommiers, a place of wonderful cheeses, south-east of Paris.
He died in 1702, and his wife, a laundress by profession, moved
to the village of St Ouen-en-Brie, between Melun and Nangis.
It is, today, a depressing village, or perhaps it just succeeds in
concealing the richness of the surrounding soil as a peasant will
hide his fortune in a miserable mattress. Many of the windows of
the church are broken, and it is one of eight tiny parishes which
are the responsibility of a single ambulant priest. I never saw him,
but I presumed that at least one of the many bicycle-tyre tracks
criss-crossing the muddy pathways must have been his. The clock
on the town hall has been broken for more years than the villagers
can remember, so that it is only accurate for two minutes every
twenty-four hours. At the time of my pilgrimage, the town hall
was only open at the time other town halls are shut, and this for
the reason that the mayor was the schoolmistress, who could only
attend to civic business during the luncheon break, and who sat in
her dark office, a pen in one hand and a sandwich in the other.

The scattered houses, with their peeling walls, stand shrouded
in mists which settle for no apparent meteorological reason, and
remain, drifting aimlessly over the cowpats and the acrid puddles
long after other parts of the plain are softly bathed in sunlight. If

it is a morose place today, it cannot always have been so. At least, at the time the newly widowed laundress settled there, some of the houses must have been new. She was evidently a resourceful and wise woman, because her only son was not only literate, but became the village schoolmaster, a vocation shared by his son later on. By the time the third generation had appeared, however, in the shape of a boisterous fellow called Jules-César, a certain restlessness had manifested itself, an eagerness to carry the advances of the family fortune a step further. He decided not to be a schoolmaster, and moved a little closer to *le beau monde* by becoming an apprentice pastrycook. He was evidently very successful at this, since before long he became pastrycook to the duc de Montmorency. The relationship of master and servant must have been rather like that between Don Giovanni and Leporello, for when the revolution struck France, they were compelled to emigrate to Holland, where the Duke was quickly out of funds. They stayed together as accomplices and eventually as friends, seeking to rectify the decline in their fortunes in St Petersburg. It was here they eventually split up, the Duke going back to France now the excesses of revolution were over and Jules-César becoming chef de cuisine to the Dutch Legation. Evidently by now his authority had extended from mere entremets to the whole gamut of culinary arts and crafts. So celebrated did he become that it was not long before he deserted the legation and was appointed 'Maître de Bouche' to the Emperor Paul I.

In case it be thought that he was extremely fortunate to find such exalted employment so soon, it is only fair to point out that to be 'Maître de Bouche' to Paul I was a little like being accredited food-taster to Nero. Both emperors spent their lives hovering on the edge of lunacy, yet were sane enough to be in constant fear of assassination, a fate which attended them both. A magnificent statue of Paul stands in the courtyard of Peterhof palace, his minute nose perched like a comma on his face, rendering his expression both proud and petulant. It is one of those rare works of official art, like the royal portraits of Goya, which seem so packed with accurate subversion that one wonders how the victims ever accepted them, let alone allowed them to be accorded pride of place.

Paul liked to play with toy soldiers in bed. It must have come as a surprise to the Queen that among her wifely duties was to be a natural feature for the toy artillery to cross as they bombarded the enemy on the eiderdown, and it was a still uglier awakening for the real troops lined up for his inspection that he belaboured them with a stick for the slightest real or imagined misdemeanour as though they had no greater sensitivity than their tin reproductions.

Any native Russian would probably rather have walked to Vladivostok on foot than accept the job of teasing the palate of such a degenerate monarch, and it took an able and resourceful immigrant with no prior knowledge of the problems to make a success of such employment. And make a success of it he did, to the extent of marrying the royal midwife, a woman of a surprisingly fragile beauty for such a massive job, if the miniatures of the period are to be believed. Fräulein Concordia Groppe and Jules-César not only survived, but virtually ran the imperial household between them, as well as finding time to raise seventeen children of their own. Jules-César gradually began to fancy the spelling of Jules-Césard, perhaps because a French condiment in the spelling gave the diner confidence, but more probably because spelling was not his strong point. And, after all, he was in good company, since as great a writer as Shakespeare could never decide exactly how his own name should be spelled. The insistence on accurate spelling at modern schools is an effort to invest a living language with rigor mortis, and to prepare a rhapsodic means of self-expression for the glacial corridors of computerdom.

Be that as it may, Jules-Césard left a book of memories in which the orthography is as erratic as the thoughts are sunlit and serene. This work is still in manuscript, in the safe-keeping of another great-great-great-grandson, Professor Fyodor Franzovich Benois, an expert on underwater soldering, whatever that may be. It describes with a wonderful ingenuousness what life must have been like at the time. I was only able to read the beginning, where he talks about his own birth as though he were a casual bystander!

'Birth of Julles [*sic*]

On the 20th of January 1770, at nine-o-clock in the morning, my good mother, after having suffered four days of extraordinary pain, albeit quite ordinary under such conditions, made a great and courageous effort. Lying on her back, and anchoring the two extremities of her body, by which I mean head and feet, raised what lay between, and by this happy initiative caused me to take the portal by which I entered the world.'

A few pages later he describes how, at the age of four and a half, he was whipped by his father. They were receiving company, which included an extremely corpulent and self-important aunt, who attempted sportingly to lower herself on to a three-legged stool, there being far more guests than chairs. Her initiative failed, and she rolled on to the floor, her legs in the air. Jules-Césard, or César, as he still was then, had learned none of the finesse which was to stand him in good stead later on. All he could think to do was to announce in a piercing voice to the crowded room that he was able to see his aunt's thing (*'je pouvais voir sa chose'*). An audible whipping was the only possible penance in those days, even for a four-year-old.

Still further into this strange little book, which would at times have brought a blush to the cheek of Rétif de la Bretonne, he confesses his remorse at having raped a few girls. In fairness to him rape seems to have been a pastoral activity, a sudden impulse and a tumble in the high grass as can be seen in the background of many Dutch, Flemish and indeed French pictures, rather than the sordid premeditated action of today. Admittedly the results are identical, but there was certainly a degree of complicity in rural sports which are quite lacking in the urban variety, hovering as they do round parked cars and lonely bus-stops. Nevertheless, whatever his motives and whatever degree of collaboration he inspired, his remorse was real enough to drive him into the confessional. He cut short his story halfway, however, when he noticed that the interest of the Father Confessor in certain details of the transaction was excessive, an impression which even the presence of a grille failed to conceal.

In an effort to purify himself without the help of the local church, he sought out his first love, hoping to turn the clock back and erase his feelings of moral confusion. The young lady in question had moved to Paris, and invited him to join her there. When he arrived, he discovered that what she had neglected to tell him in her letter was that, in the interim, she had become a prostitute. She had no further interest in him apart from an evident affection, which took the form of inviting him to observe her activities with clients through a keyhole. He acceded, one gathers, out of pure politeness, and watched six or seven performances of this kind, eventually declining to continue, 'for fear this might become a habit'. He still had seventeen children to sire, and simply could not afford to be old before his time.

He also left a rather less controversial and generally more useful volume, all the receipts of his cuisine, which was destroyed in manuscript during the German bombardment of Leningrad. The damage which the Nazis caused to the art of living will never be finally assessed.

The one of his sons who is of most immediate concern to me was an architect, Nicholas, who married Camilla, the daughter of the Italian immigrant composer Catterino Cavos. This new addition to the family brought with it the theatrical strain which enriched with an Italianate sense of drama the already present character of mischief, humility, and meticulous application to the job in hand, be it procreation or pastry.

Catterino Cavos was the son of the Primo Ballerino Assuluto of the Fenice Theatre and of the Diva of the same celebrated opera house in Venice, a distinguished lady from Perugia, Camilla Baglioni. They possessed a smallish palazzo on the Grand Canal which is today a far from smallish hotel. At the age of eighteen, young Catterino (did his parents hope for a daughter?) won the post as organist to the Cathedral of San Marco in a competition. On learning that his leading competitor was a man in his sixties, in poor health and with a large family to support, he resigned in favour of the older man. Later on, after he had become Director of the Imperial Theatre at St Petersburg, he received the manuscript of Glinka's first opera, *Ivan Susanin*, sometimes also called *A Life for the Tsar*. Acknowledging that Glinka's opera was superior to his own on the subject, he voluntarily removed his own from the repertoire on condition he be accorded the honour of conducting Glinka's première. Writing to a friend, he expressed the opinion that 'it is the duty of the old to make way for the young'. He was by all accounts one of nature's rare natural gentlemen, and one of the few artists on record who assess their own talents accurately, which is an advantage in some circumstances, and a drawback in others. At all events, he was the last in a long line of Italian composers to hold the post of Director of the Imperial Theatres, beginning with Manfredini in 1759 through Galuppi, Traetta, Paisiello, Sarti, the wonderful Cimarosa and Martin y Soler, composer of one of the tunes played by the on-stage orchestra in the last act of Mozart's *Don Giovanni*, to my great-great-grandfather, who took over in 1797.

In 1798, the same crazy Paul I suddenly banned Italian opera, with the result that Cavos began writing works on Russian subjects like *Ilya the Hero*, in 1807, and *Ivan Susanin*, a patriotic epos which must have fitted the emotional climate of 1815. When Glinka's work arrived on his desk in 1836, he explained his gesture further by a note to a friend as perspicacious as it was disinterested, written carefully in Italian, about the Russian,

22

Glinka: '*E poi – la sua musica è effettivamente meglio della mia, e tanto più che dimostra un carattere veramente nazionale*' (And then – his music is in fact better than mine, the more so since it displays a truly national character).

And yet, his music cannot have been as undistinguished as he sometimes made it out to be. In 1867, Borodin's only stage work apart from the celebrated *Prince Igor* was performed. Entitled *Bogatyri*, it was a hotch-potch of melodies, according to Alfred Loewenberg's admirable *Annals of Opera*, some composed by Borodin himself, others borrowed from Meyerbeer, Rossini, Offenbach, Cavos, Verdi, Serov, etc. Pretty good company. The work was revived in 1936 and, after a few performances, was banned by the Soviet censor, which suggests that it must have had some merit.

On a visit to Leningrad I discovered Cavos' tomb in the Lavra, an open-air cemetery which is the Russian equivalent of Poets' Corner. No member of my family had ever realized it was there, demure and undemonstrative among the tombstones of his peers, Tchaikovsky, Glinka, Borodin, Moussorgsky, to say nothing of the great writers and artists. There are quite a few weeping angels about, and weather-beaten busts, and other outbursts of petrified grief. In this quiet and damp place, Cavos is remembered by a simple black marble stone, setting off the restrained flamboyance of golden letters. Of all the epitaphs in this Slavonic Valhalla of the arts, that on Cavos' tomb is the only one defiantly written in the Roman alphabet; the language, Latin.

One of his sons, my great-grandmother's brother Albert, an architect, acquired a fame at least as great as his father by building the Maryinsky Theatre (now the Kirov) in Leningrad, as well as rebuilding the Bolshoi in Moscow after it was entirely destroyed by fire in the 1860's.

By now, practically every member of these families was expected to make a career in the arts. The Benois and Cavos families supplied a constant stream of young people who only rarely wished to enter other fields than those traditionally theirs.

My grandfather was an architect as his father and grandfather and great-uncle had been. I do not pretend he was a great architect, but he was a fine, ordered, patient and tasteful man with at least a hankering for new materials and new techniques which would have enabled him to be more daring. Above all, as Principal of the Academy of Arts he was a much-admired teacher, remembered with affection by the older generation of Russian architects to this day. When he died, in 1928, he was given a state funeral by the Soviet government, the Mozart Requiem was sung as he lay in state, and his students stood vigil in the Conference Hall of the Academy and carried his body to the place of burial, the Novodievichy Cemetery.

His brother Albert, a strikingly handsome man, with a knack for seducing the ladies while playing the violin, one of the minor art-forms which has entirely disappeared from the libertine's repertoire, was a leading member of the Russian water-colour school, with an especial predilection for melancholy sunsets, of which he produced an inordinate quantity. As with so many casually talented people, he was accused of an overriding facility, but critics often fail to recognize that no amount of fretful application would have improved those particular sunsets, and to heed criticism to the extent of refraining from painting sunsets when sunsets are your particular forte is to go the way of many facile people who scandalously betray their facility in order to work hard and masochistically at things they are no good at, while the critic who is not much good at anything himself breathes down their necks with the sterile satisfaction of a sadistic schoolmaster. Albert had too light a touch to fall into such a trap. Others might have done more convincingly with seascapes and mountain idylls, but in sunsets he led the field. His house was well known as a salon, to the extent that he often had to ask in undertones who his guests were, while his venerable housekeeper Masha kept her eye riveted on the silver. Even as an old man, when bothered by mosquitos, who, as is well known, like sunsets as much as anyone, he had no compunction in asking passers-by to fan him

24

with fir-branches while he captured the elusive moments in paint. Legend has it, however, that he preferred the mosquitos to male passers-by. He only asked for help from very young and pretty girls, of whom, according to my aged aunts, there were many before the Bolsheviks spoiled it all.

The youngest brother, Alexander, was the animator of the celebrated magazine *Mir Iskustva*, the Life of Art, designed for the Ballets Russes, art critic, historian, and one-time curator of the Hermitage. He was the most internationally known of the brothers, perhaps not entirely due to his intrinsic qualities, but also because he was by far the youngest, and therefore escaped from the fall-out of mutual admiration which is an inevitable adjunct to large families all engaged in the same type of work. Also he left Russia as his fame was beginning to spread, and designed up to the moment of his death in 1960. I knew him well, and therefore only pass him by swiftly here in order to reintroduce him on a later page as the man I loved and respected.

There were two brothers of this brood, who were not artists, and who paid the penalty. One of them, Mikhail, was a business-man who had something to do with the river-steamers which plied up and down the Volga, and was described as a silent and gloomy man. I do not know to what extent his morose nature was inspired by the monotony of his employment, but the fact is that one of his daughters married an architect, and his two grandsons are both architects in Argentina. Perhaps he should have been one too.

Nicholas was a soldier, with a rough vocational manner, and an unhappy marriage. He and his wife used to throw plates at each other in public places, with a shameful lack of accuracy for military people. He was the commanding general of the Akhtirsky Hussar Regiment, and I learned all I really know about him from a taxi-driver in Paris who turned out to have been his aide-de-camp in the First World War.

'Ah, I remember,' said the old driver, 'I remember a reception in the officers' mess. There was a minstrels' gallery, with a Cossack orchestra playing light music. After he had drunk copiously, General Benois mounted the stairs and attempted to conduct the orchestra. When he had had enough, he made signs to another subaltern and myself, which we failed to understand since they were not explicit, you see. Then he leapt into space. I thought Lieutenant Gromov was going to catch him, and apparently Gromov thought I was going to. In short, neither of us did.'

'What happened?' I asked in trepidation.

The effort of memory had been too much for the driver. The taxi slowed to a crawl in deference to his exhaustion, and his lined face became expressionless as the immediacy of his recollection faded into oblivion. There was a long pause.

'He hurt himself, I believe,' said the driver flatly. He seemed irritated, although whether it was with that young idiot Gromov I had no means of knowing.

When my father reached Leningrad in the spring of 1920, with his suitcase full of bacon and chocolate, most of these people were still alive, although hardly active. My mother, like her uncle Alexander, by far the youngest of a large family, was therefore addicted to rebellion. She was already a little more than an art student, and spent much of her time at Uncle Alexander's home, soaking up the lively debates animated by forward-looking young people like the composer Sergei Prokofiev, her cousin the composer Alexander Tcherepnin, and her uncle's son, Nicholas, until recently the head of the design department (Capo dell' Allestimento) of La Scala, Milan. Prokofiev used to try out some of his early works on my great-uncle's piano, which had survived the revolution in a better state than many of its fellows. They were a boisterous and flirtatious lot, these young people, eager to react against the existing order, endlessly jocular in manner and explosive in matter, and yet curiously respectful towards the achievements of the past.

I have always been vaguely frightened of Russian academicians, because when Russians dedicate themselves to the path of artistic righteousness, there are no people more tenacious in the pursuit of the absolute than they. Compared to the Russians, the Germans are light-hearted children, romantic and capricious where the Russians are rigorous and single-minded to a point of absurdity. The composer Taneyev struggled endlessly with fugues for string quartet, of monumental boredom and the most laudable thoroughness. The baffled and bearded Rimsky-Korsakov, who was never short of a neo-oriental melody, devoted a part of his early life, when appointed Director of Naval Music, to a painstaking and ultimately painful research into the possibilities of brass instruments which neither enriched the repertoire nor gave its composer any satisfaction. Even Balakirev, the doyen of the so-called mighty handful of nationalistic composers, amateurs all, revolted against the existing order only to become intolerably overbearing and dogmatic in his demands upon his followers. His revolution against the academic quickly hardened into an academism of his own, with new rules to replace the old, applied with identical vigour and inflexibility. It must therefore be a quirk of national character to subject oneself to impossible strictures until the spirit is almost broken. Then comes the time of liberating revolution, with its slogans of goodwill to all – a long weekend of intoxicating folly as a presage to the application of new strictures as impossible as those that have been replaced.

God was discredited with the same religious fervour with which he had been praised before. Out in the playground, there was a brief flowering of national genius in disorganized abandon. One thinks of Mayakovsky, Esenin, Alexander Blok, the Constructivists, Malevich, and of course, the young Prokofiev. Then the school-bell rang, and the refreshed school-children filed back into the classroom to find the ikon replaced by a red star, the benign picture of the little Father, Nicholas II, by the portrait of V. I. Lenin, and the lessons started afresh with the same hermetic sealing against the intrusion of doubt.

27

Everything had changed but the manner, yet the manner was all important. Even the spirit of the confessional, of *mea culpa*, *mea maxima culpa*, was deflected from the ornate robe of the priest to the frostbitten ear of the Commissar, but the spirit reigned on unchanged. We heard it with painful regularity as the brilliant composers and the magnificent writers confessed their errors of judgement to lamentable hicks like Andrei Zhdanov, and the inquisition of the people, with its condemnation of bourgeois values, continued round the clock among the potted-palms and table-runners of the most bourgeois of proletarian societies, stinking of pious hypocrisy and self-righteous indignation, of ignorance and vodka.

1920 was still a year of grace. The excesses which accompanied all revolutions were over, the vengeful arrests and the denunciations, and the rot had not yet set in under Stalin, who was well fitted for his role of dictator, having been brought up in a seminary. My father met a girl in the course of his quest for his parents, who invited him to a party that evening, where he set eyes on my mother for the first time.

It was an eventful two weeks for both of them, at the end of which they were married, but that was not all which occupied their minds. My father discovered somehow that my resolute old grandfather, disdaining many admonitions to enjoy what retirement he had left, had charged off in the general direction of the fighting to offer his services to his old regiment. It was at Pskov that he had been overtaken by the revolution, and succumbed to famine. His half-Ethiopian wife and her daughter, my aunt Tabitha, languished in a local prison, presumably because they were unable to make themselves understood. Had they spoken Russian, they would doubtless have been either free, or shot. The problem was to secure their release, but in the country which, in more affluent times, had invented the internal passport, and which had managed miraculously to combine extreme red tape with a chronic shortage of paper, this was understandably difficult.

My father was reduced to corruption – oh, not on the scale of modern industry, not in our understanding of the inflated word; a few slices of Dutch bacon and half a bar of good neutral milk chocolate. The Commissar at whom these tit-bits were aimed was none other than Ivan Maisky, later a most civilized Soviet ambassador in London, and he gracefully declined the delicatessen, producing a few herrings and some dry lentil soup wrapped in a week-old copy of *Izvestia* for my father's delectation, as well as the necessary travel document. Before shaking hands and wishing my father god speed to Pskov, Maisky sprinkled some eau-de-cologne on himself, and my father used to describe the odour of cheap perfume mixed with herring oil as one of the most ingeniously awful smells in creation, and shuddered visibly at the recollection half a century later.

He managed to secure the release of his mother and sister, and despatched them to Cairo via Istanbul and the Crimea, and at the end of that week, married my mother in church. He was dressed in long white tennis trousers and a blazer of sorts, whereas my mother wore her grandmother's nightdress, a magnificent mass of fidgeting lace and frayed ribbons, which lent both weight and dignity to the occasion.

Once again through the intervention of Mr Maisky, my father managed to procure false documents describing him as a German prisoner-of-war ready for repatriation with his new Russian wife, and the couple set sail for Amsterdam aboard a Swedish steamer.

Quite recently, some fifty-three years later, I made a pilgrimage to the house from which my parents set out on their odyssey, the building in which I was conceived. It stands in a stately yet dishevelled row of elegant town houses on the Vassilievsky Ostrov, the Basil Island, amid the Leningrad lagoons. The façades are pock-marked with rifle and machine-gun bullets, and occasionally it seems as though a cornice or an ornament has been carried away by some larger projectile, or else just fallen off in despair. A feeling of awe came over me as I stared at the dusty ochre colonnades, and felt that a moment of abstract passion somewhere among the icy corridors had set in motion a process culminating in the corpulent bearded figure who now stood meditating on its porch.

I entered, since I had heard that my aunt still lived there in one shared room. The pervading odour was that of cabbage soup, not today's, not yesterday's, but the day before's, and of all the days before it, through régimes and ukases and Imperial decrees. I recognized it as a hallmark of Russianness. Another aunt lived in Berlin between the wars, in an agglomeration of émigrés clustered round an orthodox church. Here too the cabbage soup lingered over the staircase, but mingled with incense. In spite of the intensity of the holy vapours, secular cabbage soup emerged the victor by a *soupçon*. Nothing links the generations more poignantly than aroma. The sweet smell of an old book is far more eloquent than the ancient words and eroded sentiments printed on its worm-eaten pages, and the hint of airless moisture in a dungeon or a cloister brings by way of the nostril a pang of fear or devotion as they came to people now long dead, with other criteria for fervour, different portals of pain. Here, in the cold mist of cabbage soup, I fancied my mother was still waiting to be born, as I had waited. The architecture seemed uninspired, and even illogical, as it often does when a great house has changed its character to accommodate changing times. Outside it was spring, inside winter. It was a day with a light and frivolous breeze. You would never have known it from the gales which howled under arthritic doors and through the cracks in the glass. A clearing of the throat sounded like the rumble of a distant avalanche, a cough like a congregation taking to its knees. It was too dark to read the names typed on an irregular piece of paper by a series of bells, names in a frame of orange dampness. At last, a strange shuffling, the noise of a certain Russia to go with the cabbage soup, the sound of slippers pushed along the floor like skis by legs used to immense distances. A moment after it had grown to an unnatural intensity, as though aided electronically, an old woman appeared, thin, bursting with questions and expressing in advance her misgivings at the replies.

'Who are you?'

'The son of Nadezhda Leontievna.'

'Ah, the foreigner. The actor and playwright. Have I got it right?' This without warmth, and certainly without enthusiasm.

'Yes.'

'You are no doubt looking for your aunt, Ekaterina Leontievna?'

'Indeed, yes.'

And then, on a note of triumph: 'She's not here.'

'Oh.'

'I suppose you now wish to be taken to where she is?'

Extraordinary intuition.

'Have you a motor vehicle?' she went on, and then answered the question herself. 'Obviously. You're a foreigner, with roubles. And now I suppose you want me to take you there?'

'If you have nothing better to do.'

'Better to do?' she snapped, and waited a second for the echo to evaporate. 'What on earth could I have to do that would be better?'

I could make no contribution to the conversation.

'Wait for me, I'm going to change.'

The sound of slippers receded, then, before it had really died away, it began to grow in volume again. Eventually she reappeared, wearing a threadbare coat, carrying a plastic hand-bag, but still wearing the slippers. She was ready for the April showers.

My taxi was an aged Zis from the time of the great purges, a monumental imitation of a vintage Packard with cut-glass receptacles inside for a couple of dying flowers and with a mass-produced Caucasian carpet on the floor. I encouraged her to occupy the back by herself while I sat next to the expressionless driver. Once the car was in motion, I turned to look at her. To judge by her expression, the back seat might as well have been a throne. There was no trace of surprise in her face, and in fact, she sat in the centre as though emphasizing her birthright.

'You must have had a terrible time here during the war,' I said, by way of conversation.

The chauffeur nodded in a patient, heroic, understated way. The old lady went further. She seemed to shrug it off as negligible.

'What leads you to say that?' she asked. 'A knowledge of history?'

'Not only,' I replied. 'I noticed that the building was raked by machine-gun fire . . . German bullets.'

'German bullets?' the old lady spat out. 'The Bolsheviks . . . during the revolution . . . the bastards never repaired the damage they did!'

I glanced in alarm at the driver, caught his eye in the driving-mirror, set far forward in the huge driving compartment. He smiled slightly in a way which suggested that one must be patient with the old, more especially since they have a virtual monopoly of the truth.

I felt I had a finger on the pulse of my origins.

A few minutes later, and we were in other, lighter corridors, of more recent and more miserable construction. We even went up in an elevator, decorated with lewd cyrillic graffiti by those who had spent hours incarcerated there while waiting for it to be repaired. I was encouraged to ring a bell next to an unvarnished wooden door, and once again, through it, I heard the noise of slippers gliding on linoleum. The door opened a crack, and what looked like a caricature of my mother peered up at me with amber eyes.

'Yes. What is it?'

Feeling unaccountably like a secret policeman, I prepared to reveal my true identity, but the lady who had accompanied me forestalled all my tactful preparations with a maelstrom of truncated words, explaining in detail everything that had happened up to that moment. It was clear both that the two old people were bound in inseparable friendship and that they couldn't stand each other, a phenomenon which is possible anywhere, but which reaches heights of subtle paradox more outrageously in Russia than anywhere else. My aunt Katya, whom I had never seen before, regarded me with a quiet hostility, not because she held anything against me, but because I was responsible for bringing her best friend along to plague her. Seated in the kitchen, drinking tea with jam in it, conversation was difficult. I never expected it to be easy, but what was nevertheless disconcerting was the formality of the occasion, which made me feel almost like a prisoner who had refused to reveal more than his name and number. Curiously enough, it was only when the conversation descended to the conventional level of claims and counterclaims about the Germans' bomb damage to London, to Coventry, to Leningrad and Stalingrad that it lost its imperious reserve, and acquired true, if silly, animation. The best friend watched the exchanges with an excitable eye, as though following the ball in a game of tennis.

'I don't know about England. About England I don't know,' she screeched at length, 'but over here, the Bolsheviks did most of the damage themselves, and don't try to tell me otherwise.' My aunt Katya relapsed into a patriotic sulk, while the best friend added fuel to the embers by declaring that she would stay behind to keep my aunt company after I had gone, and 'Thank you for the lift,' muttered grudgingly like a child which has been forced publicly to express its gratitude for something it neither wishes not enjoys.

I took the hint and left, kissing my aunt in a clumsy manner. The two ladies let me go, now united in a sudden complicity of silence.

On reflection, I feel that my aunt Katya resented the fact that her younger sister had left Russia, and with a 'German' at that. Her feelings were latent, but the sudden appearance of the

33

offspring of a half-forgotten union in the shape of a middle-aged man with only a few words of Russian at his disposal, and hardly any syntax at all, stirred up the old sediment.

I reached the street, and found the driver seated at the wheel, neither asleep nor entirely awake. He expressed as little as the two old ladies, and yet seemed, in some mysterious way, to realize what I had been through. Here was the patience, the sense of timelessness, which had kept people standing in line for vegetables, for meat, or for a glimpse of Lenin in his mausoleum. 'Yes . . .' he said, '. . . the old . . .' And allowed me to fill in the blanks.

We travelled from the past back into the present, and found the two in many ways identical. An old foolishness is not improved with age, nor are ancient hostilities dignified by the fact that they happened long ago. Don't you agree, dear Me?

— Ah, I was wondering when, and if, you were ever going to consult me. After all your fine intentions at the beginning of your book –

— Our book! Our book.

— We'll see about that – thank you all the same – I was beginning to fear that you had forgotten all your ambitious schemes, and were going to embark on just another autobiography, with all its self-justifications, its sensitivities (which I may add, you don't manifest in life) and its exploitations of one aspect of the truth at the expense of others –

— May I interrupt?

— Must you? You have held the floor for an inordinately long time all by yourself, and now you wish to interrupt me after only a single sentence.

— I have my reasons. There has been very little need to consult you up to now. Our story has been largely factual, and pre-natal, an area in which there is hardly any opportunity for opinion. That was true, certainly, up to the introduction of our Aunt Katya.

— Is your impression of meeting Aunt Katya any different from mine?
— Of course not. It's the same impression. My interpretation may be different.
— In what way?
— She may have been tired, or exasperated by some other, extraneous element. What do you know of her state of health at the time? You had never even seen her before, and were never destined to see her again. Was that her normal method of conducting a conversation? You noticed her arthritis. She may have been in agony.
— Now you are just being unreasonable. In order to tell a story, there must be some elbow-room, some breathing-space, some licence – otherwise you become as squeamish as a vegetarian. The truth is often painful.
— And often untrue. It is only your truth, remember.
— It is my pain too, as often as not. And my pleasure. It is not *the* story I am telling, it is *my* story. *My* story. *My* story. Not even *our* story.
— I will sit back and listen.
— Then take that smile off my face.
— On to Chapter Three, and co-existence!

- 3 -

As I have said before, I was born on April 16th, 1921, at around eleven o'clock in the morning. The event took place at a nursing home in Adelaide Road, Swiss Cottage, London. Since my parents had left Leningrad on the Swedish freighter nine months previously, I had travelled extensively in embryonic form, spending some time in Holland while preparing to make my entrance. A chance decision of a Herr von Maltzahn at the German Foreign Office apparently changed my destiny.

My mother arrived at the port of Harwich some time in February, and was immediately apprehended by the British authorities for having filled up her landing form with undue accuracy. To the question: Where born? she had answered St Petersburg. To the question: Where educated? she had answered Petrograd. To the question: What was the point of departure from country of origin? she had answered Leningrad. The immigration authorities were convinced that she was making light of the questionnaire, and I feel bound to add with a certain pride that it was only my presence that saved her from further unpleasantness. This tendency to answer official questions too literally seems to run in the family, perhaps owing to the many frontiers we all have crossed since such encumbrances were invented.

I got into similar trouble myself on my first application to enter the United States when I described my colour as pink. I was told sternly that I was white, a fact which I denied, relying upon an Embassy mirror for evidence. A great deal of time was wasted, more especially since I failed to realize the subliminal implication of the word 'pink' in those days. It speaks highly for the equitable spirit of American officials that I was accorded a visa, even if their sense of colour was somewhat slap-dash.

Once she was released by the equally pernickety British authorities, my mother travelled to London by train through a thick industrial murk, which culminated in a swirling yellow fog, impenetrable, choking, and claustrophobic. She records that she had never seen or smelt such unadulterated filth in her life. Before the names of the stations were entirely obliterated towards the end of the journey, the impression of Kafkaesque horror was increased by the fact that every station seemed to be called Bovril. It is necessary to explain to the uninitiated that Bovril was, and is, a most excellent beef-tea. Being the fruit of private enterprise in a highly competitive capitalist society, it had bright and brilliant advertisements, unlike the names of stations which, although privately owned, were without direct competition, and so tended to conceal their identities behind layers of grit and grime.

The train finally pulled in to the greatest Bovril of them all, and my mother was taken by her old governess to a boarding home run by an elderly Puritan couple where nothing was allowed except total silence. She knew, as she conversed in surreptitious whispers with Miss Rowe, who had taught her all she knew in St Petersburg, that she had made the mistake of her life in coming to this nightmare of a country with her unborn child. And yet, such is the power of acquired tastes in those of sensibility that this is the self-same country she was to die in fifty-four years later, refusing for the last ten years of her life to leave even for a brief vacation, wrapping up against the pervasive damp, making casual excuses for every discomfort, deeply involved in village life, warmed by soulless electric stoves and the great hearts of her neighbours.

The reason she was left alone to face the initial rigours of her new island home was that my father had preceded her, and was already deeply involved in his new job. She even had to be rushed alone to the nursing-home when her time came, since my father was busy hollering the contents of a speech by Lloyd George down a defective line to Berlin.

I am told I hardly cried at all as a baby, preferring to sublimate all my internal pressures into a kind of patient gurgling. I was also, as I have already intimated, almost perfectly spherical in shape, causing my parents frequent anxieties as they feared they had left me upside down, and forcing them to enter and re-enter rooms in which I had been left in order to check. I was a precocious reader, being able to master one word at the extremely early age of nine months. The second word was to follow some years later. It was, however, in the choice of word that I displayed a certain gift for diplomacy which has caused me more trouble than it was worth all through my life. The word, which I called out on top of a double-decker bus to the consternation of the passengers, while pointing a diminutive finger at a huge advertisement near Victoria Station, was Oxo. Once again I must explain that Oxo was, and once again is, as far as I know, a valid and determined rival to Bovril in the world of beef-tea, and it was a kind of tactful revenge for all my mother's early misgivings on the train that I now drew the attention of a busload of passengers to the virtues of a rival reducer of cattle to size.

It is difficult to know what one remembers in truth, and what one has reconstructed from photographs or anecdotes of loving relatives. For instance there is one event of which I have absolutely no recollection, but which I see in the mind's eye as clearly as though I had been an active rather than a passive participant, and that is my baptism.

My gently lachrymose grandmother, with her extraordinary capacity for reliving the events of the Bible as though they were headline news in the paper, wrote from Cairo, insisting that I be baptized in the waters of the Jordan, for old time's sake. My father, now enjoying himself in his new peacetime job, was properly impatient with such a jaded symbolism, and said he couldn't possibly take leave of absence for such a specious reason. Anyway he couldn't afford the fare. Backward and forward flowed the correspondence, until a compromise was reached. It was decided that the interested parties meet halfway between Jordan and Cairo. Since my grandmother's knowledge of geography was hazy, apart from Ethiopia, which she knew like the back of her hand, it was easy to convince her that the halfway mark between the two capitals lay in Stuttgart, or, more accurately in Schwäbisch Gmünd, a town a few kilometres away. I travelled there in a basket kindly lent by the White Heather Laundry of London, and I wish to take this belated opportunity to thank that excellent organization for the comfort and aeration of the larger baskets, although I must add that I have never found that part of *The Importance of Being Earnest* in which Mr Worthing was alleged to have been discovered in a handbag remotely amusing, possibly because it was too close to the truth in my case.

My grandmother advanced on Schwäbisch Gmünd from the south, clutching a stoneware hot-water bottle filled to the brim with muddy Jordan water which she had procured after a special journey by wading in the shallows, holding up her skirts with one hand and immersing the hot-water bottle with the other.

All went well until the actual christening, when the aged clergyman, who suffered from the shakes, let slip the hot-water bottle at the climactic moment of the ceremony, and it broke neatly in two on the Victorian mosaic, sending rivulets of yellowish water alive with the agitation of primitive and almost invisible river life exploding among the cracks and crevices of the neo-Gothic Bible scenes depicted on the floor. Without as much as a flicker of anguish, the clergyman promptly substituted some sterile sanctified water for the Old Testament impurities, and named me Petrus Alexandrus to lend a classical tone to the proceedings which was now lacking.

I am grateful not to have been born into a backward time where such an event might have been interpreted as the displeasure of some God or other, for I might easily have been sacrificed in a cowardly act of appeasement. As it was, my grandmother's eyes began to water whenever she clapped them on me. In less atavistic surroundings, back in London, I prospered despite this early brush with Fata Morgana.

The first nurse I remember was black, but instead of the full-bosomed, contralto, crooning warmth associated with black mammies in ante-bellum surroundings, this lady came from the Cameroons, a part of Africa formerly under German hegemony, and she possessed the febrile eye and the rasping voice of a Prussian drill-sergeant. Her name, if you please, was Fräulein Bertha, which sounds like some kinky creation of Strindberg's fevered imagination. I spent most of my time standing in the corner with a wet diaper on my head while she screamed and ranted in barrack-square German. She was caught beating me mercilessly by my father, who fired her on the spot, which caused her to feel great bitterness about white overlordship. Where she went, I do not know. Her country was now a French mandate. The hated enemy was there, as in Alsace-Lorraine. She was a misfit in a world that had changed, and like most misfits she was a splendid potential recruit for the Nazi party. She had risen to a tiny, meaningless authority through the ranks of servility, and now she was in temperament more European than the most rabid Junker. All that stood in her way was her appearance. I often think of her, with pity.

Her successor was Irish, a girl in her twenties who dressed like a woman in her fifties, in grim grey flannels, with a black hat through which a hatpin cut, seeming to pass through her head. Her hair was plaited, and she wore a rimless pince-nez which wobbled on the bridge of her nose as she spoke. She was all mildness of manner and hypocritical whispers and nursery jingles. She had a saying or a saw for every situation, but in spite of the prissy piety of her comportment, a habit she must have picked up in some convent, I spent just as much time in the corner as under Fräulein Bertha, and even more time with soggy underwear on my head. Whereas Fräulein Bertha didn't give a damn who knew of her educational methods, since she had suffered just such an upbringing and came out of it, her head high and her vocal chords higher, Miss O'R. was full of murmured threats about what would happen to me if I ever complained to my parents about what went on. Among those specified occurrences was her habit of wheeling me into the park, ostensibly to take a breath of air in my pram, a practice encouraged by my mother. We never went far, however, although we stayed out a long time. My daily constitutional took us two streets away, to a relatively low neighbourhood. Here I would be parked next to a railing, and be left to my own devices while Miss O'R. disappeared down some steps into a basement, where a door opened mysteriously to let her in.

Presumably in order to keep me quiet, a man in shirt-sleeves would emerge and place a birdcage on the steps, exciting a large green parrot inside to converse with me. There are, of course, limits to the conversation one can have with a parrot, especially when one's own vocabulary is not yet much more extensive than the parrot's. It imitated me and I imitated it, but since our relationship could hardly move much further without a slightly greater experience of life, and since the fixed and surprised expression of its eye gave me hardly any intellectual satisfaction, I soon tired of its intrusion into my privacy, and ended by ignoring it. This ritual was repeated day after day, until I began to loathe the sight of the bird, and it took scant pleasure in seeing me, remaining as silent as a Trappist.

Eventually Miss O'R. would emerge, all flushed, having taken much more colour on our excursion than me, her eye rejuvenated and flashing behind her pince-nez. She whispered her usual threat about all the horrid things I could expect if I breathed so much as a single word to my parents, and wheeled me back home.

For a while all went well for her, until I began to imitate the parrot at home. At first my parents were delighted with my performance, until it occurred to them that I could scarcely have encountered a parrot in Green Park. 'Where,' they asked me, 'did you see a parrot?' I grew red with embarrassment, and said that I had sworn not to tell. In such a manner are children prepared for the ethics of adult life, for Watergate and all the rest. My mother mentioned it no more, although she did tell my father that she had noticed that my clothes were covered in particles of soot every time I went to the park. The tentacles of justice were beginning to close on poor flushed Miss O'R.

The next day, we went around the corner as usual. Miss O'R. clattered down the steps, the man in shirtsleeves put in a brief appearance as he placed the bird in position as though it were an early morning cup of tea in a guest house. What had started excitingly as a conspiracy had now become a routine rite. I sought to break the monotony that day by shouting at the bird. The bird looked surprised as usual, as though finding these new sounds difficult to assess. We were interrupted by a presence. It was my mother who had followed the pram like a detective. That was the end of the road for Miss O'R. whose tears welled out of downcast eyes, looking for once younger than her years. She packed her bags and went, giving me a twisted little kiss on the way. She undoubtedly set the seeds in my mind for a conviction that there is nothing more boring in this world than someone else's love story, especially if you are told it by a parrot.

A procession of temporary nurses was halted by the arrival of Frieda from Hamburg. Here was a true eccentric, and she and my parents deserved each other. My mother had been an art student in Russia, and now attempted to become a fully-fledged painter. She sketched a great deal, and had acquired a very personal, rather fey, pale, stylized technique in oils. In the full flush of young achievement, she submitted one or two of her works to the New English Art Club. My father did a floral piece of his own as a joke, and submitted it also. His was accepted, hers were refused. Then Frieda arrived as a cook, and as a counterweight. She was a woman of unprepossessing appearance, one of the tragic generation engaged to a man who was killed in the war, or worse, 'missing', which word invariably introduced an element of hope into a hopeless situation. She was barely literate, and yet

42

her instincts were individual and sure, as though her schooling had failed to replace her native wit with a social efficiency less personal.

First of all she was a good cook, then a great cook, eventually a celebrated cook. Not content with this, she looked after me between courses, and as if that wasn't enough of a handful, she began to paint in a manner somewhere between Le Douanier Rousseau and Grandma Moses, and pose for my mother in the nude when in need of rest. She entered into the stormy life we shared, and was, in fact, responsible for at least some squalls.

It is perhaps necessary to give a brief description of my parents at this juncture, simply because nothing can be understood from now on without at least an appreciation of my prejudices in their regard. I do not pretend to tell the truth about them, simply because I am probably the last person in the world qualified to do so. After all, I lived with them, in the most oppressive proximity. In any case, I believe they were utterly different when they were alone, without my presence.

My father, Klop, was short, all of five foot two, and had been slight. Early photographs show him as dapper, affecting pomaded hair, cut very short, and often a monocle. I always felt he was somewhat of a ham. One can tell by the way a man will look at himself in the glass, and by the expression he adopts when posing for photographs. He never smiled on those occasions unless shamed into it by the photographer, and even then he injected a quizzical look as a condiment to his *bonhomie*. Usually he assumed a rather dictatorial look, or else one of disconcerting scepticism, hypnotizing the onlooker with an eye either all-seeing or indomitable. In short, he seemed to fancy himself as something he was really not, a man of mystery, at least not in the way he understood it.

There is a cliché which maintains that traits of character tend to jump one generation, and if such is in fact the case, it is probably due to a tendency of children to react against their parents in

43

their formative years rather than to any purely genetic reason. Klop's father became what he was as a reaction against that wicked father of his, who had made of his bed a track-meet rather than a place of rest, and whose unshaven jowls could be seen at intervals chewing on a pickle in the hallway while his wife wept, consoled by her three sons, in the town house down the street. Such scandalous comportment in a father is liable to engender introspection in a son.

Whatever Klop's father was really like, it is obvious that he was more of an age to be a grandfather to the lad, since he was turning seventy when Klop was thirteen. Klop never denied being spoiled, although he didn't care to dwell on it, making out instead that his father was a terrifying martinet, probably in order to impress me with his own relative leniency. Klop never tired of telling me, as I crept home with one of those ambiguous report cards English schoolmasters have specialized in ever since they read their Dickens, that he had been so brilliant a pupil that on leaving school in Jaffa, his name had been inscribed in letters of gold on a marble slab for all to know that Jona von Ustinov had been a scholastic *Wunderkind*.

I was less impressed than I should have been, since having my name inscribed on a marble slab has always been a fear rather than an ambition, and because other sources had told me that Klop had had help with his homework from none other than his father, eager for his progeny to shine. On the one occasion I had any help from Klop, I got lower marks than usual, and that's saying something. In case it can be thought that I blame my father for failing with my homework after all this time, I hasten to state that I do.

All this is not to say that he was in any way niggardly with his exceptional intelligence, but this intelligence was strictly post-scholastic in character, and as he would himself have insisted, superficial. His most profound visible quality was his utter belief in life as a superficial exercise, as an extent of thin ice to be skated on, for the execution of arabesques and

44

figures of fun. He lived for the day, and was, as I have stressed before, totally irreligious, perhaps as a reaction against his father's Calvinist austerity and the tasteless ecumenical excesses of the Holy Land.

It was natural for such a temperament to find real joy in the quicksilver world of journalism, which gave him every opportunity to exercise the kind of talent he possessed, and also to spend a little more than his salary on entertaining. I am convinced that I am one of the few people he knew who will remember him as a highly paradoxical person rather than as an admirable host, and I say this without the remotest implication of criticism, in the added conviction that he would far rather have been remembered as an admirable host than as a person of any kind. It was all part of his hedonistic message to mankind.

He had large and expressive eyes, the precise colour of white grapes, which were often trained on the passing forms of women, seeming to assess them with the shameless detachment of a trainer observing the finer points of racehorses. On those rare occasions when I found myself alone with him as a child, he would offer me an ice-cream or a lemonade in a café, as an exercise in public relations, or child psychology. I used to dread these moments even more than I dreaded his temper, because he would use them to scan the passing crowd and consult me as an adult accomplice on the physical qualities and shortcomings of the females present. Quite often he would become riveted on to some potential victim and would indulge in that suggestive ocular flicker which used to be described as a 'glad eye'. The victim would then either blush and appear scandalized or else wait for the next move with a suppressed confusion, as though impaled on Klop's liquid gaze. Small wonder that I became a kind of pocket Puritan, devoting the same massive attention to my ice-cream that Klop was exerting on his mesmerism, refusing to look, refusing to answer, and bursting with a sense of outrage.

At home, while entertaining, he was a master of the risqué, of the double-entendre, always galloping like a daring scout in the no-man's-land between wit and lapses of taste. Oh, his thousand and one nights would seem innocuous enough today, and he would have been as depressed with the brave show of pornography as any self-respecting rake, but in those times of nuance and pastel shades it was infinitely depressing to me to see my mother enter into the gales of laughter which greeted remarks of his, qualified gratefully as outrageous by his guests, in a pure spirit of sportsmanship.

Not that she was in the least narrow-minded. On the contrary, she was far more intrinsically unshockable than he, but her conduct was always impeccable, while his seemed juvenile even to the child that I then was.

I have always doubted that he was really the womanizer he would have liked to have been. First of all, he lacked the quality of secrecy necessary for those who lead double lives. His whole quality was public, and he shared his predilections and temptations with my mother, or, on rare occasions, over an ice-cream, with me. He needed an ear, be it friendly or merely infantile. Like Casanova, he was a flitter from flower to flower, a grazer of bottoms rather than a pincher, a catcher of glimpses rather than a patient voyeur, a man in a hurry with an avid taste for the unpredictable, the unaccountable, the sudden. At the same time, he was a real danger to no one. He had a distaste for the brutal and the cruel which was innate, and a moral courage which was at times surprising in a man so devoted to the good life. Towards the end of his life he was as surrounded by young girls as a guru, so that even then he offered a consistent amusement, an elegance of spirit, a sense of joyous irresponsibility to say the least. It was perhaps only as a father that he was sometimes difficult to stomach, and, by the same token, as a husband.

My mother was a large woman, in comparison with him, that is. She had a fine face, with the kind of natural warmth and simplicity which attracted everybody, from my father's girlfriends to homosexuals, who found in her an uncomplicated friend and mentor. She grafted her personality on to the kind of life she was asked to lead, and never showed any of the humiliation and degradation she must have felt. Basically she was a much stronger and more stable person than my father, which caused her to emerge from her turbulent existence with an illusory sense of imperious independence. When asked to paint some transitory flame of my father's, she did so with grace, and often became a friend and confidante of the young person while my father was directing his electric gaze on to some newer fly entangled in his social web.

There was never a trace of self-pity about her, nor did she ever give the impression that her life with this strange fellow was anything but normal, a fact I found bewildering and disturbing from an early age. She was expected to go on an endless round of parties, to entertain at home, and still to paint, living what was left of her time as a Bohemian in a single room. But even here, her life was invaded by Klop, who had acquired very dogmatic ideas about the arts, and who invariably stood behind her easel telling her what was wrong with her latest canvas in terms both categorical and irrefutable. She listened, often remonstrated, but on the whole acceded to his exigencies. This is not to say that she didn't stick up for herself, but since he had a mercurial temper and, at times, a wicked and hurtful tongue, much of her energy was devoted to keeping a fragile peace in the household. The family rows were far too frequent, and were obviously exacerbated as I grew older, and developed a mind of my own, and a kind of recklessness in expressing it.

On one occasion, I left for school after catching a glimpse of a picture my mother had painted. It was a very fine paraphrase of a painting by El Greco, and it struck me as a work of surpassing beauty. On returning home, I found that my mother had destroyed it, and was in fact already at work on the same canvas, painting a dish of apples. My fury knew no bounds. I surprised both my parents by the violence of my sentiments, and for the only time in my life had them both shouting at me. I banged the door of my room, and locked myself in, refusing to

47

emerge or answer for hours. Once inside, I felt a new strength I had never experienced before. It was the premature rage of an adult. There was no trace of a tear in my eye. For the first time, or so it seemed to me, I had spoken from a platform of my own, and not merely made excuses or reacted against some other initiative. From then on, I became calculatedly cold, deliberately impervious to my father's sarcasms and even to my mother's appeals for good sense. The atmosphere at home was no longer changeable, but glowering and intense.

I do not know on retrospect whether I would have the same high opinion of my mother's El Greco variant today, although in honesty, as I remember it, I think I would. As for the apples, they were reminiscent of Renoir, much beloved by my father at the time, but Renoir did his apples well enough not to need emulation. In any case, even he painted far too many apples. That awful day was a date in my calendar. I had become myself, to myself.

Before this, I had been used by my father as a cabaret, which was my first introduction to show-business. My ability to imitate had manifested itself very early on, as well as my instinctively unconventional way of going about it. After all, I had started this tendency by imitating a parrot, which is unusual, in that a parrot is supposed to imitate you. By taking the initiative, you allow the parrot no alternative but to be itself, which proves once again that attack is often the best defence. At the age of two, I apparently did a passable imitation of Lloyd George, and later on I added Hitler, Mussolini and Aristide Briand to my gallery as these gentlemen became available in the public domain. I also did a complete voyage round Europe by radio while hidden behind a curtain, which was remarkable by virtue of the fact that we possessed no radio in the house until 1936.

Fourteen years previously, during the great exhibition at Wembley, Haile Selassie had come to London to buy a few machine-guns for the Ethiopian army. My father, making use of his Ethiopian connections, invited the Lion of Judah to dinner.

Frieda cooked a great dinner for four. At the appointed time, Haile Selassie arrived at our small apartment accompanied not only by the Empress but by Ras Imrn, Ras Kassa, the Chief of General Staff, six A.D.C.s and a few princesses. Nobody in my family had sufficient faith to trust in miracles, so the German Embassy was apprised of the situation and prepared dinner for twenty, which was driven over in a fleet of Mercedes. All this took time, however, even to the chef of the German Embassy, so that in desperation I was woken up, and prevailed upon to do my entire repertoire, as well as to draw out the encores, if any. I have no recollection whatever of the occasion, but many years later, at the Ethiopian pavilion at the Osaka World Fair, I was encouraged to go and talk to Haile Selassie by his grandson, Alexander Desta, then head of the Ethiopian navy. I sat by the aged monarch and reminded him of the evening. Before I had finished my very brief résumé of the event, he had fallen into a fitful sleep at the recollection, which leads me to believe that my performance in 1924 had not been a success.

In one sense, I was eager to be called on to perform. There was probably in me a premature professional sense, a feeling I remember quite well to this day, since it has been with me for a long time now. I can best refer to it as a kind of purification of the senses, a cutting-down of non-essentials, the emotion which finds its most faithful physical expression on the face of a high-jumper about to take a stab at a record. And yet, in another sense, I dreaded these moments, because despite the laughter of my father's guests, I could discern in their appreciation a tinge of awe at the little monster I would become if encouraged to continue in this way. There was only one saving grace, and that was that I was irrevocably betrothed to laughter, the sound of which has always seemed to me the most civilized music in the universe.

At all events, these early flirtations with satire were infinitely more pleasant than another of my father's initiatives, which was to bring all his guests to come and see me in my bath. These guided tours used to burst in on me unheralded, and my father, who always considered himself a connoisseur of the arts, would compare me to this or that unfinished study by Donatello or a young Bacchus of the Etruscan school, often carrying a thick tome with him in order to prove his point.

My mother knew that I hated these intrusions, but didn't really understand why, believing it a small enough sacrifice to keep Klop sweet. Inevitably I tended to gravitate towards Frieda, who had a peppery nature of her own when my rights or hers were violated, and who never spared my father's complicated feelings. I think she must have given notice at least twice a month for the ten or more years she was with us. This was always given with extraordinary finality but somehow she never got around to packing her bags. She amused Klop, even, or perhaps especially, in the higher flights of anger, and his own heightened emotions were expressed with a malicious twinkle, laced with irony.

It was when she had finally left at the time my father lost his job, this time of course without a scene, and in an aura of melancholy – her departure was dictated by economic considerations – that I realized how valuable a domestic equilibrium she had provided. When there were only three of us again, my father's attitude towards me became more virulently critical, and his humour grew more tetchy, only really coming in to his own when there was entertaining to be done. He was, I am told, jealous of my mother's attentions towards me – she herself supported this theory, which I can neither confirm nor deny, as I have absolutely no natural feeling for or recognition of jealousy. This does not mean that I am entirely incapable of being jealous myself; that would be too beautiful to be true, but I have always regarded it as a base and fundamentally stupid vice, and I would rather be caught dead than express it. Othello, clutching his handkerchief and rolling his eyes, has always struck me as a bit of an ass, and I only began to lose my lofty sense of ignorance in the face of jealousy when I became a father of more than a single child myself, and could

50

watch human relations in their most unsophisticated form, in the nursery.

It may be true that an only child is spoiled, not so much with gifts, not with the time allotted to his problems but, believe me, there are occasions on which he wishes there was a brother or a sister to share the brunt. What is certainly true is that he tends to become self-centred, which is the outward form of self-sufficiency. He spends more time alone, and in the company of adults. He learns less about human nature faster, but I was staggered how much my own children revealed to me about the human condition, relatively obvious things which had just never occurred to me.

There were breaks in the monotonous pattern, little fragments of memory which I still possess. My parents dancing to the tune of 'Valencia' and 'Tea for Two' and 'I Miss My Swiss, My Swiss Miss Misses Me', while I was allowed to wind the portable gramophone. It was the only time I ever saw them dance together, and curiously enough for once there were no guests in the house. Then Klop bought a very early record of the Lener Quartet playing one of Beethoven's last works. I noticed that there was a tendency for the listeners to close their eyes when savouring Beethoven, so I followed suit. It seemed to me strange later on, at school, that during lessons of so-called musical appreciation, it was quite in order to shut your eyes. In fact, by this simple strategy, you quickly acquired a reputation of possessing an intensely musical nature, and yet, if you shut your eyes during Latin or mathematics, it was generally supposed that you were asleep.

Then there were the holidays, the first conscious introductions to other lands and other cultures. My mother's brother Nicholas, who had been a regular officer with the Preobrazhensky Regiment, then transferred to Imperial Russia's first and only armoured-car unit because of 'bad feet', now followed in the great tradition of émigré officers by driving a taxi in Paris. He used to fetch us at the Gare du Nord and transport us to the Gare de Lyon free of charge. It was a relief to be comfortably seated on the cloth upholstery of his maroon Delage after having spent some hours on the wood-slatted seats of a third-class compartment, even if the excesses of the Paris traffic were even wilder than they are today. The air was charged with the trumpeting of bulb-horns, forbidden today, and the torrents of abuse from driver to driver, also discouraged, but perforce tolerated as social intercourse between consenting adults.

My mother used to go to the South of France in order to paint. Her style had deepened into something altogether richer than before, a sternly unaffected impressionism. The strength of her pictures was also, to my mind, their limitation, which is another way of saying that she had personality. Everything she painted had behind it a very acute temperament, both serene and warm. Much more heart and instinct had gone into her work than thought. To paint what she saw was enough for her. What she felt would inevitably follow.

She strode across the paintable landscape wearing espadrilles, an old straw hat on her head, sniffing out the best angles and compositions, while Frieda and I followed like native porters in an African movie, carrying canvases and easels and boxes of paints. It was a curious way of spending vacations, since there was nothing else to do but to paint as well, although for me to paint what I saw was never satisfying. I could not bring myself to aim for a mere faithful reproduction, nor did any work without comment, without an edge, interest me for long. Once I remember the astonishment of both my mother and Frieda when, at the end of a smouldering day in the hills behind Tourettes-sur-Loup, I showed them my painting, the subject of which was a post-Christmas sale at Harrod's.

This event became the pretext for a family joke, which was brought out on every and any occasion, and I hope I laughed with as good a grace every time I heard it. The fact was that I did not consider it much of a pastime for a boy away from school to be sitting before a landscape nature has put together with great competence, and to seek to reproduce it on a small piece of paper. It was more of a school punishment than a relaxation, and it was useless to tell me that Cézanne had attempted to fracture light or that Seurat had reduced the universe to dots. These were men who had chosen their professions, and who had applied the alchemy of thought and vision to their paintbrushes in necessary loneliness, and who did with a discreet conviction that which I was doing only because I had no one with whom to play. In case it be thought that a note of self-pity has crept into this account of my apparent boredom, I must say that the intention was never to complain about my fate, but merely to explain the form of my protest. A Christmas sale in a department store should have been enough to convince anybody that I had no ambitions to be a landscape painter, but no, it was taken, told and retold, as evidence of youthful high spirits in someone who would no doubt settle later on, and I, social animal which I already was, laughed with the others and gave credence to the myth.

If the sacrifice I felt I was making had been of some use to my mother's career, there would have been a point to all the discomfort, but once back home, there was always the terrifying day when all these canvases passed in review before my father, and he decreed which should be exhibited and which should not. It was worse than being stopped at the Customs with contraband. He was by now not the only arbiter. There were the people from the galleries as well, and it is very probable that between the lot of them, they made the right choice, but I felt then as I feel now that the one great joy of leaving school is that you no longer have the impression of sitting for exams, and there is no excuse on God's earth for giving a grown person this lamentable impression.

I had cooled towards the visual arts, and it took a long time for my instinctive love of them to reassert itself.

— Now, dear Me, I suppose that you will tell me I have been too harsh on my father.

— Not at all. I realize that you are making every effort to recapture the emotions of a child faced by the problems

53

of growing in the shadow of a man at once dogmatic and capricious, and that your criticism is at no time the criticism of one adult by another.

— I wouldn't know how to criticize him in that way. I had known him too long and too well. I feel now that he hadn't the remotest idea how to deal with children. To him they were just inadequate adults.

— Oh, that's not true. He could be perfectly adorable, and show incredible patience with other people's children.

— Towards the end of his life that was so, but I wonder if that isn't so towards the end of most people's lives. There is a natural complicity between the very old and the very young. Children tend to enjoy the company of their grandparents, which often leads their parents into little tantrums of jealousy (Ah, I recognize it here!), complaining that their children are being spoiled. But is there not a precise biological reason for this? There is a tendency for the old to begin to remember their youth with extraordinary clarity, as though there were some metaphysical connection between the mysteries of birth and death, whereas those in the flower of life are the farthest away from those distant frontiers we all pass. They are at their most intelligent, at their most active, at their least instinctive. They brush away the reflective, the poetic, the opaque as a waste of valuable time. They read the papers with a sense of personal involvement, they fret and fume, make and lose their fortunes, carve what they imagine to be their futures out of the present which seems so permanent, and leave the foolishness to the very old and the very young.

— Yes, of course I agree, even though I might criticize your language as being a little high flown. Your own son, remember, made a most astute observation the other day. When confiding in him that you felt it was a little early in life to be writing your memories, he replied that later on you would begin to remember everything, and run the risk of being a crashing bore by a dotard's inability to be selective. The time

54

to write memories is at a time that total recall has not yet invaded the cavities of the mind left empty by the inaction of retirement.

— I remember that observation with great pleasure, although since I have not yet revealed the existence of my son, I feel I should be a little careful about running ahead of myself. I have not yet gone to school myself, in fact.

— You are lucky to have me by your side to remind you where you are in the narrative. Very well, we will forget your son for the time being, and concentrate on your father. I do not think you were too tough on him. I do not think you were tough enough.

— Oh, come on. Have you any idea how difficult it is to be a father? Children seem to regard them as infallible authorities at one time of life, and when the disillusionment comes, it is invariably painful, leading to an absurd and unhappy bitterness. Children forget that although they have no previous experience of being children, their fathers have no previous experience of being fathers. And, in any case, no one on this earth is infallible. There are no heroes, and nobody is worth the worship due to heroes.

— There you are, talking about your son again, in spite of your good intentions.

— I am talking about myself, and about my father, which comes to the same thing as talking about my son. You are right, there's no getting away from it. We all make mistakes, but at least, if we are intelligent, we make other mistakes than those which were made on us. Only if we are unintelligent do we make the same mistakes. But whether we are intelligent or unintelligent, we make mistakes, and often intelligent mistakes are the worst, since so much careful thought has gone into them.

— How about your mother?

— A remarkable woman, a sister, an aunt, sometimes a daughter, always a mother, and yet without a trace of that saccharine

55

possessiveness which traditionally marks a certain aspect of maternity. She never made me feel that the pain attending my birth was a moral debit account which could never be entirely honoured, and she taught me that independence is the rarest of life's commodities by making the fullest use of the ration she was accorded. She was always blissfully uninquisitive, which was an important aspect of her independence. She was also entirely faithful, simply because she could not conceive of not being so. My father was the one and only man in her life. She had given her word that this should be so, and the idea never occurred to her, even under the most blatant provocation, that she could go against her word. Sometimes this extraordinary uprightness was a source of irritation, simply because the insults poured on her dignity were so scandalous that decency itself called for a reaction of some kind, and yet there was no trace of self-righteousness, of holier-than-thou about her attitude. Her eyes merely became sightless, her ears deaf, her mind absent, and she concentrated with relaxed application on the highlight on this apple or the shadow in the armpit of that nude. And yet, it is humanly impossible that she did not suffer a great deal, but she probably reflected as people of such temperament invariably do that she was made to suffer because she had the moral capacity to bear suffering with a shrug, in silence.

— I asked you about your mother, and now, inadvertently, you have been as tough on your father as I wished you to have been from the beginning.

— She was, curiously enough, even tougher than I could possibly be. For years after his death she struggled with a book entitled *Klop* which was to be a eulogy and a memoir of a man she considered remarkable, the only man she had ever known. A year before her death it appeared, and it was greeted by many readers as a tribute to a remarkable man, and yet there were those even among the critics who discerned a darker side to

56

the jocular narrative, and who came to the conclusion that my father was a bigot, a snob, and an unrepentant egotist.

— How is it possible to read such different conclusions from one and the same book?

— First of all because many remarkable men are bigots, snobs, and unrepentant egotists, and secondly because the book was delightfully free from recrimination. And yet, it possessed another characteristic which was its key to those willing to look beneath the surface. It told the truth, simply and unaffectedly, because my mother was incapable of not telling the truth, simply and unaffectedly.

— And so what was sincerely intended by her as an amusing epitaph to her man became a much sadder little volume to those willing to treat it as other than pure entertainment, but as an account of events which actually occurred, recollected in cheerfulness. My mother stuck her press-cuttings into a book, including the one with the headline 'Ustinov's Father Was a Bigot and a Snob'. She made no reference to it, but did not attempt to hide it. I dare say it was probably the only act of revenge she was capable of, the only one which was not an offence to her pride.

— How touching. I know this is not really the place for such a question, and yet in the interests of equity there is no alternative to my asking it now. They were quite close at the end, were they not?

— It was during the war, dear Me, that my father suddenly declared, quite out of the blue, that he refused to live over seventy years. His categorical announcement took everyone by surprise, particularly because there was nothing about the conversation to warrant it.

— Why do you think he made it?

— I believe he felt his powers waning – not only physical powers, but his credibility as a seducer, and he refused a life of mere observation, with the promise of nothing but senility.

— You said he was totally irreligious.

57

— To the extent of fearing nothing more than eternal life. He infinitely preferred oblivion, and he prepared for it with the grace of an ancient Roman. It was sheer will power on his part that made him die four hours before his seventieth birthday.

— Incredible. It sounds as though he didn't merely die, he gave up the ghost.

— Asking nothing in return. Towards the end of his life, he sulked like a child who had been denied eternal youth. This attitude, utterly bereft of volition, irritated my mother, who tried unsuccessfully to instil a little zest into him. But he knew what he wanted. And he left instructions that he was to be cremated. He wished to disappear. My mother cringed at the idea of cremation, but we obeyed his wishes. Then, once he had gone, my mother gradually wilted into the same baleful inactivity she had found so annoying in him, as though in obedience to some signal from beyond the grave. She faded away exactly as he had done, only coming to life momentarily on the publication of her book. At her death, she left instructions to be cremated, the idea which had always horrified her. I placed their ashes together in the same village graveyard in Gloucestershire.

— They were reunited.

— They had never really been separated. That is to say there was a difficult period just after the war in which they lived apart, he in a bachelor flat in London where he cooked his rich but succulent dishes for the delight of his guests, or guest. Later they were reunited, first of all in London, later in the country.

— Was the breach between them a real one?

— I don't know. It wasn't a breach, you know, it was an absence, a physical absence. After my mother's death, I found huge piles of letters from one to the other, all graded by vintage and kept together by rubber bands. At a glance, they were talkative, informative, benign, and confidential. But there

58

were those among them which gave me the feeling of being an eavesdropper, since they seemed to go beyond privacy into what was practically a private language. In this way, they are certainly love letters pure and simple, and I have no desire or inclination as yet to penetrate into their secrets. I have merely kept them in neat piles, as she left them.

— And they are from the period during which they were not living together?

— Many of them, yes.

— Has it occurred to you that perhaps it was you who injected an element into their relationship which they had never foreseen?

— At the time they were not living together, I had long before left home. I hope what you suggest is not true.

— I am not blaming you, merely the fact of your existence.

— The fact of my existence?

— How could Tristan and Isolde have survived if there had been a child, or Romeo and Juliet? All the poetry would have been lost in irritation at feeding time.

— I do not think my parents were lovers in that sense. What they created was something far less ambitious and far more profound. And Wagner would have been the last one to set their story to music. Offenbach perhaps, or Mozart. Nor would Shakespeare have been right, as an author. Feydeau on good days, Chekhov for the rest, with a little help from Tolstoi and Michael Arlen, but most of all, themselves. – Me.

— Well, whatever blame we must take for our existence, dear me, I think it time we accorded them a little privacy. It is time for us to go to school.

– 4 –

Mr Gibbs' Preparatory School for Boys occupied a house in Sloane Street in London, 134 to be precise. Whereas other British schoolboys wore caps which fitted fairly tightly to the head, and which boasted a multiplicity of colours, with coats of arms or monograms in evidence, the boys of Mr Gibbs' wore caps curiously like the shape of that favoured by Lenin, and what is more, cherry red without any heraldic symbol. Mr Gibbs himself was a fairly burly old gentleman, who was extremely cordial, and also extremely absent-minded. He seemed to have some difficulty shaving, since, apart from his immaculate white military moustache, his jaw was often decorated with tufts of bloody cotton-wool. He also sang a great deal, as though the cherished privacy of his bathroom travelled with him. What he sang were not so much recognizable tunes, as a kind of personal parlando set to melodies very much his own, reminiscent of Schoenberg, by negligence rather than design, for he was not very musical. He imparted news in this manner, both pleasant and unpleasant, rather like the town-crier in his own little city.

'Oh, Oosty-Boosty,' he would chant as he saw me, 'can't tie his shoe laces . . . Come over here . . . Mr Gibbs will help him, won't he . . . sit down, fatty,' all this in a high tenor like the evangelist. A far lower register was used for news unfavourable, although the quality was as doggedly in advance of its time.

'Thompson minor deserves to do a hundred lines . . . come and see me after school.'

I learned at Mr Gibbs' how to survive by emphasizing the clumsy and comic aspects of my character, and to hide my secret ambitions for fear of challenging those better equipped by nature too openly. For instance, I was often encouraged to play in goal during football matches, partly because I was not the fastest of runners with the ball, and partly because I was large, and therefore occupied more of the goal-mouth than a slender boy, the theory being that there would be a greater chance for me to deflect the ball unwittingly simply by being hit by it.

During the summer I was introduced to the game of cricket, and felt my inherent foreignness for the first time. The ball is far too hard for my taste, a lethal projectile left over from some long-forgotten battle. (I have always imagined cricket as a game invented by roughnecks in a moment of idleness by casually throwing an unexploded bomb at one another. This game was observed by some officer with a twisted and ingenious mind who devoted his life to inventing impossible rules for it.) The genius of the British lends itself not so much to the winning of games as to their invention. An astonishing number of international games were invented by the British, who, whenever they are surpassed by other nations, coolly invent another one which they can dominate for a while by being the only ones to know the rules. Whoever thought up cricket deserves a special commendation, since here is a game so doggedly peculiar and dangerous that no foreign nations, apart from those of relatively recent independence, subjected to an English type of education, have ever adopted it. The Americans, as a reaction against the indignities of the redcoats, grew tired of the sight of stumps on their village green, and took up baseball, which is more adapted to a country of vast spaces, with fewer architectural features to damage; whereas the French and Romanians, who think nothing of flinging themselves at each other in the wild excesses of rugby football, would be bored stiff on the cricket pitch, faced by hours of languor punctuated by the mean crack of ball on bat, and a bit of choreography.

It is against this background that children in British schools are taught to lose gracefully, often at the expense of winning. The real encounter is won in the changing room after the event, in which the extraordinary grace of the loser makes the victory seem hollow and even vaguely indecent to the winner.

No wonder that old colonels have been heard to bark, 'Play the game, sir,' or 'Gad, sir, it isn't cricket,' referring to events far from the playing grounds, nor is it surprising that an authority on aggrandizement and gamesmanship such as Cecil Rhodes once gave the following advice to a nervous young officer about to police a bit of empire, 'Remember that you are an Englishman, and have consequently won first prize in the lottery of life.'

Well, it was at Mr Gibbs' school that boys were issued with their tickets for this lottery, and although I was still technically von Ustinov, I was given the benefit of the doubt, and slipped my ticket when not too many people were looking.

There were occasions on which Mr Gibbs must have wondered if he had not been too free with his tickets, as when an Argentine boy and I were caught picking flowers instead of fielding during an important cricket match against another school, thus allowing the opponents no less than seven runs, simply because neither of us could find the ball. We were violently upbraided by a master, our bunches of wilting daisies still in our hands.

I redeemed myself later, however, when it had been admitted that cricket was hardly my forte, and perhaps for that very reason I was made the scorer for another vital match. The rival school also had a scorer, a small, anaemic and impressionable lad who looked hard done by. I was very agreeable with him, and he became almost pathetically grateful for a conversation absolutely devoid of threats or taunting, eventually being so immersed in it that he quite neglected to fill up his score-card. As a result of this extremely relaxing afternoon, my school won the match by the smallest of margins in spite of having far fewer runs, a victory greeted with disbelief by our opponents, who only had to check the figures of their scorer, gratefully copied off my score-card in the last moment, to see that it was unwise during matches against Mr Gibbs' school to judge by appearances, above all if I was the scorer.

Mr Gibbs hugged me with exceptional warmth after this most unexpected win, and it seemed to me that in his heart he knew that, thanks to him, I had at long last learned to play the game.

Among the other teachers, there was Mlle Chaussat, a slightly deformed spinster in her fifties, small and frankly frightening to look at. Her malformed back made her walk half-crabwise, and her broad-brimmed felt hat, which she never took off, gave her the aspect of a Hieronymus Bosch creation, a hat with legs. To add to the sense of menace exuded by poor Mlle Chaussat were a mouth which never stopped moving as though endlessly assessing and reassessing some outrage, a sallow face from which her defiant brown eyes shifted angrily above a spatulate nose and an explosion of moles, and a pair of open scissors which dangled from a satin cord down where her knees must have been.

Bless her heart, she was the one subversive element admitted into a classroom which was dominated by a large print entitled 'The Boy Scout's Oath'. In it an evidently bewildered boy scout was led by the hand by Jesus, who, with his other hand indicated a map of the world on which the Empire was lit by a strange, unearthly radiance. She often glanced with sheer hatred at this work of art, and shook her head at the gratuitous expropriation of Jesus by the Protestants. Whenever the national anthem was played, Mlle Chaussat remained seated, her twitching increasing, and her gaze showering the assembly like water from a hose. Her actions were never questioned, and she never amended them. She did, however, invite me to tea, which was the first gesture of friendship she had been known to make to anyone.

Our tea took place at M. Debry's Confiserie in Knightsbridge. I was plied with the most delicious chocolate cakes, and a host of

63

other goodies. In contact with M. Debry, Mlle Chaussat's entire character changed. She became playful and even ribald, passing remarks both salty and Gallic. I hardly recognized her as the grim French mistress who wore her scissors as a sword.

Then followed the reason for the tea, which was a temptation rather than a treat. With a surreptitious step, heeding the traffic with more than usual attention, she led me across the road to a French convent, which turned out to be her lair. Here, under another Christ as biased as the one showing such an unnatural interest in a boy scout and the British Empire, this one on his cross, but with a painful smile reserved for the French, the advantages of Catholicism were shamelessly exposed.

'*La Protestantisme, ce n'est pas une religion,*' Mlle Chaussat spat out with contempt, to the smiling embarrassment of a group of nuns with gold teeth and suspect skins. I smiled back at them. '*Ce n'est que dans le Catholicisme qu'on trouve la vraie foi!*' On and on it went. Only a layman could afford to be as categorical or as wild. The nuns offered me more tea, a mournful lot of plain buns with the same scrubbed look as they, after the sensuous opulence of M. Debry's éclairs. I declined as politely as I could.

'*Le petit a déjà mangé,*' snapped Mlle Chaussat, suggesting that a glimpse of Satan was intended to make the cold clutch of Mother Church more desirable. I hid my thoughts in the guise of deep spiritual reflection, much as I had suggested my love of music by shutting my eyes during Beethoven. To this day I have never been subjected to as shameless a barrage of religious propaganda as on that sunny London afternoon, when Mlle Chaussat attempted to force her way into Heaven, using me as a battering ram. The only moment of my life commensurate with this one occurred many years later, when a Russian Orthodox bishop told me, with the relish of the trainer of a sporting team, 'Yes, we are making headway everywhere, mostly at the expense of Catholics.'

Events like these make me wonder if there isn't something in the attitude of crusty British colonels, and that it isn't all a game after all, and may the best church win. I avoided giving

Mlle Chaussat any hope whatsoever, but from that day on, she searched my face for signs. Every smile on my part was regarded as an indication that grace was beginning to seep into my soul through cracks in my defences, whereas every negligence on my part was sensed as a local reverse for the truth at the hands of the infidel. Relations with Mlle Chaussat could no longer be normal, since we were never alone. There was always Jesus, or Martin Luther, or both to complicate the issue.

At the beginning of my scholastic life, the mothers were expected to attend school in order to help their fledglings with the written part of a history exam. The history we learned was, at that time, entirely English, as though children of very tender years were too fragile to be exposed to the existence of foreigners and their past, except when they appeared briefly as enemies for the English to defeat. The standard text was a fat book, printed very large as though children are half-blind, and about as silly an introduction to reality as one can imagine. Alfred and the cakes was a shining example of its probings into the past, presumably to explain the English indifference to the culinary arts, and I remember a coloured illustration of a Pre-Raphaelite Boadicea gazing into the distance with determination, while the flaxen-haired warriors around her seemed distinctly worried. My poor mother, who had mastered everyday English by now, but who had had little cause to probe into the Arthurian twilight, was compelled to take down my dictation, as I attempted to make sense of the comings and goings of Uther Pendragon, of Hengist and of Horsa, and of King Canute, who told the sea to back, and who had the good sense not to be surprised when he got his feet wet. It became clear before my essay on Ancient Britain was half over that my mother didn't know what I was talking about, and was beginning to entertain doubts about the standards of education in England. Since they could hardly punish me for my mother's spelling errors, I came out of the exam relatively well, but it was the last personal appearance my mother made at school except for an eventful day at the school sports, held on the eve of the long summer holidays.

Not only my mother, but exceptionally, my father turned up at one of these, wearing his monocle. One of the items was a so-called Fathers' Race, in which the fathers of boys were supposed to demonstrate their spirit of sportsmanship by lending themselves to a curious flashback to their own schooldays over 100 yards. I asked my father to uphold my honour by running. He declined my offer with the usual mixture of humour and blarney. He was bound, he affirmed, to be in the lead, since he had been inordinately fast at school. At that point, he would also be bound to lose his monocle, without which he could not see the course, and naturally the monocle would be bound to be trampled into destruction by the stampede of other fathers battling for second place. Since monocles were expensive and necessary items, he preferred not to take the risk of running.

My mother understood my evident disappointment, since we both knew that my father could see rather better without a monocle. He had them for both eyes, incidentally, and wore them when the spirit moved him. She now made the great sacrifice of entering in the Mothers' Race, and I wish to this day she hadn't. My father was outraged by her initiative, but she could be very stubborn at times, especially when it had nothing to do with her painting. For the first yard or two I thought she had a chance, but then she began falling back, handicapped by her own explosion of laughter at the absurdity of the situation. It must have been one of the slowest 100 yards sprints on record, with my mother entirely alone at the tail end of the copious field of cantering maternity. She must have come in over five minutes after her departure; in other words she would have been wiser to walk. The actual time is, thank heavens, not on record, but I do remember that she was still running when the next race began, and, despite her enormous lead, she didn't even win that one, which was for the under-sixes.

The humiliations of the day were not over yet, however, since the final event of this joyous festival in an era of snobbery and privilege was a chauffeurs' race. It was impossible for me to redeem my misfortunes, since we had no car, and even I recognized that it would have been an absurd luxury to have maintained a chauffeur specially for the yearly race without having anything for him to do the rest of the year. My best friend at school was the son of a celebrated banker, and with the instinct born of comradeship he read the distress on my face. Taking me aside, he informed me in a whisper that his father had two chauffeurs, and felt sure he could prevail on daddy to lend me the slower one of his stable. My pride had been wounded sufficiently for me to decline his generous offer. It would have been hard to stomach a third setback, with borrowed personnel to boot.

My first attempts at acting occurred at Mr Gibbs', but I was averred by the mistress in charge of dramatics to have but little talent. As a consequence, I was compelled to make my debut masked, playing the role of a pig in some dramatized nursery-rhyme, which I did adequately according to the school reports. I have had many bad notices since, but I do not think one can argue that one started one's career from the bottom with any more eloquent proof than to produce a document stating that one was adequate in the part of a pig.

When finally unmasked, I was to be type-cast in the part of Friar Tuck, and my first apotheosis, or perhaps farewell performance, was as one of three nymphs tempting Ulysses from an Aegean beach. I was the one with blonde tresses, stage left, who sang flat. Ulysses wisely passed us by.

On the whole, my stay at Mr Gibbs' was a happy time for me. During the day, at all events, I was away from the pressures and problems of home, and although I still made my scheduled appearances in pyjamas at dinner parties to give my imitations, the intrusions into the privacy of the bathtub were now few and far between. Contact with other boys of my age gave me a release from my introversion, although a certain timidity has stayed with me to this day. I was, I believe, fairly popular with both the masters

67

and boys, and even if certain subjects like mathematics, algebra, and up to a point, Latin, gave me great difficulties, I was always top in geography, and near the top in French, history and English. Mr Gibbs was a charming old gentleman, in spite of his belief in corporal punishment and the sanctity of the boy scout movement. He used to invite the senior boys to camp in the grounds of his house at Goring-on-Thames, and drove us down there in his copious Austin tourer. His absent-mindedness made of him a very dangerous, very slow driver, and since I was often seated next to him, he was known to change gears with my kneecap, then failing to understand why the engine raced or stalled. We would stop by the roadside while he examined the carburettor, attributing to it the fault which was his own, and mine, I suppose, for having kneecaps which resembled the gear-lever of an Austin Heavy Twelve.

Everything within this academy was safe, and sunlit. The values were as certain as they had been for years, and even if they seemed vaguely ridiculous, they had longevity and usage to speak for them. Nobody questioned the rectitude of King or Country, and both Jesus and the Boy Scout seemed in place, as indeed did those portions of the map coloured red. The only questioning gaze (it was not even a voice) was that of Mlle Chaussat, and what she had to offer as an alternative was merely the same thing again in another guise, the map painted green, a President with a tricolor sash, Marianne in a Phrygian cap, a Jesus with drops of blood where the crown of thorns had bitten into the skin, the bees and eagles of L'Empereur.

Because of that 'von' before my name, I was often taunted about the defeat of Germany in what was then the Great War, but when my colleagues felt they had gone too far, they flattered me about the cleanliness of the German trenches as compared with the unmitigated filth of the French ones, which seemed the only message which their fathers had learned from the holocaust. Once again, when Caracciola won a race in his supercharged white Mercedes-Benz, I was congratulated as though I had been at the wheel, whereas when the team of green Bentleys won, I received formal condolences. 'Hard cheese, von Ustinov' from my acquaintances, 'Better luck next time, Oosti' from my friends.

I was, for some reason, the acknowledged expert on motor-cars, being able to tell many makes by their sounds alone. In fact, in my younger years, I was a motor-car, to the dismay of my parents. Psychiatry was in its infancy then, both expensive and centred on Vienna. There was no one yet qualified to exorcise an internal combustion engine from a small boy. I know to this day precisely what make of car I was, an Amilcar. Why I chose this spindly little vehicle, with its look of an angry insect, I do not know, but I suspect it was a wish-dream for a tubby little fellow constantly teased about his nascent corpulence to transmogrify himself into a svelte and insubstantial *bolide*.

At one period of my life, I switched on in the morning, and only stopped being a car at night when I reversed into bed, and cut the ignition. It was an admirable escape. I avoided answering questions, and every other contact, rational or unreasonable. It was a luxury I could afford in a safe and immobile world.

It was only during the holidays that the anxieties began, with evidence of another, unhappy part of existence, away from the handclasp of an Anglo-Saxon Jesus, the lime-flavoured water-ices, the smell of new-mown grass on the cricket patch, and the reassurance of Mr Gibbs' uncertain bel canto.

When I was seven years old, we went to Estonia for our summer holiday, my mother and I. No paints were taken. Estonia was then, briefly, an independent republic on the Baltic. Its capital, Tallinn, better known under the Russians and the Teutonic Knights as Reval, was and is a lovely city, compact and crenellated, redolent of the commercial acumen of medieval and pre-medieval northern traders. The country people came to town and walked about barefoot, carrying their shoes in their hands to show they were the proud possessors of such marks of civilization, while, in the neighbouring countryside, horses would still bolt at the sight of motor-cars.

Our purpose in coming to this attractive little country was that my mother's father, Professor Louis Benois, principal of the Academy of Arts in Leningrad, was allowed by the Soviet government to leave the national territory as far as Estonia for a period of one month, in view of his advanced age and contribution to the Soviet arts. We stayed in a datcha in the middle of a forest, and lived a pre-revolutionary Russian life for a while. The raised wooden verandah with its peeling paint and splintering steps, which groaned and creaked at every footfall, was straight out of some Chekhov stage set. The forest whispered, sighed and sometimes roared. It was infested with adders and mushrooms, both poisonous and edible. To be lost in it was to be lost in a fairy-tale, an impenetrable continent of unidentified noises and lingering menace, a taunting, chattering, cajoling prison which seemed to move with you and trick all sense of orientation. Through it, with luck, one could find the sea, a grey primeval shore of clay and boulders washed by fussy waters. It was possible to sculpt with the clay of the beach. Most people bathed and sculpted naked, only dressing again to meet the hazards of the forest and the journey home.

The pervading odours of the datcha were those of mushrooms and of apples drying in the barn, a sweet and pungent mixture which I can recall instantly to this day.

My grandfather made a great impression on me, since he exuded severity and balance despite his age and ill-health. I saw him feebly swatting some flies which circled in great number over our bowls of milk, some of them left to turn to yoghourt. He explained to me that flies were the harbingers of disease, and that it was man's duty to protect himself against these harmless-looking annoyances. I took the fly-swat from him and began laying about me with all the vigour of my young years. After a short while he indicated it was time to stop the chase. Disappointed, I asked him why.

'Because now you are beginning to take pleasure in what you are doing, and killing can never be allowed to become a pleasure.'

'How about the disease?' I asked hopefully.

'Better we should become ill than that we should take pleasure in the death of living things,' he replied quietly, and that was that.

My mother had a toothache one day, an abscess I believe, whereas the engine of my Amilcar was in particularly fine fettle. I changed gear on every conceivable occasion, revving up as I came to every bend in the road, and hooting with my simulated klaxon to warn oncoming traffic of my presence. Suddenly my mother could bear it no more.

'For God's sake, shut up for a moment!' she cried from the depths of a yellow cloche hat.

Her father, who was walking slowly with us, held up an admonishing hand.

'Never shout at him!' he instructed his daughter quietly. 'I know it is irritating, even without a toothache, dear child. But don't think of it as the sound of an automobile, but rather as the sound of his imagination developing, and then, you will see, it will become bearable.'

I understand now why he was known as a great teacher, and I felt even then an immense empathy for him and his undemonstrative wisdom.

Back in London, I agitated for a tie other than the one cherry-red school one which I had to wear on every occasion. I longed for a multi-coloured striped or polka-dotted one like my father. Eventually my mother surrendered and gave me a little money. I went to Harrod's department store with Frieda, and unaccountably returned wearing a black tie. I found my mother in tears, having received a cable ten minutes before my return that her father had died peaceably in Leningrad.

On later holidays, we were compelled to go to Germany so that my father could report to his directors, a Herr Dietz who

71

lived in Cologne, and a Herr Heller, who lived in Berlin. I remember little about those people except the rasping sound of German when it is spoken in the intolerant, dogmatic voice of officialdom, and the querulous diapason of the ladies when they add what they imagine to be a human or sentimental note to the necessary noisiness of the men. I do recollect having to go to the toilet at the house of Herr Heller, who had a reputation for stinginess. This was confirmed when I discovered that the toilet paper was composed of quartered sheets of typing paper with holes in one corner, through which a piece of string attached them to a nail arbitrarily driven into the bathroom wall. These pieces of paper were covered in messages printed in violet ink, many of them marked 'Secret' and some of them 'Most Secret'. How much simpler a method of disposal than all the latter-day complications thought up by those involved in the activities of C.I.A. and F.B.I.! And they say we have advanced in technology!

On that same day, there was a ticker-tape parade in Berlin for a fearless aviatrix of the period called, if I remember rightly, Elly Beinhorn, who had flown from somewhere to somewhere else without incident, thereby advancing the cause of German technology. I watched the parade from Herr Heller's window, and saw Hindenburg himself, yellow and immobile in his car, looking as though he had been inflated like a mattress.

On my grandfather's death, his widow received permission from the Soviet government to emigrate to Berlin, where her daughter, my aunt Olga, lived as an X-ray technician in a hospital. My mother and I visited them in 1933, when I was twelve. Germany was already in a turmoil. Truckloads of horrid-looking men, packed like sardines in a complicity which had something obscene about it, drove through the streets shouting '*Deutschland Erwache!*' (Germany Awake!). If groups of grown men could find no better pastime than that, it boded ill for the rest of us. Jewish shops had already had their windows smashed by the more ardent of these idiots, and the public was weary of the complications of

72

an increasingly impotent democracy. Everything was ugly and ill-natured.

Naturally my aunt went out of her way to find friends of my own age for me, but unfortunately it is no easier to impose friends on children than it is on adults. She found me the son of a neighbour, a brawny little fellow with his hair cut in a 'Berliner Schnitt', rather long on top and shaved to above the ears, the most inaesthetic of all coiffures. He introduced me to his best friend, who was Jewish. It was a few days before the Reichstag fire.

We went into the Grünewald to play, at what I had no idea. As we strolled among the trees, we talked politics. The young neighbour was a convinced Nazi, and spoke highly of the new Germany which would rise from the shameful embers of Versailles. What he said, and also the way he said it, seemed imitated from a source both authoritative and obtuse, probably his father. He also made some long-winded declarations about the purity of the race, and explained how from time immemorial the Jews had infiltrated into the lifeblood of the German people like an amoeba, and that the time had come to remove this foreign body. Surprisingly enough, the Jewish boy agreed with him, nodding the while and assuring me it was all true.

The wood seemed full of young people training German Shepherds, throwing sticks, shouting, making signs. In flurries of leaves these bounding dogs would appear, almost fall over in their dripping eagerness to obey, and leap out of sight again, gripping some object in their fangs. Far from being a place of sylvan repose, the Grünewald was a training ground for some of the wild excesses yet to come. The Shepherds were immense, of heroic mould, and bent to the will of the sheep who exercised them. A group of youths stamped by, singing an old folk-song, now syncopated in the rhythm of a march. Not boy scouts, I was told, but Wandervögel, and their kindly light was beginning to glow from a thousand braziers in Nürnberg.

My two imposed chums lit cigarettes stolen from home, and

73

they told me they did it deliberately to excite the attention of the forest-watcher, who was a pervert seeking any excuse to tie small boys over an ironing board he kept in his forest hut, and belabour their buttocks with a rattan cane. While he flagellated them, he would lecture them on the evils of smoking, or masturbation, or whatever else he had caught them at. After this explanation, the boys offered me a cigarette they had kindly stolen for me, an offer I gratefully declined. I nevertheless kept my eyes open for the forest-watcher, since I was rather less enthusiastic about his hobbies than the two boys, who explained the delights of being flogged with many lurid details, although they admitted they had never been caught, nor did they even know what the evil forest-watcher looked like. It was all part of the underground folklore which fitted all too well with the regimented hounds and the militarized Schubert in the innocent frame of the German forest.

What happened next was to sicken me for good and all. Laying the ranting and the erotica aside, they passed from the theoretical to the practical. They realised they would have to part, like star-crossed lovers, since the weight of race and geo-politics lay too heavy in the balance; mere personal affection had to make way for great historical realities. They had come to a secluded spot for their pale variation on the *Liebestod*, inventing a ritual both repugnant by its ambition and risible by its inadequacy. After they had sworn eternal brotherhood, whatever destiny held in store for them, they proceeded to cut their veins with a rusty kitchen-knife in order to allow their bloods to mingle in an irrefutable gesture of union. Since I had no reason to suppose they knew the difference between veins and arteries, and more importantly since I felt I was going to vomit, I ran all the way home, defying the angry perplexity of the dogs, which were all of a kind to be excited by rapid motion.

'Butterfingers' cried the angry spectators as I dropped the ball for perhaps the thousandth time during one of my last games of cricket at Mr Gibbs'. I could smile. Everyone knew in their hearts now that I was going to drop the ball anyway, and nobody expected me to be able to play the game. Foreign origin, you know. They also failed to realize for far too long that away from the whimsicality and absurd charm of Mr Gibbs' playing fields, others of foreign origin were beginning to invent other games, played to other rules, and eventually, to no rules whatsoever.

5

I had the choice, said my parents, who couldn't afford either, between St Paul's and Westminster Schools. The former wore straw hats, like Harold Lloyd; the latter, top hats like Fred Astaire. I thought that once I was to look ridiculous, I might as well look utterly ridiculous, and opted for Westminster. Officially I was not yet quite of a height to warrant a tail coat, but since I was believed to be still growing, I was spared the ignominious bum-freezer reserved for smaller lads, a kind of black bolero with a collar spilling over the top like froth from a Guinness. As the greater of minute mercies I was given the clothes of an undertaker, together with a furled umbrella, in order, so the school brochure explained, to distinguish the boys from City of London Bank messengers. The final mockery on the head of a fourteen-year-old boy was a top hat, a crown of thorns if not a calvary, especially if your daily way to school took you through a virtual slum.

But there, for a year and a half, my parents wanted me both at home and away, the clearest indication of a love-hate relationship, and so I was sent away to school, not where my lungs might fill with ozone or my skin might burn in the wind, but a tuppenny bus ride away from home. Of all possible compromises this was the most ludicrous and for me, the most onerous. Far away I might have become used to new surroundings much quicker, and revelled in a relative independence, become what they like to call a man, but this was frankly impossible in the shadow of Big Ben, with a bus-stop just underneath the window of my dormitory, and my bus stopping there every five minutes.

Westminster is an exclusive school which has advanced rather happily with the times. It comprises both day-boys and boarders, and nestles in secrecy amid the ecclesiastical surroundings of what might be called the Kremlin of Westminster Abbey. There are arches galore on which to hit your head, steps of time-worn irregularity on which to break your neck, portraits of dead clerics before which to lose your faith. Owing to the proximity of Church House, the quiet bit of greenery known as Little Dean's Yard was invariably the striding ground of deans and bishops in couples, discussing some new posting or administrative detail in terms of opulent secrecy. And there was endless choir practice to rend the air, some of the most appalling sharps and flats ever, emanating from the unbroken voices of unhappy cherubim behind stained glass, evilly lit.

When all the boys were awaiting the daily morning prayers in the Abbey, we looked like a migration of crows which had made a haphazard landing in a field. The pervading atmosphere was doggedly morose and gothic, and our faces began to show the premature signs of that nervous affectation which passes for breeding. This impression was enhanced by the fact that many sons of Members of Parliament were sent to Westminster, so that, whereas their fathers were gripping their lapels in portentous and jowly gravity a stone's throw away, in the House of Commons, the offspring were busy imitating their fathers in school debates, waving notes instead of order papers, and bending their treble voices into all the respectable mannerisms of British oratory.

'Indiah – ' some piping voice would declare, and pause, while its owner, stooped with a premature bookishness, would scan the listeners for signs of inattention – 'Indiah' it would repeat, to drive home a point which needed no driving – 'Indiah cannot be accorded home rule at this – ah – time.' And a groan of 'Hear, hear's' would rise from the audience, punctuated by solitary bleats of 'Shame' from enlightened boy sopranos. I

77

understood very quickly the purpose of education such as this when I was called aside by a master to tell me that I would be involved in a debate, in order to second the motion that 'The Death Sentence should be retained as a deterrent.' I informed the master in charge of debates that I was categorically opposed to the death sentence in all its forms, on moral grounds.

'That may be,' said the master in a silky voice, 'but you are still seconding the motion in favour of retention.'

'I don't understand, sir – '

'You will,' he chanted quietly, and left.

I realized then that this was a school in which lawyers, diplomats and businessmen were formed and there was no room here for the sloppy thinking of those who wished to change society.

I made what I deemed was an excellent speech against the death sentence, but such was the bloodthirsty temper of the times that there was an overwhelming vote in favour of retention, and my reputation as a debater rose in spite of what I had said. My eyes met those of the master. He was smiling slightly and nodded his congratulation at the victory of my side. I was being prepared for life, in more ways than one.

When new boys arrived, they were entertained at tea by the headmaster, who was at that time a clergyman of advanced age with a permanent grin of considerable intensity on his face. I have no doubt that the Very Rev. Dr Costley-White was a good man, but he was also a big man, who walked quickly, so that the wind would make his black gown billow behind him, while the tassel on his mortar-board spread over his face like a claw, and he frankly terrified new boys. When, during that initial tea-party, he called out, 'Will no boy select the chocolate éclair?' there was no response, because no boy dared. 'Oh very well,' cried Dr Costley-White, and ate it himself.

After that benign and warm-hearted introduction to my new school, my hopes rose, in spite of being what was known as a 'fag' (not to be confused with the modern American usage of the word as a camp description of a homosexual. A fag in England was either a cigarette, or else the nearest thing to a slave since William Wilberforce, a small boy at the beck and call of a big one). I was serving some kippers to the prefects in the medieval dining-hall, which was one of the functions of fagging, when Dr Costley-White swept into the room, his landing flaps down and his hat at a jaunty angle. His smile was spread from ear to ear as usual.

A pin-up photo had been discovered, he bellowed, a pin-up of a woman in a bathing costume, clutching a beach-ball. He wished the perpetrator of this filth to own up at once. There was, of course, silence.

'Very well,' he declared, as his smile attained even more extraordinary proportions. 'When the culprit is found – and found, he will be – I shall beat him!'

And then, very gently, as a summer breeze after his squall, 'I am in the need of exercise.'

As he turned to go, his gathering speed caused his gown to billow once again. I had the feeling he would take off as soon as he was out of sight.

Of course, what constitutes filth and the mysteries of sex have always been a cause of contention in British schools. An old friend and mentor, Sir Clifford Norton, told me about sex education in Rugby before the First World War. The headmaster, who must have been an enlightened man, summoned all the boys who had reached the age of puberty to his study, and after reassuring himself that the door was firmly secured, made the following brief announcement. 'If you touch it, it will fall off.'

The boys were then invited to file back into their classes, now equipped to face adult life.

Many years later, Britain was still irked by this elusive yet fascinating subject. Arriving at a theatre for a performance of a play of mine, I ran into a fellow actor of our troupe, Cyril Luckham, a true friend and magnificent performer who happens also to have very fair skin and hair. He gave every evidence of having wept. It is always disturbing when grown men are reduced to tears, so I took him aside and asked him tactfully what was the matter. He replied that nothing was the matter apart from laughter which had been racking him intermittently for the past couple of hours, and of course laughter and tears leave very similar after-effects, especially in those of fair pigmentation.

He let me in on the cause of his joy. It was, apparently, the first day of a new term at his son's school. The headmaster, obeying the instructions of a government by now aware of the dangers of ignorance, was compelled to explain the facts of life to those of a certain age-group. The poor man had been rehearsing his speech all through the summer recess, and eventually, in a panic of prudery, unable to bear the sniggers he could already hear in his head, he was reduced to composing a pamphlet, published at his own expense, which every boy found lying on his desk as the new term began.

This pamphlet began with the following seven words: 'You may have noticed, between your legs . . .'

This unreal atmosphere pervaded Westminster School, but the sheltered charm which had characterized Mr Gibbs' had gone for ever. Von Ribbentrop was the new German Ambassador in London, and as a good Nazi, hoped to send his son to Eton, perhaps in order to take photographs of the playing fields, and find out exactly what Wellington had meant when he had alleged that Waterloo had been won there. Eton, jealous of its secrets, refused young Rudolf. The ambassador, in a rage, demanded that the youth be taken at Westminster. Perhaps he had already bought his top hat, since these were worn in both places. At all events, the British Government, in its habitual dither of appeasement, exerted pressure on Westminster to accept the lad, and lo, a huge white Mercedes with external exhaust pipes panted its way into Little Dean's Yard every morning, picking its gargantuan way among the parked mini-cars of visiting bishops, and disgorged him, dressed like the rest of us, but with the Nazi party youth badge, swastika, eagle and all, prominently and incongruously displayed in his lapel. For a moment he and the embassy chauffeur engaged in hushed conversation, and then both leapt to attention, lifted their right arms as though a military marriage was being celebrated beneath them, shouted 'Heil Hitler!' and Rudolf hurried in to morning prayers while the chauffeur picked his way meticulously into the open traffic once again.

He was an overgrown and shy fellow with glasses, reddish hair and freckles, who kept very much to himself, and yet it was impossible not to notice a smirk on his face as he walked past on the one day in the week devoted to the parade of the O.T.C., the Officers' Training Corps. Britain's well-bred youth were in training then, but if you were to ask what we were training for, I would be compelled to answer that it was for Dunkirk and a series of military disasters in the best tradition.

I stood stiffly to attention in my 1914 military uniform, my puttees either working loose, which occasioned a sense of relief, or else so tightly tied that all feeling had long since departed from my legs. My cap was pulled very low over my eyes, which is in the tradition of the Brigade of Guards and is supposed to give soldiers a correct military stance, although I privately believe it is to make the men share the blindness of their leaders. In my hand I carried a rattle, like those used by spectators at football matches. The reason for this was twofold; not only were there insufficient rifles to go round, but I represented an entire machine-gun company by myself.

Once a week, I lay in the wet bracken in Richmond Park, swinging my rattle, and killing thousands and thousands of adversaries and occasionally, owing to my bulk, which was difficult to camouflage, being killed myself. In this way we were preparing for the next war to end wars, alive to the most modern battle techniques, and ready to 'hit the Hun for six'.

It was almost a relief to get back into the absurd costume of every day after these military masquerades. At least I could look von Ribbentrop in the eye. Not far away, at the German Embassy, my father was in trouble with his father. By now promoted to the rank of Press Attaché, Klop was more and more frequently reprimanded for not distorting the news at source, but giving the editors in Berlin all the trouble. He was reaching the end of the line. With the help of Sir Robert Vansittart, he applied for British nationality secretly, printing his mandatory intention of doing so in a Welsh language newspaper which defied the expertise of German Intelligence. One morning he walked out of the Embassy, never to return.

At precisely that time, young von Ribbentrop entered the school art competition with an atrocious triptych depicting ancient Germans encamped before a blazing dawn, their horned helmets silhouetted against the red and mauve of the empyrean, while the breastplates of the flaxenhaired women were aglint with hateful optimism. This huge work was entitled 'Armed Strength', and was, of course, totally devoid of mystery.

I earned my first money thanks to von Ribbentrop, which was perhaps justice, although hardly poetic. I wrote a piece about his artistic efforts, an original manner for a young party-member to emulate his Führer, and sent it to the *Evening Standard*. They printed it, having altered it somewhat, I thought for the worse, and they sent me a letter asking if seven shillings and sixpence would be adequate remuneration. I forgot to answer their letter, and they sent me a pound, thereby rewarding both my malice and my procrastination.

There was an immediate upheaval at school. The German Embassy was, apparently, absolutely furious. The housemaster, a retired opera singer by name Mr Bonhote, called me into his study. The school, as usual, was thoroughly ill-informed about the most recent events, and believed my father still to be an employee of the German Foreign Office. Mr Bonhote asked me, in confidence, to bring the matter to my father's attention, in order to trace the identity of the culprit. The *Evening Standard* had evidently already refused to cast any light on the origin of the leak.

I didn't think the matter was of sufficient urgency to warrant my disturbing my father's peace of mind, and so I merely allowed a couple of weeks to elapse before returning to Mr Bonhote in order to tell him that the most thorough investigation had failed to reveal the name of the villain. All I was able to confirm was that the German Embassy was, indeed, furious.

Mr Bonhote grunted. 'I can't help feeling that whoever is responsible will go far in life. Damned clever.'

'Yes,' I agreed gravely. 'Still one doesn't want to encourage that kind of thing, does one, sir?'

'No,' he replied, and then added with a twinkle, 'of course, some people don't need encouragement.'

In a short while von Ribbentrop returned to Germany and became Foreign Minister, and Rudolf departed with his father to complete his preparations for the conquest of the world.

My father had, meanwhile, fallen on evil days. I was withdrawn from the boarding section of the school to become a day-boy, because it was cheaper, and even then I had the uncomfortable feeling that my school bills had remained unpaid. The school behaved with exemplary elegance, however, never making me feel that the penury mattered, or making my parents feel that their plight was in any way out of the ordinary.

Jobs were offered my father, but he couldn't hold them down. At one point he became art critic for the *News Chronicle*, and I knew perfectly well from his ranting behind my mother's easel and his inflexibly epicurean opinions that this could never last. At the end of his first week he poured scorn on a sculpture of Henry Moore's in his jocular and punning fashion, and was amazed at the uproar which ensued. That was that. He was then employed as an accountant at the Vaudeville Theatre. From his inability to help me with my homework, I could hold out no greater hope for this venture, and, indeed, it too lasted a week.

I felt immensely sorry for him, since he was humiliated by his inactivity, which took the form of fits of anger interspersed with periods of sullenness. He considered my reports from school a disgrace, he continued to harp on his own prowess as a scholar, and he called me lazy, which was undeniably true. I had foolishly gone on the modern side as opposed to the classical side in school, simply because two or three of my friends had taken that course, and now I was faced by mathematics, physics and science on a scale unprecedented before.

Of physics I could understand nothing at all. Why imaginary wheels should gather speed running down hypothetical slopes, and create friction, I could neither understand in the terms in which it was taught, nor care about. As for chemistry, the acrid smell of the lab made me queasy to start with, and I was always distinctly nervous of spilling any substance smelling stronger than water on my fingers.

The master in charge of science was called F. O. M. Earp, from which his nickname of Fome, or Foam. He was a man so utterly dedicated to the abstractions of science that he would often point a finger between two boys and tell 'that boy' to see him afterwards. Since he never managed to aim at anyone in particular, nobody ever came to see him, and by then he had forgotten the incident anyway. Once he mixed a couple of liquids in a test-tube. There was a most resounding explosion, breaking several panes of glass in the lab. When the smoke cleared, there was no sign of Fome. He had disappeared, as in a fairy-tale. There was an audible gasp from the boys, caught between shock and laughter. Then, slowly, he emerged from behind his desk, black, singed, and dishevelled. 'What did I do wrong, you?' he said in unemotional tones, pointing between me and my neighbour.

The whole classroom broke into a roar of relieved laughter.

Fome did not even smile.

'Come and see me afterwards, the boy responsible for the laughter.'

Needless to say, I didn't, and nor did my neighbour.

Owing to the shortage of teachers even then, Fome was

supposed to teach not only chemistry, but also divinity, of which he knew very little. He got around this difficulty, which might have daunted many less inventive spirits, especially in such unrelievedly ecclesiastical surroundings, by proceeding to explain most of Christ's miracles scientifically. It was clear from his attitude that even if he had mustered a little faith in Christ, he had absolutely none in the miracles. I do not remember in detail every one of his explanations, but do recollect him attributing the illusion of water turning into wine to the surreptitious addition of permanganate of potash, which could quite easily have bamboozled a crowd of simpletons.

In the field of sports, I had put my name down for tennis, the only sport for which I felt any real affinity, but this was refused owing to a limited number of courts available, and I was made to row. This seemed to me a monotonous and draughty pursuit, and somehow wasteful to be making all that effort in order to be going in the wrong direction. It is, in any case, never very reassuring for a young person of my weight to be seated in a boat seemingly made of cigar wrappers, and overlapping its sides.

I eventually took an inadvertent revenge on my tormentors during a 'friendly' encounter with the second, or third eight of another school. The old boy who had presented the school with the boat I was rowing in was bicycling along the riverside pathway bellowing incomprehensible instructions to us through a megaphone. He was in his sixties and affected the dress of a schoolboy in order to give us the garbled weight of his experience. Meanwhile the other school slipped gradually from view. At first I could see nine men out of the corner of my eye, then eight, then seven, eventually nothing but a little disturbed water.

Then came an end to my misery. The fragile little seat beneath me was derailed, and fell sideways. I immediately 'caught a crab', and in attempting to resist the pressure of the water on my oar, I pushed the wheel of my seat through the hull. We began sinking, and there is no sight more ludicrous than eight men with a small ninth the size of a jockey facing them, settling gracefully into the

85

water in Indian file. The veteran on the shore, who had spent a lot of money on the boat, moaned, but since the sound of his distress was distorted by the megaphone, he became as grotesque as everything else. We drifted helplessly into the side of a Dutch ship moored in the Thames, whose crew, far from helping us, bent over the rail and laid bets as to which of them could hit us squarest with gobs of spit. After that, miraculously, room was found for me on the tennis court. I learned yet another lesson.

I could at times beat members of the school tennis team in unofficial games, but I was only once in the team myself, and that was as a reserve. I came to the conclusion that there was something disconcerting about my personality as far as games masters were concerned, and that the undefinable quality which consistently got me out of trouble also kept me from being taken seriously as an athlete. Although I had inherited my mother's gifts as a sprinter, and had insufficient breath for the mile, and though my elevation and projection were entirely inadequate for jumps high or long, I was and, dare I say it, even am, surprisingly quick around the tennis court. In other words, when I see the point in moving quickly, I am capable of it.

In order to restore my morale, which was rather low at this time, I entered a tournament at a wonderfully nostalgic organization called the 'Anglo-Russian Sports Club', where septuagenarian Czarist officers would lob each other to a standstill in immaculate whites. There was an aged sergeant-major in charge of the changing-room, bald as an egg, with a pointed white beard and a fixed pair of blue eyes, who would click his heels at the end of every curt sentence. He would take orders for kasha, blinis and pickled herring in the canteen as well as leap at you with hot towels as you emerged from the tepid shower. Life was good on the *Potemkin* before the mutiny, at least for the officers. I won my little tournament, and a pile of ashtrays in various colours which I still guard jealously as though they were *objets* by Fabergé.

The reason my morale was low was not only due to frustrations, both at home and at school, but also to the ominous hurdle

My great-great-grandfather.
Michael Adrianovich Ustinov.
who lived to 108, building 16 churches
and leaving 6000 serfs

His son, Gregori Michaelovich Ustinov.
who enjoyed dissipation for
just over 50 years

Catterino Cavos, who wrote operas
in the Italian manner on Russian themes

Rescued by Lord Napier, after the Battle of Magdala:
in centre, my Ethiopian great-grandmother holding my grandmother

Engagement picture of my
father's parents, Venice 1885

My father appears

A few Benois at the
starting-post. My mother is
the small able-seaman
in the foreground

My mother's parents,
in the country near
St Petersburg

My father
and his aeroplane
in the Great War

My father and his brother Peter preparing to be Red Barons

As my mother saw me

As the camera saw us both

My daughter Andrea, aged 8, in front
of my mother's portrait of me, aged 4

Fred Astaire in
preference to Harold Lloyd

I was sketching
Yehudi Menhuin,
Sir Robert Vansittart
and Bernard Shaw,
my elbow resting on
an unknown Archbishop

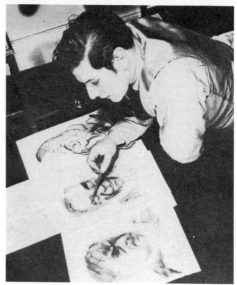

Igor Ustinov,
my son, sketching
a carriage some
years later

The Goose Steps Out

With Isolde in
Green Park the day
after the opening
of *House of Regrets*

Sir Bernard Miles, Walter Crisham, Vida Hope, Peter Ustinov
in Herbert Farjeon's *Diversion,* the only non-nude show
in wartime London for a time

Peter Ustinov, John Byron, Edith Evans.
Joan Haythorne in *The Rivals*

of examinations, called 'O'-levels today, but called the School Certificate then, which plague youths in all countries and at all times. Rumours abounded then as they abound today. You couldn't even get a job as a dustman without one. In case of war, it meant permanent relegation to the ranks. The majority of suicides in Japan were occasioned by a failure in exams. And so on and so forth.

There was little or no hope of my passing them, at least on the modern side. Despite my prowess in certain subjects, I was absolutely without a vestige of hope in the general field of science and mathematics, and that was going to ruin my chances of advancement. At home, I hardly received any encouragement, although, to be fair, I doubt whether encouragement would have done much good.

My father's temper had become a little more equitable as he became used to the new situation. His counter-attack against misfortune expressed itself in different ways. Once every few months he would declare that he was writing a novel. There was to be no noise in the flat. He settled in the living room while we tiptoed around the small space left over. At the end of the day he would emerge with a single page of foolscap, as full of corrections, scratchings, and emendations as a manuscript of Beethoven. He would then read the first page to us. When we had laughed – the style was unrelievedly epigrammatic – he would then read this page to visitors and guests over the next six weeks or so, until the novelty had worn off, when all would be quiet until the start of the next novel, and history repeated itself. It is not so much a matter of literary record as of interest to the *Guinness Book of Records* that my father wrote six or seven of the shortest novels ever.

When inspiration flagged, he involved himself in art-dealing, an area in which he was at first more enthusiastic than knowledgeable, but he quickly revealed something perhaps even more important than mere knowledge, which was flair. Although he made many minor errors of judgement, he would, on big

87

occasions, take an atlas of the British Isles and a pin, and sit there like a medium awaiting a call. When he heard it he stabbed the atlas, put on his hat, took his walking-stick, and left the flat in silence.

As a result of these mysterious celestial communications, he returned from Tewkesbury of all places, with a Rubens study for the Farnese bull in sanguine, which he then sold to the Rijksmuseum in Amsterdam for £1,000, a very modest figure even for those days, but a magnificent windfall for him. He would then remain inactive apart from perhaps a novel or two until the money ran out, when he would once again reach for the atlas and the pin. Other jaunts into the English countryside produced several little oil sketches by Hogarth for Butler's *Hudibras*, long lost, to say nothing of a Bonnington or two, a few Constantine Guys, a Daumier, and eventually a collection of Renaissance bronzes.

My mother seemed less affected by the events of the day than either of us, since it was she who kept our ship on a relatively even keel. Her reputation as a painter was established, and she was even represented in such reputable galleries as the Tate and the Carnegie Institute. Apart from her sale of pictures, she was known as a designer, especially for the ballet. Her work for the Ballet Rambert included 'The Descent of Hebe', 'Bonnet Over the Windmill', 'Lady into Fox', and 'Dark Elegies' for Anthony Tudor. When this last work was produced in America, under the extraordinary system then prevailing, her designs and costumes were attributed to the distinguished American designer Raymond Sovey. When, many years later, I performed my play *Romanoff and Juliet* on Broadway, I used the sets of M. Jean-Denis Malclès, a leading French artist. We were permitted to use the sets on condition there was no acknowledgement whatsoever of their origin. I have never understood how a professional union could have so little respect for its own dignity or integrity to make rules like that. Are stage-designers so much lower a species than painters pure and simple? If not, then why do the same ridiculous rules not apply to painters? Why are the Michelangelos in the

National Gallery in Washington not attributed to Ben Shahn, or the Velasquez to Jackson Pollack?

In any case, these are reflections out of context based on a very ancient sense of outrage. At the time, I was merely shocked by the fact that my mother's work could not be appreciated as hers in the United States. She spent more and more time in the theatre, doing many sketches in the wings of the Compagnie Quinze, the French avant-garde troupe run by Michel Saint-Denis. He had just emigrated to England in order to open a drama school. My mother, who after all came from the Benois family as I have said, a clan who would have flinched had they thought for a moment that one of their scions was destined for the Stock Exchange, and have suggested sculpture as a safer profession, now looked the facts squarely in the face. She recognized with a greater sense of reality than either Klop or I that I was not going to pass the School Certificate, and that it would cause the most terrible commotions in the household when the news of my failure was known. Why should I be put through this moral mangle, she argued, when I had no intention of being a chemist, or a doctor, or even a chartered accountant? Had I not held the attention of small audiences with my imitations? And what is the difference between small audiences and large ones except their size?

My father raised objections, of course, for the sake of form, but his energies were more and more taken with the inevitability of war. Distinguished Germans came to the flat to listen to Hitler's latest speeches, and lament at the blindness of the Western democracies. Even at school, the ominous atmosphere made itself felt as the Spanish Civil War was going badly for the legitimate government of Spain, while the German and Italian dictatorships were being encouraged by our benign negligence to go from excess to excess.

There were mock elections in my house before I left Westminster, encouraged by the headmaster under the guise of citizenship. We all made speeches and campaigned, and whereas it was natural in such a school that the Conservatives would win, there was a feeling of shock and even of dismay at the showing of the Liberals and Socialists, especially when we united in a kind of Front Populaire to form what was called the United Front of Progressive Forces, or Uffpuff. The headmaster met our delegation to reassure himself that we were neither subversive nor undemocratic in spirit, and when he found we were merely exasperated with the smugness of the Conservative majority, he blessed us with one of his more extravagant smiles.

I mention this with absolutely no wish to attribute any importance to our activities, but it is rather remarkable on retrospect that feelings ran high in one of the nobler seats of learning as early as 1937, and that the young were almost equally divided between unflinching support for the appeasement of Mr Chamberlain and a desire to resist aggression before it was too late. There were those, young and inexperienced and foolish in many other ways, who were wise before the event. I did not participate in many of the subsequent arguments, because I took an audition at M. Saint-Denis' Academy at Islington. Typically, I failed to understand the terms of the audition. One of the stipulations was to choose a page of any celebrated drama and learn it by heart. It did not occur to me that I was supposed to learn a single part, and that the other parts would be read by senior students, so I just took an arbitrary page of Shaw's *St Joan* and learned all the parts. My procedure seemed to amuse M Saint-Denis and George Devine, who was one of the other professors, and I was accepted even though they considered me, at sixteen, to be on the young side.

My mother begged them to take me, adding that, in her opinion, I had eyes very like M. Saint-Denis.

The great man studied me shamelessly through the swirling smoke of his pipe, and agreed.

'He has good eyes,' he said, in his French accent, and then added, with a sense of drama – 'But, you realize, Nadia, that there will be divorce, there will be unpleasantness, there will be scandal, but *it must be like that*!'

His eyes lifted heavenward to await confirmation of his

mystique, and I was launched into the world of adults, even if I was a little on the young side.

— You have been quiet for a long while now.
— I have been reflecting on various aspects of your story, and reflecting mainly on the kind of tricks which memory plays – not memory perhaps as much as time.
— Have you spotted any inaccuracies?
— Oh, inaccuracies there are bound to be in the story of one man, because after all, most things in life are matters of opinion. No, it is not that which disturbs me. Take Westminster School, for instance, and Mr Gibbs' Preparatory School for Boys. Did we hate them or love them? Or perhaps, were we indifferent in the main?
— There were days on which we loved them, Gibbs more than Westminster perhaps, and days we hated them, Westminster perhaps more than Gibbs, and yet on the whole they were ways of life, inevitable, boring, routine which we had no strong feelings about.
— Indifference then?
— Not indifference exactly; you can't live in the shadow of punishment or indeed reward and be indifferent.
— D'you remember that horrid boy who used to stick a rusty hypodermic needle into his victims?
— Indeed I do. Lived in Markham Square.
— Absolutely correct. Name of –
— Quiet! He's probably a high court judge by now, and utterly respectable. That dangerous needle may have been his first and only, and perhaps even necessary, contact with crime.
— You never can tell. Remember that timid boy, Wakeford, with an inability to pronounce his 'r's? Victoria Cross. Heroism in battle.
— Exactly. And that joyous little gnome, Wedgwood Benn? And

Michael Flanders, agile and slim in pre-polio days? Only Donald Swann hasn't changed at all.

— Well there you are. We know what we feel about these colleagues now. What did we feel about them then?

— Much the same as we feel today. Remember that fellow, such a great buddy of yours at school, who burst into your dressing-room at Boston, and turned out to have become saturated in alcohol?

— Yes, of course, I remember, since he didn't confine himself to Boston. He burst into your dressing-room in Toronto and London as well, lamenting that he'd just lost his job with the airlines.

— What was he?

— A pilot, I believe.

— Yes, well there you are. Among my matters of reflection while you have been busy with your narrative are friends. Contrary to general belief, I do not believe that friends are necessarily the people you like best, they are merely the people who got there first. Most of my friends have faults which are all the more blatant because of their proximity, and yet they are people you are never out for if they ring. Even with your drunk, you let him into your dressing-room on three different occasions because you were animated by ancient and guilty feelings of friendship. And yet there are many people you meet casually with whom you could be the best of friends if only you had met them sooner. All in all, I don't believe you choose your friends any more than you choose your parents. After all, if you were able to choose your friends with the same application and caution with which you choose your wife, you'd have antagonized most of them years ago, and lost them. No, no, you drift into friendships, and there is no divorce. You are stuck with most of them for life. And friendship revives quickly even after a long absence, often with people who are entirely reprehensible, unreliable and even spiteful.

— Does that mean you are opposed to friendship?

— On the contrary, I wouldn't know what to do without it. Sometimes a friend will ask, usually after making a normal gesture to which he wishes to attribute abnormal or even charitable characteristics, 'After all, what are friends for?' I'll tell him what friends are for. They are there to remind each and every one of us of the imperfections which surround us, of the vagaries of human nature, the unpleasantness of which man is capable, the meanness, the narrowness, the hypocrisy of society; and they also teach us to forgive, but never to forget. We would all be lost without friendship.

— How about pets, what are they for? Our *dumb* friends?

— They remind us that whereas man is an animal, alas, animals, thank God, are not men.

— With all that liveliness in you, how can you even discuss indifference?

— You cannot have opinions about everything under the sun. You cannot be interested in everything. There just isn't the energy. And one aspect about living which psychologists too often ignore is stamina. Why is only the object you are looking at in focus? It would be too exhausting to have everything in your field of vision in focus all the time. Why do you daydream? To recover your strength – permanent attention is impossible. Even the eyelid blinks. And so it is with our emotions. There may be a time to love and a time to hate, but most of the time is spent doing neither. Indifference is restful when it is negative, insulting when it is positive. It can be cultivated. Voltaire could have said '*Il faut cultiver son désert.*' I would be willing to swear that more tragedies are due to human indifference than to human engagement, and yet, it is the guardian of our balance, the bandage round our ills, the refuge in the maelstrom.

— Are you indifferent then?

— I can be passionate now about that which I treated with indifference then.

93

— Why?
— Perhaps because had I spent my passion on such people, places, or events long ago, I might have been left with only indifference today. It's all a question of stamina.
— Stamina?

6

It was a new and invigorating experience to go to school dressed as I wished. Since I only had one suit, however, bought from an organization of lunatic optimism called the Fifty Shilling Tailors, this solitary mark of independence constituted a uniform of a kind. It was not until I had scraped together enough to purchase some grey flannel trousers and a tawdry blazer that I felt the full flush of liberty. I, who was unused to the problems of choice, was often minutes late for class, largely because I couldn't decide which of my two outfits to wear.

Money was, of course, yet another problem. Earlier, in an unaccustomed fit of paternal munificence, my father had solemnly proclaimed that the time had come for me to receive pocket money. He then produced a shilling out of his pocket, and told me that this would be my weekly salary. I was, not unnaturally, as delighted by the gesture as I was disappointed by the amount. As an avid listener to my father's novels, I could have spared myself my emotions, however, since this shilling was the first and last pocket money I ever received. Whenever I reminded Klop of it, he either denied that a week had yet elapsed since my last payment (What payment? Don't be impertinent!), or else he told me in no uncertain terms that I was a spendthrift and a wastrel, which was a little like telling Gandhi he was overweight.

It was not that he was in any sense stingy, it was just that the possession of money did not seem to him an important step on the way to civilized living. Once he did not admit the perils of poverty to his own well-being, there was no reason why he should admit them for those less gifted than he in the refusal of reality. It was for that reason that I sometimes wished he would realize that he was poor instead of being that most nerve-racking of phenomena, a rich man without money. And yet, one could hardly blame him for looking facts in the face, and seeing nothing. Even if it gave me moments of anxiety, there was always the consolation that he was affected not at all by penury. Humiliations, real or imagined slights, indignities, offences, all took their toll of him, but when short of cash he merely slapped his pockets as though trying to trace elusive assets which had never been there, and expressed irritation that other people had no sense of order. Then, his wallet empty, he went shopping and invited people to dinner.

Naturally, anybody with any financial sense at all will realize that I couldn't have survived on no money whatsoever, especially as my drama school was at the other end of London. It was, of course, my mother who gave me what she could from secret funds – the sale of a picture, housekeeping money, dribs and drabs – God only knows how she made sense of it all, puffing away at her easel with incredible serenity, cigarette smoke coiling up to the ceiling, closed by now even to my father's counsels. Perhaps it was the Revolution which had taught her to live for the moment, without ever succumbing to the temptation of living in moments past as did so many other émigrés.

My requests for money were never exorbitant. I had too much respect for the difficulties of living for that, but of course, quite apart from my new-found freedom of dress, I was for the first time plunged into the world of girls.

I had been to dances, where I had been an active and determined wallflower, believing that the bodily contacts of waltz and tango went for naught once the mind was fully occupied in chopping out a complicated rhythm. In other words, I was not a natural dancer, by shape or inclination. To me, it was more mathematics than choreography, and the penalty for an error was more palpable and eloquent than it had been at school, a tearing of delicate material or a howl of agony. I even found the courage, at a later date, to decline a charming invitation to dance with the Queen (or should it be a command?), by warning her of the physical dangers attendant on such an initiative. British democracy having matured over the centuries, my distress was greeted with a gracious smile by Elizabeth II, whereas under Elizabeth I it would no doubt have cost me my head, although, to be fair, I would have had less compunction in trotting out a gay galliard with Elizabeth I, since the volume of her clothes would have made it an act of positive malevolence instead of one of mere incompetence to have flattened her royal toes.

I had even, on holiday, bathed naked in mountain pools with girls and women, under the aegis of a nature-loving godmother, whose hiking habits invariably ended in some glacial mountain torrent as an act of communion with the earth, but here again, the numbing temperature of the water took the same precedence as had the rhythm in the dance, to the exclusion of all other possible emotions.

Here, at drama school, I was for the first time exposed to the permanent presence of a veritable battalion of girls, all dressed on the first day of term in black bathing costumes – all that is, except one, a Canadian girl called Betty – I will refrain from identifying her further – whose black costume had not yet arrived, and who crouched among us in salmon-pink bloomers and a bra, looking like a Rubens nymph who had wandered into a sinister witches' coven by mistake.

Real life had begun, very late in life, and in the happy absence of my father, my eye could wander over the graceful features unguided and free from extraneous comment. I needed pocket money as never before.

I was not irresistibly drawn to the drama. It was an escape road from the dismal rat-race of school, but I never understood how actors learn all those lines, and, I must admit, I do not understand it to this day, any more than I understand how a pianist remembers all those notes. I had, however, started writing plays at school. The first one, I remember, was a comedy-farce-melodrama-tragedy involving Chicago gangsters in the English countryside. It was fifteen pages long, and designed as a full-length play. There were four or five deaths per page, which meant that it had a huge, expendable cast. I was caught writing it during a maths lesson at Westminster, and punished by being forced to stay in late. Since I was the only boy so punished on that particular day, the master in charge of the punishment class felt himself victimized, and left me to my own devices, which merely meant that for once I could continue writing under virtually ideal circumstances. The school had the last laugh, however, since the play was lousy.

After that, I had written others: a play called *Jackson*, a somewhat Priestleyish affair about an average man, but as I knew nothing about average men, it turned out rather peculiar; a Pirandello-like drama entitled *Uneasy Lies the Head*, in which the characters created by a reprehensible dramatist come to life and badger him into an introspective suicide; a drama in verse about Maximilian of Mexico called, unavoidably *La Paloma*; and the most indicative if not the best of a particularly poor lot, the only autobiographical work I have ever written in the guise of fiction, a play called *Trio* about a father, a mother and a son, in which there was more bickering and more mental and physical disorder than in *Look Back in Anger*, and, of course, far less dramatic discipline as well.

If it did nothing else for me, my work on this play, which was never finished, convinced me that my one aim in life was to leave home. I did not for a moment wish to run away. I am not the type, and in any case, it was too late for gestures. I wished to continue the contact with my parents, who fascinated me, from a position of dignity and independence. I also felt, rightly or wrongly, that my absence would enable my parents to rediscover what they had first seen in each other during the brief nine months before I arrived to complicate things.

I had been treated as a child-like adult for so long that

I had an enormous impatience to be responsible for myself, and to be professional. I admired my mother's application, her staying-power, the ability to outlast a problem which must have been the heritage of centuries of artisans, from architects to pastrycooks, from court-musicians to makers of cheese for family consumption, each function as important as the other, a balance to be found between logic and inspiration in infinite patience and infinite pains, the state of grace which comes with utter concentration.

At the same time, I mistrusted my father's facility, his mercurial and whimsical changes of direction as his mind was blown weightlessly hither and thither during the social banter in which he so excelled. He was a delight to his friends; perhaps even more so to his acquaintances. It was only in company that he flourished with an impermanent radiance peculiar to him, merely to relapse into an ill-tempered, querulous gloom when the last guest had departed.

I knew that I had both these elements within myself, the dogged and tenacious as well as the urbane, and with the earnestness of youth, I set about consciously making the best of the turmoil of my natural inheritance. Already at Mr Gibbs' School I had become sickened by my own cowardice, my squeamishness in the face of pain, my panic when confronted by strange dogs or flying cricket balls, and I had deliberately, to my watching mother's horror, entered the school diving competition without knowing the first thing about it and climbed up to the highest diving-board. With all the school and all the parents watching, there was no way back. From up there, I saw the green water below which looked much like a stamp on an envelope, and I wondered what guarantee there was that I would not miss the water altogether and end up, a red smudge on the gleaming tiles. Taking myself by surprise – it was the only way to do it – I made a graceful gesture in the air, rather like the Rolls-Royce mascot, and fell, a tangled ball of flesh, until I heard a tremendous explosion, and fingers of chlorine bored their way brutally into my nostrils. My stomach felt as though it had been unzipped. 'You must remember to keep your feet together,' called out the expert, but I could hardly hear him over the wailing sirens in my ears.

Nobody was to know, in spite of their amused smiles, that what had really occurred in that swimming-pool was a victory which I had won over myself, even if I brought myself and my house no glory. Now I had another kind of timidity to conquer, the absurd and the unnecessary one in the face of girls. I felt for the wretched Betty, crouching like Susannah in her salmon-pink lingerie on the first day of a new life for us all. It could not have happened to a less fortunate victim.

Whenever we had to read from classical texts, she was invariably selected for the interpretation of amorous or, what was worse, suggestive poetry by the saucy giants of the past, and even discreet references like 'the sweet disorder of her dress' caused the unhappy Betty to stammer and to giggle, turning a deep accusing red, and casting a veil of embarrassment about her. Her calvary came in a play of Beaumont and Fletcher when her partner in a dramatic text was supposed to say 'Then will I pay a visit to the Low Countries,' in a thinly disguised reference not to the Netherlands so much as to the nether reaches of the human body. This was too much for poor Betty, whose convulsive giggles eventually turned to bitter tears. I hope she is happily married, far from the coaxing reach of libertine poets, for she helped me to realize that my problems were negligible compared with some.

Michel Saint-Denis, a tweedy Frenchman with a short Roman nose, nostrils flared like those of a nervous horse, teeth gripping a dribbling pipe, short yellow hair covering his huge head and lapping his neck like little waves, was a formidable figure, dedicated to the theatre as a priest is dedicated to his God. There was permanent amusement in his eye, a lip twisted to accommodate the pipe, and the dangerous look of a minotaur assessing the quality of the human sacrifices offered up for his gratification.

For one whole term, we were asked to be an animal of our

choice, in order to 'broaden our imaginations'. The more ambitious and energetic pupils selected wild predators or gossamer victims, according to their temperaments. Poor Betty trotted around, an elk from her native plains, entangling her antlers with imaginary thickets and being hunted by erotic braves, while a South African girl with acne outran Betty in both speed and archness as an okapi. She ended the term pounds lighter and in a depressed frame of mind.

Gifted with my habitual foresight in the face of the unusual, I decided to be a salamander, and just dozed comfortably in the sun for three whole months, occasionally tilting a quizzical eye at the members of the faculty, and darting out my tongue to ensnare an unwary fly. This exercise certainly revealed more about my character than it did about what goes on in the heads of lizards.

There was, at the beginning, a great and salutary emphasis on physical suppleness, an art in which we were instructed by a little lady called Gerda Rink, who worked on my discordant limbs as though I had the makings of a Nijinsky. Her patience and kindness were rewarded as far as I was able, which was not much, although I did become aware of the possibilities of physical co-ordination, and recognize its importance for an actor.

A Mr Scott and Miss Iris Warren worked hard on our breathing and our voices, my own gradually increasing in power from the inaudible mumbling which my natural shyness had imposed upon me. I made slow yet perceptible progress in the purely physical branches of my chosen art, but the reports were perhaps more penetrating and unkind than any I had yet received at Westminster or Mr Gibbs'.

'Has a long way to go', 'He is still lamentably stiff', 'He seems to find great difficulty in walking, or running, or jumping', 'His mind wanders easily during gymnastics', 'His voice is unresonant and very monotonous' – there was no end to the well-meaning but stern prognostications about the dimness of my prospects, and my father, who had by now abandoned his monocle for glasses for fear of appearing Prussian, read these remarks with growing alarm.

'At your age,' he would say, 'I was supple as a willow, I jumped, ran, and walked most outstandingly, my mind never wandered whatever the subject, my voice was powerful and sparkling with colour. Nothing will come of you. Nothing.'

He had gained in assurance since he had now found employment, the nature of which was so secret that it was obvious. There were often strange visitors in our flat, English colonels with so little to say that their very appearance seemed like an uncrackable code, foreign gentlemen who darted meaning looks at each other, then quickly pretended they hadn't. An aura of the unspoken and the unspeakable hung over our home, and I was exhorted to ask no questions, ever, which, of course, automatically gave me half the answers.

When my father had left the German Foreign Office, several important Englishmen, including Sir Roderick Jones, the head of Reuters', had declined to sponsor my father's application for British nationality, on the grounds that such an initiative on their part might have 'offended the German government'. Sir Robert Vansittart had no such scruples in the face of Nazi sensibilities. Consequently when Klop left the German Embassy for the last time, he did so with a British passport already in his pocket. The immediate reaction of the Bendlerstrasse was to order him to return at once to Berlin in order to 'report'. This cable from the Foreign Office was followed within half an hour by another one from the German General Staff, telling my father as an ex-officer and holder of the Iron Cross, on no account to return to Germany. This fact is an interesting reminder of the temper of the times.

One day, as late as 1938, when I returned home from the drama school, I found Klop in an unusual state of agitation. There were glasses on the table, a bottle of champagne on ice, a box of cigars, open.

'You're late,' he snapped.

I began to think of an excuse.

'No time for that,' my father barked. 'You are to go to the cinema.'

'What do you want me to see?' I asked. Sometimes, when I was younger, we had gone as a family to see a film deemed suitable, usually something like *Tabu* or *Trader Horn* which gave me nightmares for weeks afterwards, but never had my father sent me to the cinema.

'What do I care what you see?'

'Well, I need some money.'

'Again!'

The last time had been in 1934.

Irritated, he rummaged in his trouser-pocket and came up grudgingly with sixpence.

'It costs more than that.'

'There's no need to take an expensive seat, you know.'

'The cheapest one costs more than that,' I murmured.

'Since when?' he cried, as though I had announced the outbreak of hostilities.

'About two years,' I said.

'What is it now?'

'Ninepence.'

'*Ninepence*!' he shouted.

My mother came to the rescue with threepence, and I was sent on my mysterious mission.

It was evidently too late. We lived on the fourth floor of a Victorian building without a lift. As I reached the second floor, I was forced to flatten myself against the wall to make way for a procession of elderly gentlemen who were climbing the stairs laboriously, some with bowler hats, some with green trilbies, grunting and wheezing like a group of mature elephants on the way to a watering-hole. They seemed oblivious of my presence as they concentrated on the business at hand, looking upward every now and then to see if there was still a long way to go. At long last the rearguard passed me, and I was free to leave.

I no longer remember what film I saw at the local, but when I returned it was dark. I climbed the four flights of stairs and was greeted by a blue haze of cigar smoke. A thin bar of light from under the living-room door and a murmur of hushed conversation suggested that it would be imprudent to enter. I brushed my teeth and went to bed. Next morning, neither of my parents was awake. I made myself some tea, and went to work, quickly forgetting the whole incident.

It was several years later, during the war, that it suddenly came back to mind for some reason, and I asked Klop about it. He was in an expansive mood. Apparently the German military attaché, Major General Geyr von Schweppenburg, had telephoned him from a public phone box, complaining that Ribbentrop, during his tenure at the Embassy, had so alienated British opinion that now all contact was lost with people of influence.

'My dear von Ustinov,' the general had said, 'you are the only one who can still help us, and whatever your feelings towards us, you cannot deny us this request. We simply must convince the British to stand firm at Munich. If they give in to Hitler now, there will be no holding him. Now is the moment, more especially since we are far from ready for war. Even a relatively simple operation like the annexation of Austria showed us the tremendous gaps in our equipment and our capacity for staff-work on a large scale.'

'What do you want me to do?' Klop had asked.

'If you can organize a meeting between the British and German General Staffs, our people will all take leave on different days, and make their way independently yet indirectly to London on private airlines,' the general had replied.

For the historically minded, the meeting in question took place on the fourth floor of No. 134 Redcliffe Gardens, London S.W.10, while I was at the movies. And the outcome?

'The British declined to co-operate, believing there to be a risk that the whole thing was an elaborate German trap,' said Klop, and the facts are confirmed by General Geyr von Schweppenburg's memoirs, published in Germany after the war.

A while later, when war had already broken out, I identified one of the silent British officers at the flat as Major Stevens, one of the shrewdest of the shrewd. A couple of days after I had seen him, he appeared at a secret rendezvous at the Dutch-German border in order to take possession of a top German defector. The British General Staff did not believe this to be an elaborate German trap, but this time it was one. Instead of taking possession of the top defector, who turned out to be non-existent, Major Stevens was himself spirited away into Germany, and spent four long and undoubtedly heroic years being as silent there as he had been here.

After these débâcles, I was no longer encouraged to go to the cinema. I was merely asked to tell no one about the comings and goings at the flat. What was curious, however, was to watch how Klop, who once had fancied himself as the dapper German officer, had now shed these mannerisms to become more and more British. He even began to stammer on certain words, and indulge in a host of oratorical mannerisms which were the hallmark of Conservative politicians. Klop even referred to the British fleet as though he had vested interests in it, and eventually, when exhorted to write a book of memories, declined to do so, because he did not wish to mention any of his more interesting activities for fear of, to use his own words, 'letting the side down' – and this after every general with half a star the world over had revealed all, and after Philby, Burgess and Maclean had 'let the side down' irrevocably and thoroughly. In his gratitude for his acceptance by the British, he became loyal to a point of touching absurdity, believing that any scrap of ancient information could still bring comfort to an enemy utterly discredited, destroyed, and scattered to the Bolivian and Paraguayan winds.

While odd occurrences continued at home – I never knew who or what I would encounter on the staircase – at drama school things were mercifully less dramatic. I began to find some little favour among one or two of the teachers, John Burrell, and in particular George Devine, who was in charge of improvisations.

Whenever forced to concentrate on pure gymnastics or vocal exercises, I still lagged behind the others, but when I applied what I had learned to a dramatic, or more especially, a comic text, I showed great improvement. At all events, I became at last deeply concerned with the job in hand, and work, for the first time in my life, became a pleasure. Even if the theatre had not been a vocation, at least it was becoming a profession.

I was strengthened in my resolution by a letter from Alexandre Benois, my great-uncle. He had directed the Molière and Goldoni plays in the repertoire of the Moscow Arts Theatre, amid frequent quarrels with Stanislavsky about the exorbitant rehearsal time accorded the actors to deal with the palpable mysteries of these texts, which could only be unravelled with the help of an audience. Stanislavsky insisted on treating every work of art by the norms he had established for Chekhov.

Once, in a rage, Benois was calmed by Artëm, the venerable actor who created the role of Firs in *The Cherry Orchard*.

'Don't excite yourself,' counselled the old man. 'Do what I do. Pretend. Stanislavsky believes he has converted me to his method. In fact, I am doing precisely what I always did in the old Imperial theatres.'

Now Benois wrote me a memorable letter of welcome to professional life. 'For two centuries', he began, 'our family has been sniffing around the theatre. We have designed for it, we have composed for it, we have conducted in it, we have applauded and we have slept. At last one of us has had the incredible audacity to clamber upon the boards himself!'

Even if not quite accurate by its neglect of his great-grandfather the ballerino and his great-grandmother the diva, this gave me the most enormous confidence in dealing with my quandaries.

His example did not end there. Over my desk there hang three designs for *Petrouchka* intended for a revival of his masterpiece. They were executed when he was eighty-seven years old, and the draughtsmanship is as crisp and sure as ever.

I was greatly helped in finding a kind of personal focus by the fact that for the first time I felt an attraction for a girl. At last, painfully late, instead of being compelled to confirm or deny my father's impressions of a passing female, I was doing the staring and the manœuvring all on my own, instinctively and evidently not too badly. I noticed her on the very first day. She wasn't obviously pretty or beautiful. She belonged to no particular type. She held mystery for me, and that was enough to cause indescribable confusion in my thoughts and feelings. I found myself planning to sit close to her, or in her eyeline, or behind her. Eventually we just drifted into one another's company.

She was Isolde, the daughter of a playwright, Reginald Denham, an amusing and eternally youthful man. He was no longer married to Isolde's mother, a delightfully vague and splendidly proportioned lady who had formed an attachment with a Scottish military gentleman, and shared his house in Highgate. The atmosphere in this house was somewhat strained, since the Scottish officer kept his tin hat from the Great War and a loaded revolver from the same conflict suspended from a hook on the bedroom door, threatening to use the gun on himself if ever his mistress should leave him. The expression in his bloodshot eye when aroused tended to confirm his sincerity.

The mixture was further enriched by the presence of his two large boys from his former marriage, one of whom had formed an unhealthy passion for electric guitars, and the languorous music of Hawaii caressed the ear, interspersed with howling atmospherics. Apart from Isolde, there was also a younger girl, the issue of another marriage of Isolde's mother, a gawky and very amusing child of twelve or thirteen called Angela Lansbury, and male twins who are now celebrated producers in America.

And if this disparate and ill-matched household needed a symbol to crystallize its discordancy, it received it in the shape of a bloodhound puppy which had acquired the attractive habit of placing its paws on your shoulders while it peed on your legs.

'He's not yet fully grown,' barked the Scottish officer in evident satisfaction.

It was clear that poor Isolde had even more reason to leave home than I, and with the discovery of our mutual secrets and penury, a solid and comforting bond was formed between us.

I have never derived much satisfaction from working for myself. There must be some deeply patriarchal side to my character, an atavistic need to be responsible for a clan or family, which sometimes contrasts with my desire, my habit, of being alone. Whatever the truth of this, it is undeniable that my work improved owing to my attachment to a single person. I was now working for a purpose, building something, showing off discreetly to my chosen partner, a champion in a mental joust.

Our relationship had its ups and downs, but in spite of depressions, I clung to it as though my life depended on it. We both still lived at home, and were as chaste as Puritans. During the summer holidays, I appeared before the public for the first time at a small theatre in Surrey called the Barn Theatre, Shere. Probably in imitation of Michel Saint-Denis and George Devine, who both smoked pipes as though they were badges of rank among the high priests of the theatre cult, I bought myself a pipe, hailed a taxi for the first time in my life, and drove to Victoria Station in order to take the train for my first engagement. Inside the taxi, I lit the pipe, and said to myself that I was now an actor, on his way to work. I sat back and ruminated magnificently until my head began to swim, and I managed to suppress an urgent desire to throw up. My forehead was covered in an icy sweat as I paid the cab. The pipe was evidently not my mark of masculinity.

My first appearance on any stage before a paying and anonymous audience was in the role of 'Waffles' in *The Wood Demon*, the first version of *Uncle Vanya*, by Chekhov. I was on stage as the curtain rose, seated in my grandfather's smoking-jacket and pretending to eat ham. The overture was the 'Polonaise' from Tchaikovsky's *Eugene Onegin*, and I can still remember my feelings of controlled panic as the record neared its end, the hiss of the rising curtain, the sudden blinding light isolating us on the stage, and the vague outline of heads, like cobblestones on a wet night.

My role was not an easy one, since I spoke roughly once in every twenty speeches, and experience tells you that it is easier to play someone who speaks frequently than to maintain an intense concentration 'counting bars'. I came through my baptism of fire not too badly, however, and by the second night, I felt I had done it most of my life.

In the next play, the first performance in England of *Mariana Pineda* by Federico Garcia Lorca, translated by Charles David Ley and directed by John Burrell, I played a very different role, that of a lecherous Spanish Chief of Police offering the heroine the kind of crooked deal Scarpia offers Tosca. In the Chekhov it had been all twilit impressionism; here it was Andalusian symbolism, blinding white and rhythmic as the stuttering of a guitar, all of which was far outside my experience, or, for that matter, outside the experience of anyone connected with the production. John Burrell brought us some books to look at, with pictures of rows of sullen gypsies sitting outside their caves in Granada, and of crowds of functionaries, a priest and a surgeon or two, all jockeying for position in the photograph of a newly expired torero. Everybody was smiling for the photo with the exception of the dead man and the Virgin Mary on the wall, both of whom seemed rather less enthusiastic. Far from opening any doors for us, these bits of evidence only served to make Spanish folklore even more hermetic, and I launched myself into a text of which I understood not a single motivation, not a single image. It was difficult to comprehend why lust should be so talkative, although it is undeniably a tremendously valuable adjunct to an actor to be able to cope with a text in which he simply doesn't know what the hell he's talking about, while his expression must imply that he has a vital message to impart.

The Times was, as ever, cautious in its assessment, and small wonder. Lorca had a great reputation, augmented by the tragic circumstances of his death. He appeared as a lyrical variation on the Che Guevara theme, and yet the translation of his burning mysteries into marbled words of English was bound to be difficult, especially in the hands of dramatic students. The first press notice I ever received from a national newspaper said that 'Peter Ustinov gave the part of Pedrosa a sinister restraint which was acceptable.' It was a great moment for me; in retrospect even greater than I could imagine at the time. Never since have I been called either sinister or restrained.

During the course of the two-weeks run we received the visits of Charles Laughton and Elsa Lanchester. He always blossomed when surrounded by youth, since he had something of the major prophet in him. At that time, he had a strange tree-house not far away, and we were all invited there for tea. I picked up a pine-cone which had fallen on to the front steps, packed it in a parcel, and sent it to Isolde, who was holidaying on an Irish island. I hoped it would bring us both luck.

Not long afterwards I went to see *The Sign of the Cross* in London, in which Laughton was playing the part of Nero and in which Claudette Colbert took her famous bath in asses' milk. I sat through the film, and came out into the early afternoon, worn out by the fustian and blinded by daylight. I walked across Green Park, ruminating on ancient Rome and its influence on the architecture of the Empire State Building, of which I had seen photographs, when I suddenly found myself face to face with Laughton again. To my amazement, he recognized me, and asked me to walk with him. I was too overwhelmed to refuse. He talked a great deal in his meticulously authoritative way, flooding his eyes with acute expression, then letting them flicker away to a pained docility, while his mouth expressed a voluptuous pleasure in its own disgust. What he said was invariably intelligent and precious, breaking platitudes to you as though they had been announced to him by a passing archangel, and as though you were the only person privileged to share such knowledge. He then wearily announced that he was going to give me a treat. I thought this might take the form of a drink, or at least a cup of tea. Too late I realized that we were heading back to *The Sign of the Cross*. Before I could react, Charles had called out the manager, asked him to look after me, and left with the airy wave of someone who is sure of himself, and pleasantly warmed by his own generosity.

I didn't dare tell the manager I had seen it a couple of hours ago, more especially since he gave me a seat I couldn't possibly have afforded. Every time I looked round for a chance to escape, I found him still standing there.

'There's nothing like spectacle, is there?' he said.

'No,' I agreed.

'What a lovely man Mr Laughton is.'

'Yes,' I agreed.

'I mean the very idea of going out of his way to bring a young student here – it's an education, you know – and you're never going to forget this!' he almost threatened.

I saw Nero scowling at me from the screen, and believed the manager to be telling the truth.

At the London Theatre Studio, we began preparing for the end of term. Michel Saint-Denis directed us in *The Alcestis* by Euripides. I, wearing nothing but a tiger skin conceived by the Motleys, made a lot of noise in the part of Herakles, or Hercules. I suppose you might refer to the reasons for the noise as labour pains. At all events, M. Saint-Denis treated the drama as a bold imperishable monolith until, shortly before we were to open, he called us together telling us he had made a vital error, since he had treated the play as though Sophocles had written it, whereas it should be full of Euripidean ironies. We all said we understood, then performed it exactly as we had previously, and he said how much better it was played that way, and what luck he had discovered his mistake in time.

Since there was a great shortage of men, as always at drama

schools, all the lads had several parts. I was cast in the role of Branwell Brontë in that archest of plays, *Wild Decembers* by Clemence Dane, a lady who entered rooms like a yacht in full sail, her mouth for ever puckered as though savouring some inspirational ambrosia. She gave me one of the choicest fruits of her meditation when the wretched Branwell, exhausted by the incessant comings and goings of his blue-stocking sisters Charlotte and Emily across the blasted heath, to say nothing of the inane complaints of his father, the reverend, suddenly rushed to the door, announcing to his family that he too was going for a prowl on the moor now that the weather was bad enough, and, as an afterthought, delivered himself of the following piece of beastliness: 'But you needn't try to stop me – nothing can. Not the grave itself nor the devils who sit on the tombstones on the other side of the wall and grin at us on winter nights!'

With that, I rushed into the gale, thankful to be out of the cottage. Unfortunately I never once got that line right at the time, and now, nearly forty years later, I can't forget it.

I was, of course, utterly unsuited to either part; Herakles, eager to clean out Augean stables, and Branwell, eager to be listened to with nothing much to say, were both beyond my reach. The third part I played, Sir John Moneytrap in *The Plain Dealer* by William Wycherley, was one of those Restoration bundles of gripe and style which submerge any but the finest actors in a haze of filigree. Altogether, as I often suspected, the parts selected for students at such academies are never designed to procure them work in the commercial theatre, but rather to drive them out of desperation into tiny temples of true art, making their own masks and coffee in chipped mugs, in the belief that, because money corrupts, poverty must therefore be equated with integrity.

I once said to a Belgian dramatist, Herman Closson, who had started with the Compagnie de Quinze, playing in villages, that I believed its motto to be: '*Nous vaincrons parce que nous sommes les plus faibles.*'

He corrected my impression by saying '*Cher ami, c'est pire que ça; nous vaincrons parce que nous sommes les plus pauvres.*' The whole quasi-religious aspect of our activities became clear. If we were very good we would be elevated to the position of apostles, if not we would be thrown out into the impure world of scribes, Pharisees and Philistines, and the eye of the needle would shrink to nothing from the triumphal arch it was to those willing to follow glowing ideals in mute subservience.

Michel Saint-Denis was a man of great and persuasive charm, with the finely honed cruelty due to a minotaur. Once, during the rehearsals of a French play, he told me that the way to express fear was to contract the buttocks. I didn't understand how such a muscular change could be conveyed to the public, especially to those seated far away. A little later he stopped the rehearsal to ask me why I was waddling instead of walking. I explained that, according to the text, I was still very frightened, but that it was extremely difficult for someone with my lack of experience to walk while contracting his buttocks. He nodded dangerously, savouring my semi-conscious sarcasm as though it were *pâté-de-foie gras*, a qualified declaration of independence, and for a little while longer I was allowed to express fear by more personal methods.

At the end of the second year, he sent for me. The interview was an awkward one, he maintaining that I was not yet ready at the age of eighteen to face the rude, unscrupulous world of money-lenders – 'I don't know what kind of parts you can play,' he said coolly – 'Shakespearean clowns *à la rigueur*, and then . . . Shakespearean clowns are not wanted every day . . . there are others, with experience. Take my advice and stay here another year.'

My yearning for freedom was too great. I told him, as steadily as possible, that I wished to try my chance.

He attempted to outstare Judas.

'The decision is yours,' he said, disguising his disappointment with difficulty, and added, somewhat sourly, 'You will – if by some chance you succeed – fall into the world of tricks, like Charles Laughton.'

For a moment, I had the illusion that I was being taken to see *The Sign of the Cross* for a third time, but this time by Jesus Christ himself.

I didn't answer. I rose to go, and said goodbye with some emotion.

It was a school which had taught me a great deal, especially about voice and movement. Aesthetically I quarrelled with much it had to offer, but this was even better for me, since I had to work out in my own mind reasons with which to back up my instinct. Deriving from Stanislavsky, it was much given to analysis, making the smallest gesture the pretext for lengthy discussions. My instinctive quarrel with the so-called method, valid to this day, is that so much of what is said, done, and more importantly, thought, during rehearsal is untranslatable into dramatic terms. This leads to the all-too-frequent phenomenon of actors who have reached devious and impractical conclusions about their roles, doing incomprehensible things with an aura of self-satisfaction and even authority, which not unnaturally tends to alienate an audience.

As with every artistic movement, it is necessary to examine the style against which it rebelled in order fully to understand it. Stanislavsky and Chekhov cannot be entirely appreciated without being at least conscious of the melodramatic style of acting against which they reacted. The husband, finding love-letters from another man to his wife, would stagger back a couple of paces unsteadily and raise his hand to his forehead as though warding off one of destiny's blows. 'Life,' affirmed Chekhov, 'is not like that,' a sentiment faithfully echoed by Stanislavsky. A man finding such letters usually does not react at all, at least visibly. His immediate concern is to try to capture a kind of diabolical initiative by leaving the letters exactly as he found them so that he has all the time in the world to study his quarry and to decide on his reaction. After all, he doesn't wish an accusation of snooping to lessen his moral ascendancy.

Naturally each man would have his own reaction to such a

situation, as would each theatrical character, but what both Chekhov and Stanislavsky were sure of was that only a ham actor, obeying the instructions of a conventional dramatist and a workaday director, could totter back the two statutory steps and bring his left hand up to his eyebrow. Chekhov thereupon set about showing up the false by a poetic mobilization of all that is inconsequential and wayward in human intercourse, with the result that his plays are not so much dialogues as many intertwined monologues, plays in which people talk far more than they listen, a technique which illuminated all the bittersweet selfishness and egotism in the human heart, and made people recognize, if not themselves, at least each other.

Not without reason, the new introspection of the Stanislavsky method coincided admirably with the new introspection of Chekhov. Actors were encouraged to work by themselves with a growing disregard for external problems, and consequently they were invited to be as egotistical as the characters they so brilliantly played. The fame of the Moscow Arts Theatre was built on Chekhov, and it is indicative that its forays into Molière, Goldoni and even Maeterlinck made much less of an international mark. It is therefore to be suspected (and indeed confirmed by my great-uncle) that this modern and revolutionary technique did not lend itself all that happily to the interpretation of the classics.

It is not difficult to understand why this was so. Since Chekhov, the journeys into the depths of realism and beyond have been accomplished more thoroughly if not more profoundly by the cinema. Now, the theatre has once more sought to break out of its frame, where it had been consigned by naturalism and gentility. It is the one dramatic art-form left which exploits a living audience, as does a sport; a living audience, for which the canned laughter of the television is but a corrupt and artificial substitute.

As a consequence of this reversion to its fullest potential, I submit today as I have always submitted, that the theatre is basically a sport, based on integrated team-play, with, as in

room for improvisation and the opportunities of
~~~~~ment, and very much dependent on physical and vocal
~~~dition. Whereas the so-called Method tends to slow down
reactions by giving precedence to the intelligence at the expense
of instinct, I believe that the duty of the intelligence is merely
to correct the instinct in cases of emergency, and that speed of
reaction is all important.

The driver of a racing-car maintains a loose grip on the
steering-wheel, and uses it merely to correct the car when an
emergency looms. The rest of the time, he 'feels' his car round
the course. So it is with acting. The mental processes are too
fast to intellectualize at every curve in the road, and grip the
steering-wheel as though your life depended on it.

Once again, one has seen actors of a certain school seeming
to take themselves by surprise by strange and sudden inflections,
by hesitations so exaggerated and external that they appear to
be a caricature of naturalistic behaviour. Once again one must
invoke the sport. I am not, to quote Ken Tynan, smitten by
Bull Fever. There is nothing in this world uglier than a bad
Corrida, and I have insufficient intellectual power to enter into
the realm of Mediterranean tragedy or Minoan antiquity and be
totally indifferent to the unpleasantness which accompanies the
thrills. Nevertheless, there are aspects to bullfighting which have
a direct bearing on the art and craft of the actor.

The great torero minimizes his movements to the uttermost.
Why? To give a scale to the map of our vision, without which
nothing can be clearly understood. The bull is a clumsy and
unconcentrated animal. A fly, entering the field of its vision
even at the height of its agony, is liable to deflect its attention
from its tormentor. The loss of tension is immediately felt by
the public. To regain the attention of the bull, the torero
makes a brief, curt, studied movement. He has to compete
with the wayward fly. His movement must have some meaning
to the bull. How can he ensure this? By being as still as
possible the rest of the time. Stillness is one of the prime

adjuncts of the actor; to be able to maintain tension by total immobility.

Even the game of cricket, which I have spoken of without love, has revealed sufficient of its mysteries to me for me to understand that it is also one of the 'rationed' sports in which much of the excitement is produced by anticipation, and a stillness on the field to give importance to the sudden outbursts of activity. It is this stillness which furnishes the scale of the map, and enables us to calculate the exact meaning of the outbursts of hitting and running. The stillness is, once again, all important. As it is in conversation, and since dialogue is but organized conversation, the same rules apply to both. People have been heard to remark time and again that the art of conversation is dead. Pessimists with a profound if erroneous historical sense will maintain that there has been a gradual decline since Dr Johnson.

To believe this is to misunderstand one of the most important prerequisites of conversation, which is the ability to listen. Whenever Dr Johnson bellowed an irrefutable 'Sir!', all conversation stopped at once while the great man pontificated. He did not need to listen all that closely. After all, he had Boswell to do that. And Chekhov's characters did not need to listen either. They had Chekhov to do it for them. But actors simply must not only listen but show that they are listening. As in a sport, you cannot score every time. There are moments, and many of them, when it is important to pass the ball so that a colleague may eventually score. To be aware, and convincing, it is absolutely essential to listen to everything, with the sensitivity and sensibility of an insect, and not just confine yourself to inner voices. It has, of course, taken a long time and much experience to arrive at such conclusions with any degree of lucidity, but they are merely formulations of a direction which my instinct had been urging on me from the very beginning, from my drama school in fact.

* * *

I left M. Saint-Denis' office and prepared to face the world. I had written a few letters to agents, and had had no replies. All doors seemed to be closed. I had blotted my copybook as a potential apostle, and now discovered there was no room even for a Judas. The cock crowed twice, and I was given another chance. Saint-Denis was about to do an all-star production of *The Cherry Orchard*, with Edith Evans as Mme Ranevskaya. He had previously done a memorable *Three Sisters*, and it was the kind of play he did best, in which there were no great claims on visual imagination or decorative taste. Now I was offered the understudy of George Devine, who was going to play Lopakhin, which was not bad going for a Shakespearean clown in retirement before the start of his career. I accepted, and made plans to leave home at the first pay-day. Unfortunately that master of the dramatic, Adolf Hitler, opened before we even had a chance to go into rehearsal, and with him as impresario, I slowly prepared to play a part I was totally unsuited to, for the worst pay, in a run lasting over four years. Fortunately for me, I was allowed a brief whiff of freedom before going back to school in the army as what is so ironically, so inhumanly, so inaccurately called a Private.

7

Looking back from this nuclear age, our preparations for survival in 1939 seemed both charming and pathetic. My mother and I pasted strips of adhesive paper over the windows in Union Jack pattern to prevent them from shattering. We placed blankets in readiness to be laid at the foot of the living-room door in case of a mustard gas attack, and we read the pleasantly archaic instructions of what to do in the case of any particular form of German initiative. A mustard gas victim, according to the handbook, was to be taken to a zone outside the contaminated area, wrapped in blankets, and administered hot, sweet tea. Nice clear thinking to thwart the holocaust.

War was declared at eleven o'clock on a particularly fine Sunday, and within half an hour the sirens wailed, announcing the first air attack on London. Far from running for our shelter, we opened the window wide, and clambered out on to our tiny, sooty balcony to see the dogfights. Every balcony in the street was similarly occupied. So much for government handbooks and their instructions.

Within a few minutes the enemy raiders had been identified as a flock of gannets with no recognizable markings on their wings. It was a fine start to the Phoney War.

I was still at home with no immediate prospects. I had outgrown the room which had housed me for seven or eight years, and I tried hard and miserably to stay out of the way of the mysterious people who still clogged the stairs. My father was in a far better frame of mind, since there was to him more than a trace of the adventurer, and he really seemed to come to life now that the boil had been lanced, and the war was definitely upon us. He was as bitterly opposed to Hitler and all that constipated stridency as anyone in the world. Once, on returning home from Westminster, I had found my father in tears, a rare and embarrassing occurrence. It was the day of Mussolini's attack on Ethiopia, and Klop was weeping on behalf of his Ethiopian antecedents. He never told me about them in his determination to be as English as possible, and carrying the touching charade so far as to believe that I would be adversely affected by the knowledge of 'a touch of the tar-brush'. Even my mother, in her book, did not reveal this guilty secret. She must have believed also that it would be 'letting the side down'.

At all events, now that Mr Chamberlain was discountenanced, and that the war was irrevocably under way, Klop was cheerful enough even within the immediate circle of the family to suggest that instead of waiting around idly to be called up, I might join Military Intelligence. He even went so far as to arrange an interview for me, which was to take place outside Sloane Square Underground Station. I could scarcely believe my ears that fact should follow fiction quite so slavishly. I was to go up to a man who would be reading the *News Chronicle*, and ask him the way to Eaton Square. He would ask me what number I wanted. I was to reply Number Nine, after which we would go for a walk together.

I arrived at Sloane Square Underground Station at the appointed hour, and saw a man holding a copy of the *News Chronicle* in such a way that it was evident that he was not actively reading, but merely waiting. I could just see the top of his homburg hat over the top of it. 'Could you please direct me to Eaton Square?' I asked. He lowered the paper, and studied me as no man ever studies another unless recruiting him for the secret service. 'What number was it you were wanting?' he enquired. He was obviously a man of few words.

'Number Nine.'

'Very good,' he snapped, forcing the paper into his macintosh pocket. 'I will indicate the general direction for you to follow. If you will kindly walk with me . . .'

As we walked, he never looked at me, and I consequently didn't trust myself to look at him.

'I know your particulars from your proud parent,' he said. 'Education, hobbies and the like. I will therefore just ask you what makes you think yourself to be suited to this work?'

'I don't really know,' I replied. 'Good memory. Language.'

'*Sprecken see Dutch?*' he enquired.

'*Ja*,' I replied, and he seemed extremely impressed, even out of the corner of my eye.

'*Parlez-vous les français?*'

'*Oui, monsieur.*'

'Good man . . .'

After a while, he looked at his watch, and remembered an urgent appointment. He left, and I took care not to follow him. I don't know why, but I had an idea people like him simply hated being followed.

The result was a disappointment for my ambitions as a budding James Bond. I was told I was unsuitable since I did not possess a face which could be lost easily in a crowd. Yet, on reflection, the very element which made me inadequate as a spy gave me a curious confidence as an out-of-work actor. Klop, on the other hand, was somewhat saddened by my latest failure, as though I had in some way declined to take over the family business.

Among those who had for years been assailed with my party performances was a Miss Babs Ortweiler, now Mrs Hilton, a friend of my parents who arranged an audition for me with Leonard Sachs, a South African actor who ran a Victorian cabaret called The Players' Theatre.

I did a monologue for him based on a real visit to Westminster of a decrepit colonial bishop, who delivered himself of a sermon in the Abbey demonstrating the onward march of Christian

Soldiers in the heart of darkest Africa, the climax of every moral example being rendered in Swahili. The old cleric either forgot, or else did not think it necessary, to translate his words of wisdom into English for the betterment of English boys. I rather cruelly adapted this octogenarian's sermon for my own nefarious purposes. I passed my audition, and began to appear at the Players' in company with Alec Clunes, Bernard Miles, and others of great achievement.

Klop, far from being entranced, sighed a deep and fatalistic sigh, and uttered the words 'Not even drama . . . vaudeville!'

This crushing verdict was quite inadequate to detract from my joy at earning my own money, even if it only amounted to £5 a week, and then only intermittently, since I was only engaged every now and then. I was told that I should work on another monologue, which is how I came about the idea of Mme Liselotte Beethoven-Fink, an ageing Austro-German lieder singer, who sang bits of unknown Schubert – that is, unknown even to Schubert – such as 'Der Musenvater'. She was a sort of blowzy Malaprop – in order to clarify Schubert's tangled family relationships, she cannily half-closed her mascaraed lids and cattily proclaimed there to be 'a little bit of insect in that family'.

She became a veritable triumph, attracting the kind of critical acclaim reserved for the newcomer. James Agate and Ivor Brown, the two leading critics, were full of the most elaborate praise, although neither went as far as Herbert Farjeon, the genial writer of revue material, who was at the time the critic of the *Tatler*. He wrote, quite baldly, that Liselotte might have been the work of Edmund Kean in a lighter moment, entertaining friends.

I enjoyed my success to the full, especially since I had made a small breakthrough without the overwhelming assistance of Shakespeare and one of his incomprehensible clowns, and without ever having had to understudy or to carry a spear in Laurence Olivier's *Macbeth*, which some of my chosen contemporaries had had the privilege of doing. My pleasure was increased when I observed my father and friends tiptoeing into the back of the auditorium just as my act was starting, and leaving again before I re-emerged into the auditorium as myself. Agate, Brown, and Farjeon had given me my only unmitigatedly good reports since I had first gone to school at the age of six, and now Klop was evidently becoming resigned to Vaudeville once it attracted critical acclaim worthy of Drama.

Once again, my engagements were intermittent, and I earned pocket money rather than a wage which allowed me to go my own way. In the interests of experience, I accepted an engagement at the Aylesbury Repertory Theatre at £2 10s a week. There was just enough for my digs and a single chocolate-covered peppermint cream bar per week. I played a French professor in Terence Rattigan's *French Without Tears*, a German seal-trainer in Robert Morley's *Goodness How Sad*, Colonel Higgins in *Pygmalion*, the Robertson Hare part in *Rookery Nook*, and the depressing doctor in that superb piece of far-flung Empire kitsch *White Cargo*.

I had to make an appeal for medical magazines from Blighty in this latter play, so that I might keep up with the latest trends in Vienna, Harley Street, and the Mayo Clinic in spite of the sweat, heat, and filth of tropical existence. A copy of the *Lancet* arrived at the stage door, with a letter from the editor, saying that he had been so moved by my appeal that he had despatched the latest copy forthwith. Not another notice from Herbert Farjeon, perhaps, but as heartwarming in its own way. I still have the copy, which is by now as out of date as the play was then.

The Londoners had begun to recover from the first impact of war, and although the bombing had begun, this had only strengthened their resolve instead of breaking their spirit. Norman Marshall, who had successfully run the little Gate Theatre, which performed plays by Steinbeck and Maxwell Anderson for the first time in England, now conceived a revue starring, among others, Hermione Gingold and Robert Helpmann. I was summoned for an interview, and engaged to appear in the West End of London for the first time in my life. My salary was considerably augmented, and flushed with this success, I went flat-hunting, Characteristically I found a tiny penthouse in Dover Street, one of the centres of traditional British hypocrisy, high-class commercial addresses by day, low-class commercial addresses by night. Normally such a little apartment would have cost the earth to rent, despite the fact, or perhaps because of the fact, that my next-door neighbour was a distinguished prostitute. Now it cost very little, and I grabbed it as though it were a rare bargain. It never occurred to me that with its large expanse of glass roof, it afforded very little protection from the German bombers, and required a very thorough and meticulous system of black-out curtains.

The décor was nothing short of awful, with a false Venetian negro youth holding a trayful of dusty glass grapes at the entrance, and other bits of camp and chi-chi cast like confetti over the blood-red interior. The flat had belonged to a high-strung homosexual who had committed suicide very recently when crossed in love, and his mother, a plaintive and tearstained lady, insisted on looking after me with all the care she had lavished on her son. I am afraid I was a considerable disappointment to her, for although I listened to her woes with patience, I was hardly mercurial enough to replace, even for a few minutes every day, the comfort she had lost.

My appearance in the revue was not at first the success I had hoped for, since I wrote new material which tried to widen the scope of what I had developed, and in doing so, lost the esoteric audience I had acquired. A lesson learned, which I have had to learn over and over again. My original text I can no longer remember, nor can I even recollect the nature of the character I conceived. All I do know is that I almost immediately replaced it with a Russian professor who was jealous of Chekhov's success, and this creature had sufficient contradictions in him to be interesting. He was both pathetic and basically frightfully unpleasant, which set my mind exploring along the lines of dramatic paradox. It must be understood that the British theatre of the period was beset with distinguished elderly actors and actresses who were determined to be liked by the public even if they were playing totally unsympathetic characters. The stage was cluttered with semi-sympathetic performances of disreputable people, and the audience was beset by little signals from such performers, signifying that although they had just killed their wives or husbands on the stage owing to the exigencies of a particularly silly script which only the difficulties of the times had made them accept, they were not really like that in life at all.

I suspected then, as I believe now, that the most interesting parts to play are those in which there is a wide span of often divergent characteristics, so that the reactions are unpredictable and only consistent at the end. After all, the stage can hardly hold a mirror up to the nature of all theatrical characters, because these must expose their complexities within two and a half hours, and have therefore to be simplified to fit within the rigours of convention. Chekhov solved the problem by suggesting a constellation of unsaid things, Pirandello spelled out the paradoxes with glacial precision. Shakespeare gave his actors more elbow-room than they really needed. What is known in technical terms as a well-rounded character really means one with insufficient mystery, one with theatrical life at the expense of human credibility.

The Russian professor was so academic that the need for mystery totally escaped him. His quarrel with Chekhov was based on such alleged absurdities as Irina's phrase 'I want to be a seagull!' He shrugged his shoulders in denigration.

'For me . . . physical impossibility,' he said.

It was during the run of *Swinging the Gate* that I was married to Isolde Denham at the Marloes Road Registry Office. She was nineteen years old, so was I. My father expressed no opinion about the advisability of such a marriage, and nor did my mother. They were probably both too shocked by my precipitate departure from home to have fully recovered yet. Through the good offices of a remarkable woman, Lady Norton, who was my *de facto* godmother, Isolde's mother was able to leave for America in charge of a group of evacuee children, which included her offspring. By this well-timed action, she avoided the reprobation, or indeed the bullet, of the Scottish military gentleman, whose passion was easily deflected by patriotism.

Isolde knew a little about the realities of adult existence, I absolutely nothing. Had I realized for a moment how little I knew, I would doubtless have been more cautious about plunging into marriage. It is not my intention at this late stage to level any accusations or attribute any blame for this curious situation, which astonished my mother many years later when I dropped a hint about its existence. The fact is that an entire dimension of my life had been lacking ever since my precocious introduction to the dance and counterdance of adult seduction. The antics of men assessing women I found annoying, whereas the response of women went as far as sickening me. It is even extremely difficult for me to write about this today, two marriages and four children later, since it requires a real effort of honesty and the most intense recollection to place myself once again in the sterile prison from which I escaped so long ago.

I developed such a streak of puritanical frigidity that whereas love and affection were at no time excluded, the idea of their physical expression just did not exist for me; or at least I imagined that a remote instinct, which had not manifested itself to any great or puzzling extent, would, at the required moment, take over everything, initiative, aggression, know-how. I could even, like so many others, exchange lascivious jokes with a splendidly relaxed air, and yet I knew nothing other than that which others told me with the same easy assurance.

There is in existence a photograph of me at the age of a year holding a Russian toy comprising ten wooden women, one within the other, from a great bulbous earth-mother to a woman the size of a pea. I am brandishing two halves of this educational toy with evident pleasure. It apparently occurred to me at an early age that a pregnant woman had another pregnant woman inside her, and then another one right down to the smallest. I don't think I ever really suspected that this smallest might be a baby. I like to believe I did, simply because I like to believe I was what the Americans so depressingly call 'bright', but in my heart I consider it more likely that I believed the embryo to be a very small woman indeed, dressed, of course, in peasant costume.

The truth of this probability is given further credence by the fact that when my mother informed me of the facts of life at an embarrassingly late stage of my youth, my father being too shy to talk about men, although more than willing to banter about women, I underwent a long moment of utter incredulity. My first reaction was one of horrified claustrophobia. I didn't understand how I had survived nine months of incarceration in a belly without a breath of fresh air. Then I got used to the idea, and quickly accepted such a process as being distinctly odd, but no odder than some of the other phenomena which had been brought to my attention.

It seems to me that I was always half a step behind the others, having no brothers or sisters, and being brought up in an atmosphere of rare sophistication without any of the basic hurdles so essential to mental and physical balance. It was as though my cerebral diet were composed entirely of delicatessen, and vintage formula.

I was, if anything, over-prepared for a life of inconsequential refinement within extremely narrow horizons, and absolutely unprepared for choppier seas and fresher winds. I did, however, recognize from the beginning the nature of my shortcomings, but it was only when I had children of my own to appreciate and to study that I finally realized the full extent of the distance I had travelled.

However people may carp or cavil about what has become known as the Permissive Age, I believe that free communication, even if pushed to excess, is infinitely preferable to the murk of ignorance. Better a generation which has come to terms with its physical existence than one in which a lack of knowledge is veiled by social propriety and the hypocritical grace notes of piety and breeding. Even pornography, which is the antithesis of the erotic, and which has now settled on us as a garish consumer-orientated commodity, is, in its early stages, a liberator from the greater evil of social censorship.

It may seem strange that I can write with evident feeling about a battle which today is won. I do so only to remind the incredulous that it was not always so; that whereas men and women have always found a way, up to relatively recently there were prejudices, both parental and institutional, which made subjects of vital interest to human happiness a taboo.

Thrift was the first necessity brought home to me, and we moved out of the penthouse into a basement flat in Redcliffe Road, a fall from mincing grace to workaday gloom which had about it a symbolism worthy of a medieval morality. Virtually our only possession was a small spaniel dog we had acquired, which soon began having epileptic fits in the cavernous darkness of our new abode. The gas fire was supplied by a meter into which shillings could be fed, or, in moments of penury, pennies. The pervading odours were those of damp and cats. The one advantage of these sordid lodgings was a garden, a sombre Victorian-looking patch of balding grass, in which all the greens seemed a couple of shades darker than natural, and the broken trellises appeared to sag under several coats of immovable dust. There was a shattered and unvarnished table with a hole in the middle, which had accommodated a parasol in happier days, and a couple of white wickerwork chairs on legs of different lengths which were unwinding themselves suicidally. It was not the ideal place for a honeymoon. But then, it wasn't the ideal time for a honeymoon either.

The great daylight raids had begun. The sky was filled with hundreds of planes. The climax came on one glorious summer day when the Italians, in wooden aircraft, ̶ ̶ ̶ ̶ ̶ in their effort to annihilate the R.A.F. We ̶ ̶ ̶ ̶ and drank tea, feeling like privileged V.I.P.s and ̶ ̶ ̶ ̶ immense drama enacted above our heads with ̶ ̶ ̶ ̶ fascination of royalty. There were flames, trails of black ̶ ̶ ̶ ̶, metal glinting in the sun, the noise of a thousand dental ̶ills, even parachutes drifting sideways in the wind, and yet, try as we might, we could not associate these conventional scenes of war with the many human tragedies enacted within our field of vision. Thanks to the movies, gunfire has always sounded unreal to me, even when being fired at.

Swinging the Gate was now off, and my father began a series of dangerous trips abroad. My mother moved to the country, to the Cotswolds, where she was to spend the rest of her life, with one brief interlude in London. I began to be solicited by the films. It all started with a semi-documentary called *Mein Kampf – My Crimes* in which I played Van Der Lubbe, the half-witted Dutchman blamed for the burning of the Reichstag. I had a wax nose to give me the syphilitic look, and a boil on my cheek only added to my appearance of listless guilt. My next effort was a preposterous short film called *Hello, Fame!* in which I performed a monologue of mine, and then climbed one of a series of star-spangled rope-ladders, and waved at Jean Kent, who was rather nimbler than I on another one. We were supposed to be a lot of young people on our way to the top of the ladder, you understand.

The third was a really serious film called *One of our Aircraft is Missing*, directed by Michael Powell, and boasting some of the most distinguished of British actors, such as Godfrey Tearle and Eric Portman. I was selected, probably because of my un-English look, to play a Dutch priest. The fact that I look un-Dutch didn't seem to matter a great deal, especially in time of war. Much of the little I had to say was in Latin, a little less in Dutch, and there were a few words in English.

I had so often been warned by well-meaning elderly actors

...angers of overacting, most especially on the screen, ...t I approached this important first serious venture into film acting with enormous circumspection. Britain had already supplied Hollywood with a whole battalion of elegant understaters, immaculate actors of the Du Maurier school, who, as I have already intimated, were able to play anything from cuckolded husbands to dainty blackmailers, and from chiefs of Scotland Yard to masterminds of underworld gangs without their assumed characters in any way being allowed to affect their performances. One such paragon was the late Hugh Williams, at once heroic yet vulnerable, but at all events perfectly groomed and impeccably mannered. He watched me rehearse my Dutch priest with an acuity which made me singularly uncomfortable. Eventually he came up to me, and asked, with commendable politeness, 'Excuse me, young man, what exactly are you going to do in this scene?'

I struggled to find words to adequately express my devotion to this school of acting.

'I don't really know, Mr Williams,' I replied, and added, hopefully, 'I thought I'd do nothing.'

A trace of hardness entered his eyes and voice. 'Oh no you don't,' he said, '*I'm* doing nothing.'

I reminded him of this incident many years later, and he laughed in merry disbelief. We had all changed with the times.

Still, that did not solve my problem then. Discovered in my evil act of poaching nothing, I had to find something to do. In desperation I clung to the one element which separated me from the others, and became almost unbearably Dutch, seeming to understand little that was said to me, yet attempting to exude a vocational glow of compassion which the lower orders of the priesthood are encouraged to wear as an integral part of the uniform. The film company had in addition engaged two technical advisers, both priests and both Dutch, who happened to be in temporary exile in London. Both of these fathers were no doubt excellent, as a couple of fine Swiss wrist-watches may be excellent, even if to consult them both may be unwise.

Since the two fathers outshone me in radiance, it was quite a relief that they had not much time for each other, never being present on the set at the same moment. When one was there, the other was in the canteen, and vice versa. They also were in utter disagreement about whether I should wear a cross or not, although the conflict never came into the open, but was conducted in ferocious whispers with the director. The result of this painful schism was that every scene involving me was shot both ways, with cross and without. Thanks to them, I worked twice as many days as I had been engaged for, with the consequent economic advantage. Amen.

I next put in an appearance as a dialogue director in a very broad adaptation of one of J. B. Priestley's most accessible books, *Let the People Sing*, in which I also played an elderly Czechoslovak professor, and finally I played a brilliant pupil in a Nazi school for spies in the farce *The Goose Steps Out* starring the celebrated comic Will Hay. For the first and practically only time in my career, I played a man younger than myself. Before this sudden involvement with the cinema, however, I had undergone a fallow period, which corresponded with the height of the blitz. All the theatres were shut, with the exception of the famous Windmill, inventor of the immovable nude to thwart the censorship of the times. Its proud boast, only understandable in the context of the air raids, was 'We Never Closed', and evidently no nude so much as flexed a muscle even under the most intensive bombardment. At that time, fear of the censor far exceeded fear of the Germans.

Herbert Farjeon, once again my benefactor, saved my bacon by inviting me to participate in a daytime revue called *Diversion*, which was to include Edith Evans, Dorothy Dickson, and Bernard Miles, and was to do for the dressed what the Windmill was doing for the undressed. I performed Liselotte Beethoven-Fink, and also gave impressions of three different directors to whom I had been exposed, the Continental with a sense of mission, the Communist doctrinaire of the time, and the Semi-Precious. I also appeared in supporting parts in other scenes, notably an Edwardian bathing party, in which two mashers attempted to seduce a couple of beauties by discreetly splashing them. The other moustachioed gallant was a young fellow called Dirk Bogarde, with whom I shared a dressing-room.

Sir Bronson Albery was the owner of the lovely Wyndham's Theatre in which this daily matinée performance took place. He was a rubicund gentleman who had been old for so long there were rumours that he was immortal, and other rumours which claimed that when the pipes in the theatre burst in midsummer, it was his cold feet which were to blame. Actually, he was not so famous for his reticences as for his uncertainties, and for his extraordinary capacity for talking to himself at full volume, contradicting himself, scolding himself, agreeing with himself, and in general coming out of such arguments moderately well. I can't imagine that he ever felt a pang of solitude, or that he ever needed an assistant.

Trying to cast a play of mine later on he decided after a lengthy conversation with himself, in which of course there was absolutely no room for any contribution that I might make, that a certain elderly actor would be ideal for a role, especially since he had, with commendable prudence, never asked for more than £20 a week. He ascertained the name of the actor in question, and lifted the receiver of the telephone. At this juncture, he had a moment of reflection, and replaced the receiver with the simple reminder to himself, 'Of course, he's dead.'

I was not dead, and whereas Bronny Albery was willing to offer a dead man £20 a week in the knowledge that certain obstacles would stand in the way of his generosity, there was no such guarantee in the case of the living, and he consequently offered me £5 a week to appear in the West End with two solo acts in which I had also written the material, with, as an added temptation, 1/2% of everything over £2,000, which came to just over £1 during one bumper week. I was so astonished by this magnanimity that I accepted. I had no choice. The week previously, squatting in the basement during an air raid, we had fed our last penny into the gas-meter and watched it flicker to nothingness. I announced my intention of swallowing my pride, and running round the corner to borrow a few pennies from my parents.

'Do be careful,' said Isolde, as the bombers droned overhead. The British had built street shelters, which were not designed to withstand a direct hit but which afforded protection against that greater danger, bits of our own shrapnel which flew around looking like modern sculpture. I set off at a steady canter. Our anti-aircraft guns were firing away, and the sky was lit with searchlights as at a Hollywood première. Suddenly there was a formidable crackle of gunfire and I sprinted to a street shelter, just having time to notice another dark figure running and entering the shelter from the other side. We met in the pitch darkness somewhere near the centre of the edifice. It was my father, who was short of cash, and who had swallowed his pride to come and borrow some from me. We laughed until our eyes were full of tears, and the bombers had gone home.

In January 1942, I received my call-up papers. I had made enquiries earlier about the submarine service, since I had once read a book by Lowell Thomas which had fascinated me, but I had been told I was of more value where I was, in the only entertainment running in London apart from the static nudes. Why on earth I should have been attracted to submarines I cannot now understand at all. After all, for a small boy to have felt an acute pang of claustrophobia when told the facts of childbirth would not seem to be conducive to the selection of a steel womb for military service. I am very glad they turned me down.

At my selection board interview, I was asked if I had any preference as to the arm I wished to serve in. I told the officer I was interested in tanks (once again, the lure of the airless womb!). His eyes blazed with enthusiasm.

'Why tanks?' he asked, keenly.

I replied that I preferred to go into battle sitting down. His sparkle faded abruptly, and I shortly afterwards received a letter ordering me to report to an infantry regiment. I arrived in Canterbury on January 16th, 1942, and was allowed to keep my own clothes a day or two in the absence of anything to fit me. For me, if not for the Allies, this date marked a turning-point in the war.

8

— Before we hear once again the cannon's belch, and the bugle's sour note, perhaps you'd care to say a word.

— Had I wished to say a word, I would most probably have said it.

— Would you?

— You're right, probably not. As we are about to embark on our military career, we must take care not to talk. Words are always misunderstood in the army, at least intelligible ones. They get you into trouble. They commit you.

— Not really. Hardly anybody ever understands them. I got the impression that most of the non-commissioned officers had a vocabulary of ten words, used in an infinity of different ungrammatical patterns.

— And the officers?

— Somewhat fewer, but they had a vast selection of distinguished grunts to fall back on.

— You are talking of the regulars, of course.

— Of course. The conscripts came armed with words, and even sentences, but they had nowhere to put them, nowhere to practise them, so they gradually surrendered them and as they ate the food they were given, they likewise used the words they were given. Only the thoughts they were given they rejected solemnly, in the silence of the night.

— Remember Sergeant C.?

— Is it out of forgetfulness you don't call him by his name?

— Out of disdain. He was only twenty-eight years old, and had lost all his teeth, not fighting, you can be sure of that, but out of ignorance. He munched on gums, like an old man, and had a predilection for cake, soft crumbly cake he could assimilate. He would watch parcels arrive and make a mental note as to who were their recipients. It was about as complicated a mental note as he was capable of. Then he would prowl around, asking in a thin, sinister voice: 'Any cake?' At first, the timid would give in and share their cake with this monstrous young fellow. Then they got wise to the fact that surrender only led to obligation, not to consideration, and whatever the parcels contained we would inform him that we had some excellent toffee to offer him. His cratered face would twitch with irritation. 'Fuckin' date,' he would rasp, 'you fuckin' well knows I can't fuckin' eat fuckin' toffee,' and he would slink away. The monotony of his conversation was remarkable even by the standards set by his colleagues.

— I recognize the first word, of course, as well as I recognize the fourth, the ninth, and the eleventh, but what is a 'date'?

— I never found out. It is, I suspect, an Edwardian term of derision, perhaps deriving from the conquest of the Sudan, or some other place with oases. Do you further remember that extraordinary parade conducted by Sergeant C., during the course of which he made a graceless and terrible exit from our life? False teeth had been ordered from the Army Dental Corps round about 1936, but with the usual administrative complications, they did not arrive at the right mouth until the late spring of 1942. His gums were suddenly separated by two sets of gleaming white castellated fortifications, while his cheeks were stretched unnaturally, so that his murderously pale eyes reposed on wet, red carpets, like a bloodhound. He croaked and barked his incomprehensible orders as usual, but with a hideous assurance. Suddenly, a particularly grating yell turned into an unearthly wail. We all dared to look, and saw him stagger. After a moment, blood streamed from his mouth. Unused to his new embellishments, he had bitten right through his tongue, and now was near to fainting with pain and panic. A corporal rushed to the rescue, and we saw him leave the parade ground, not to return during our time.

— Will I ever forget him? His greatest love was soldiering, his greatest fear, active service. In retrospect, his bite really was worse than his bark. And do you remember Company Sergeant-Major R.?

— Anonymous for similar reasons?

— What other? Charity, perhaps. He had been a boxer, and was now what is called punch-drunk. He was incapable of looking you in the eye without dancing on toes deadened by stamping, ducking his head, bobbing and weaving to avoid your imaginary blows. Among his multitude of nervous tics was his repeated litany of 'Stand Up Then,' even if people were lying patiently by their machine-guns. This maniac had a seven-day leave due and we all counted the hours. The morning of his presumed departure, he was still there. He was still there in the afternoon and evening and the next day. He utilized his leave to spy on us and put us on charges without the restriction of other duties. On the seventh day, I had the courage to ask him why he had not gone home. He feinted, blinked and steadied himself on the bar where his tenth beer stood half-finished.

'I'm a Comp'ny Sar'nt-Major, i'n I?' he asked, and when no answer was forthcoming to this question, which I presumed to be rhetorical, he wheezed dangerously, 'I'n I?'

'Yes, you are,' I acknowledged.

'My dad, 'e's all I go' left, i'n 'e?'

'Yes,' I agreed.

'An' I'm all 'e's go' left, i'n I?'

'Yes.'

'Yes what then?'

'Yes, sir.'

'That's fuckin' be"er. Well, my dad, 'e's a Regimental

Sar'nt-Major, and I ain't never goin' 'ome on leave till I can talk to the old bastard as an heequal, go' it?'

'Yes, sir.'

'I got my rights, i'n I?'

'Yes, sir. Indeed you have, sir.'

'Right then. Fuck off then, afore I lose me temper.'

'Yes, sir.'

A fiendish grin lit his face.

'Tell you what you can do afore you go. Buy me hanother beer.'

Not even Dickens could have invented such a lyrical flow of rustic awfulness. We had been moved from a dramatically overcrowded billet into a new and better one. Shortly afterwards, I met him in the street.

'Stand up then,' he said, and added: 'Ow's the new billet, U'nov?' (The last word is my name.)

'Oh, much better sir, thank you,' I replied. 'It's much less congested.'

'I know,' he snarled, as though I had uttered an unworthy imbecility, and then, on reflection, he added, 'More room too, i'n there?'

Yet another time, he held aloft a plastic grenade, the latest fruit of British ingenuity, a weapon which did no great damage, but which made a most deafening noise. 'I want you to look at this 'ighly careful,' he said mysteriously, holding it aloft. 'This grenade I got 'ere is 'ighly detrimental to henemy morals.'

When his remark was greeted with a titter of laughter, he bobbed and weaved as never before, pointing a tremulous finger at the esplanade of the seaside town we were stationed in, which was visible through the window, and yelled: 'Laugh, will you? I'll 'ave you all runnin' hup an' down the hescapade with full packs on till tomorrow mornin'. I don't care, I got time, i'n I?'

'Yes, sir,' we all chanted.

Many years later, the odious fellow was admitted to a lunatic asylum. His unquiet spirit had led him into the habit of beating up new recruits in camera, and he chanced on a better boxer than himself. The shock was too great, and he lost all co-ordination.

— Tell the story we first heard on entering the service, and after that, you're on your own. I haven't thought of all this for so long, it fills me with a sense of awe that it should have happened at all, to us of all people, in this lifetime.

— How well I understand you. The story we first heard on going in? Ah yes, an illustration of the sensitive ironic soul's existence beneath the veneer of incomprehensible shouting and stamping which constitutes the outward show of military efficiency. It happened at St Margaret's Bay, in Kent, a resort a few miles east of Dover, where a pebble beach nestling at the foot of the famous white cliffs is the target for innumerable Channel swimmers in times of peace, it being the closest landing place to France, a fraction under twenty miles away.

In time of war, it was melancholy indeed. The bungalows on the beach were deserted, and had been used as part of a street-fighting course by the military. Complicated barbed-wire constructions to a height of over ten feet added to its desolate hostility. Up on the cliffs was the village itself, and countless holiday homes, now largely taken over by the army. Dominant among these was the Granville Hotel, a white building with slatted verandahs, redolent of distant summers and sweet idleness.

Here I stood in my civilian clothes, together with a few other depressed recruits, staring into a roaring fire, under the penetrating scrutiny of an old sweat who had remained a private soldier for nigh on forty years. He had lived totally without ambition, with a clear, precise concept of his position in society. The coming of war had prevented his retirement, and now he studied us and our civilian sadness with eyes both critical and kind.

'I'd 'ave to cast me mind back forty years and more to put myself in your shoes, an' yet I remembers it as though it was yesterday,' he mused, and then, with a sudden buoyancy, he added, 'There was an old sweat like myself to greet me the day I said goodbye to civvie street, and I'll tell you the story he told me to cheer me up, see. The story went as follows. Once upon a time there was two private soldiers engaged in latrine fatigues. It was autumn, and they was sweepin' the bits o' soiled toilet-paper into piles for incineration, see, when a gust o' autumn wind come along, and sent one of these bits o' bumph up in the air like a leaf, just out o' reach o' the two men, and before they could do anything about it, it 'ad gone in the Colonel's window. Now one of the men says to the other, "Listen, you go on sweepin' up. If there's any questions asked, I've been taken short. It's only 'uman, isn't it? Meanwhile, I'll go in there and try to get that bit of soiled bumph back. The old man's quite deaf, short-sighted an' all, 'e may not notice me." After a couple o' minutes, 'e's back, see, and the other private, still sweepin' away, says, "Well?"

'The first private shakes 'is 'ead, gloomy-like. "I was too late," 'e said. " 'E'd already signed it." '

The comfort which this piece of folklore imparted was inestimable at that moment. It suddenly humanized the conspiracy which seemed bent on destroying the human spirit in the interests of an illusory efficiency. Amid all the hoarse yells of the morons who rushed around us like sheep-dogs, nipping our ankles, shoving and threatening while our bleating mass stamped hither and thither on the parade ground, there was the solace of this ancient legend, dry as the season in which it was set. Its final wisdom lay in the fact that the man who told it was, with all his simplicity and the lowness of his rank, more literate, more poetic than any of the non-commissioned officers who identified the voice of even the most slow-witted of officers with that of God.

It is, of course, possible that I was abnormally sensitive to the brutalizing effects of military life because I already considered myself destined for better things than being a successful robot, and it is not without reason that I have entirely overlooked a date of primordial importance in my life. It was 22nd June, 1941, the day on which Hitler launched his fatal invasion of the Soviet Union. At that time, I was not yet in the army.

While appearing in *Diversion* at Wyndham's Theatre, I had written a play, partly in my dressing-room, partly at home during the nightly bombardments. It was written in pencil in a couple of school exercise books. When I deemed it to be finished, I rather shyly gave it to my habitual benefactor, Herbert Farjeon, who took it away to read. Four weeks passed, and I heard nothing. I began to believe that it had either displeased him or else that he had mislaid it. Although it was in manuscript – I have never learned to type, nor could I, at that time, afford to take it to a typing agency – I was not convinced that it was a very great loss. Whenever I saw him, and dropped a hint of my impatience to know his opinion, he was subtly, smilingly evasive.

Then came the weekend of Hitler's greatest initiative. I was down in Gloucestershire with my parents when the news broke. The village postmistress, Miss Pitt, rode recklessly over the somnolent Sunday-morning landscape on her ancient bicycle, shouting 'Russia Invaded' as though selling newspapers in a crowded thoroughfare.

We seized the papers and began speculating about all the imponderables an event of such magnitude automatically turns up. I even toyed with an old radio, capturing garbled voices in a hail of static which we imagined was both Russian and hysterical. It was only after lunch that I settled with the interior pages of the Sunday newspapers to find out what had been going on in calmer backwaters. In James Agate's column of the *Sunday Times* I glimpsed a headline, 'A New Dramatist', and felt a pang of envy. The foremost dramatic critic of the day had seen fit to bestow his accolade on some fortunate soul; good luck to him.

Then I read the article. The new dramatist was none other than myself. I re-read it several times before daring to impart my secret to my parents. Now I understood the mischievous smile on Farjeon's face, the cool, uncharacteristic evasiveness. He had had the play typed at his own expense, and given it to Agate. The article was superb. It ended with the following words:

'When peace permits the English theatre to return to the art of drama as opposed to the business of war entertainment, this play will be produced. Let not the ordinary playgoer be dismayed at the prospect before him. This tragi-comedy is funny to read and will be funnier to see. Yes, a new dramatist has arrived, and his play will be seen.'

I showed it shyly to my father as though it was an item which might be of vague interest to him, and I must record that he took the news remarkably well.

It is hard to take the rigours of military life when you have been so flattered, and yet this unique happening also gave me a glow of serenity, even when the sergeant-major was lavishing his choicest obscenities on me. There was, I remember, an odious procedure called kit-inspection. All one's kit had to be laid out in prescribed geometrical patterns, with the socks somehow arranged in square shapes, flanking the oblong greatcoat on top of the blankets. Now it is all very well for square people to have square socks, but once they have been worn by round people, they faithfully adopt the shape of the wearer. I did what I could to hammer them into the squareness demanded by military protocol, to no avail. The moment I left them alone, the wool expanded slowly into a voluptuous rotundity, and they lay there like buns on a breakfast tray. The sergeant-major entered my room in a fairly jovial mood, but when his eye fell on my socks, I fancied I saw smoke emerging from his flared nostrils. He just had time before the appearance of the inspecting officer to promise me the direst punishments in the nastiest of manners.

The officer entered the room. 'Shun,' screamed the sergeant-major, his expression fixed on my socks with a kind of satanic premonition. The officer didn't even glimpse the kit. He came straight over to me and asked me if I was indeed Ustinov. I confirmed it.

'I read about you in James Agate's column,' he said agreeably, and then spoke warmly about the theatre for about ten minutes. He had, apparently, been assistant stage-manager at the Shakespeare Festivals in Regent's Park, and found military life intolerable. He was, he confided, near a nervous breakdown. I told him I understood him only too well. He agreed that it was of some consolation to him that it must be worse for me. We both laughed, and he went out. The sergeant-major came over to me with a perplexed expression.

'What'e say?' he enquired.

I looked at him in quiet, compassionate triumph.

'He said that he had read about me in James Agate's column – sir!' I said.

'What the fuck's 'e talkin' about?'

And he followed the officer, murmuring about the decadence of the modern army, owing to the influx of civvies.

As one of the coldest winters on record gave way to one of the hottest summers with hardly a hint of spring in between, life became more bearable, even under these circumstances. As a result of one of the innumerable administrative breakdowns to which all armies seem to be prone, we welcomed to our ranks a Polish Jew who could neither read nor write who spoke practically nothing apart from Polish and Yiddish, and who stood five foot in his socks. Even before the arrival of the computer to add chaos to society, it was practically impossible for the army to undo a mistake of this order once it had been made. Consequently the powers that be were forced to improvise, and our padre, a Welshman who looked like Beethoven but with a predilection for dull hymns sung in unison, appealed for anyone capable of speaking Yiddish to come forward. One man stepped forward, but he was a gypsy with an earring, who thought Romany might do the trick. It didn't. Eventually I asked to be able to try German. For the first time a tiny ember of recognition flickered in the eye of the newcomer. It was not his favourite language, of course, but Yiddish is merely a distortion of medieval German mixed with a few onomatopoeic and exotic elements, and a bridge of sorts was created.

With the help of the padre, I was given moments of compassionate leave in the regimental canteen, or rather my new friend was, and I was instructed to help him decipher love-letters from his wife, who could not read or write either. These letters, written by a neighbour I never met and was never meant to meet, were extremely touching by virtue of their ingenuous eroticism, and my mind was broadened considerably in struggling with the replies to his dictation.

On parade, human contact was less easy to maintain. The British Army at the time formed threes rather than fours, so that whichever direction a platoon turned, the central file was always somewhat hidden from view. It was therefore normal that the two of us were relegated to this central file, and I received formal instructions to translate the orders into German out of the corner of my mouth, so that seconds after the body of men accomplished their movement, we would follow suit. Since he was not sure which was left or which was right, it stood to reason that *links* and *rechts* didn't mean much to him either. He, however, was saved by his five feet, whereas I was more prominent. After a while, tired of getting the blame for his sake, I gave up my German whispers, and told him to just do what I did, which he succeeded in doing with increasing artfulness, sometimes even forestalling the rest of us by guessing correctly whatever was going on in the drill-sergeant's mind. When we eventually obeyed the order, he had already done so, and was even manifesting impatience.

At about this time, somebody decided that I was potential officer material which meant that I was put in temporary charge of a position which dominated the western cliffs of St Margaret's Bay. This position was an earthwork imitation of a pillbox, part of a rapidly improvised system of front-line defences linked by a path which snaked hither and thither on the edge of a precipice, and which no self-respecting mountain goat would ever hazard, leaving such wild risks to boys of the British army festooned with obsolete equipment. Inside the dank and perilous position there was room for three men to squat and peer into the unpromising darkness through tiny slots. It was a place ideally suited to study the habits of seabirds but hardly adequate to stem the attack of a German division. In the centre, on a small trestle table there was a wooden box full of the phosphorous grenades which had been described as detrimental to enemy morals, presented as a huge and rather austere selection of liqueur-filled chocolates, and in one corner lay a small aerial bomb, bright yellow in colour, and covered in technical information in red, with next to it, a wooden ramp. We had the orders to push the bomb manually down the ramp and over the cliff edge in case the Germans got a foothold on the beach.

The powers that be gave to me two men to hold this position with, one a Berkshire farmer with a face purple as beetroot, and a pair of joyous and bloodshot eyes to match. The other was the inevitable little fellow from Poland, who had nowhere else to go. We each were armed with rifles, of which mine was the most modern, dated 1912.

The beach, which we often had to patrol at night, was a sinister and even tragic place. Apart from the noise of the sea on the pebbles, there were rodents under the duckboards and bats in the eaves of the mined houses, and endless bits of flotsam landing, a burned aviator's cap, a few sodden pamphlets exhorting the French populace to fresh efforts which had missed their mark and been blown back, crumpled and twisted pieces of metal and charred wood from sunken ships, even a shattered case full of dripping erotica, the life's savings of some solitary voluptuary, which landed at my feet on a blanket of boiling surf early one morning, and caused me to call out the guard.

Rumour had it that before our arrival, a German commando had abstracted the entire guard of the regiment which had preceded us, leaving no trace of their absence apart from the mugs of spilled cocoa and the vague signs of struggle. True or not we were armed with four grenades each, which hung from our belts, as well as sub-machine guns, recently arrived from the United States, so that to the military this was clearly a position of some sensitivity.

It was against this background that the invasion alarm sounded one night, a wail of sirens. There had not been much sleep in any case. The R.A.F. was bombing the French coast, and there was the crisp bark of artillery as well as the rumble of war, an indefinable noise like a magnification of silence. I struggled into my equipment, and ran blindly along the clifftop path, my grenades beating a tattoo on my uniform as they danced on my belt. I had no faith in the damned things. All I saw was a child's drawing of conflict. There were fires burning near Calais, and the sky seemed to have a scarlet pulse. In the inky Channel, I noticed spasmodic lines of tracer bullets, which suggested there was some kind of engagement between motor torpedo boats. Perhaps this was it, what we had been led to expect. I plunged through the canvas curtain at the entrance of my strongpoint. The farmer was already there, his goofy chuckle echoing against the dank walls. The little Pole was there too, fingering the glass grenades, and shaking them in his hot little hands as though they contained cough medicine.

'Little bugger got 'ere afore I did,' giggled the farmer, 'an' I reckon I'se a fast dresser.'

I was less concerned with the Pole's uncanny ability to forestall events than with his reckless handling of the odious little grenades, which had been known to explode when held or shaken in the hand.

'*Das müssen sie nicht anrühren!*' I cried. '*Diese Handgranaten sind mit Phosphor gefüllt! Die können in ihren Händen explodieren!*'

In a sudden rage, I understood why we were being invaded. Hitler, in two minds about whether to try his luck, had received information from a spy that the British position nearest to the French coast contained two private soldiers who could only communicate in German. Immediately the adrenalin began to flow. He slammed his fist on a map of the British Isles and shouted to his entourage: '*Meine Herren, Wir fahren gegen England*!'

My lightning reverie was interrupted when the Pole put the grenade back in the box, and complained that he had found it difficult to sleep.

'Why?' I asked, incredulous.

'*Zu viel Lärm*. Too much noise.'

As is often the case in the army, before you have the time to savour one absurdity, it is already replaced by another. The sergeant-major burst through the curtain and held it for our Company Commander to enter. In the dim light of a torch, I could see that the officer was wearing pyjamas, over which he had flung his greatcoat, a mapcase, a revolver and other martial accoutrements. He was a paunchy but energetic man, his hair in an iron-grey crew cut, and a moustache bristling chaotically on his upper lip. At the moment, he blinked furiously. The coolness notwithstanding, he was perspiring freely, and the prickly drops flowed in a continuous stream into the corner of his eyes.

Despite the agitation on his face, he spoke softly and calmly, with almost a tinge of melancholy.

'Men,' he said, 'I can now reveal to you that we are a suicide battalion. Inland there are massed mortar and artillery batteries trained on this beach. In the very nature of things, some of the shells are bound to fall short. Good luck. Good luck. Good luck.'

He shook all three of us by the hand, and bowed his head to sweep out, and carry his message of great joy to those still blissful in their ignorance. The sergeant-major screeched again, and followed the Company Commander.

The farmer laughed serenely. 'I never seen the old man in such a state,' he observed, amused. 'All that sweat . . .'

The Pole was less reassured. He didn't much care for handshakes under such circumstances. '*Was sagt er?*' he asked.

I heard my own voice, as though from far away, speaking in immaculate German: '*Der Herr Major hat soeben festgestellt, das wir ein Selbstmord Battalion sind.*'

147

Before I had time to elaborate, and explain about the *'Minenwerfer'* trained on the beach, our diminutive friend had decided to carry his questions to a higher level. Sinking to his knees, his face turned to the humid walls, he began a religious chant as old and as lacerated as time itself.

Naturally such a sound in the midst of battle had all the non-commissioned officers running hither and thither like hens on an arterial road. The quizzical whistle of shells and bombs, earth-shaking explosions, the barking of incomprehensible orders – all that was natural, but the lamentation of a tiny Jeremiah whose forehead was streaked with mud where he had beaten it to claim attention – that was a disruptive influence in the midst of a grand show of sterile manliness.

I could not silence him, nor did I see much point in it. He was merely expressing what I felt, an exasperation with mortal folly, and making his point much more eloquently than I could ever have done it. Two sergeants couldn't budge him an inch, tugging with all their might. It was only after silence had fallen over the seascape that he consented to go with his captors. It had been either a false alarm, or else a sortie in strength to test our defences. We never fired a shot. The yellow aerial bomb and the tray of phosphorous bombs lay tidily where we left them. We returned to our palliasses, removed our equipment, and set out to sleep through the little that was left of the night.

It was impossible. From far away, the guardhouse no doubt, thin and pure as a flute, the strains of an ancient Hebraic song permeated the midsummer night, and gave no less peace than the sounds of war. At dawn it ended. Shortly afterwards, the Pole was released from the army, to go back to his craft of tailoring. He, with the help of a few prophets and of God, had taken matters into his own hands, and had convinced the British army that he was not for it, and therefore that it was not for him, and all this without knowing a single word of English, simply by singing songs.

Months later, on leave, I crossed Piccadilly on foot. Who

should I meet on an island in the centre of the thoroughfare but the hero of St Margaret's Bay. On his arm was a dumpling of a woman, an inch or two shorter than he, a grin wrapped halfway round her head.

'*Wie geht's?*' I asked.

He answered in English.

'Diss my wife.' I nodded. 'Tings moch better. I now make ooniforms,' he said gravely, in the knowledge that at last his full potential as a man was being tapped in the interests of the war effort.

I was happy for him, and yet somehow saddened that he had become so much more ordinary. The purity of his gesture could not possibly be renewed. He was interpreted into a new society, and was busy acquiring the colour of his surroundings. Soon he would share its prejudices and its small-talk as well.

Not long after this incident, we were marched away from St Margaret's to make way for elements from another regiment. We passed our successors, whistling the same silly songs of masculine loneliness, as they marched towards the pretty little village we had just left. They seemed robust and jolly chaps, as they chanted, 'She'll be coming round the mountain when she comes,' and I thought to myself, 'There, but for the grace of God, goes a suicide battalion.'

Our next duty was to try and capture the town of Maidstone from the Home Guard, that civilian task force of veterans and the infirm who were supposed to harass the Germans in case of a landing, and hold vital positions until better-armed units of the army could be deployed.

We were, on this occasion, supposed to be German. As soon as the battle began, I detached myself from my unit, and advanced alone to the centre of the town by the simple expedient of knocking on people's doors. When they were opened, invariably by men in pyjamas or women in nightdresses, for it was a little before six in the morning, I would explain the vital nature of the manœuvre, without ever revealing which side I was on. Flushed with patriotism, the good burghers of Maidstone forgot their annoyance at being woken so early, and let me through their houses, and into their gardens. Here I would climb into a neighbouring garden, and knock on the back door of another house. These people would then let me out of their front doors. Looking both ways, I would then race across the road and knock at another front door, and the process would repeat itself. It took me over two hours to penetrate into the centre of the city at right angles, as it were, to the traffic.

There, I suddenly found myself before the Home Guard headquarters. A choleric general emerged. I aimed my rifle at him, and fired. Since the rifle was empty, it only produced a click, which neither he nor the umpire, a very stout lieutenant, heard. I consequently shouted 'Bang!' and then informed the general, politely, that he was dead.

Death was the farthest thing from the general's mind, and he spluttered, 'Don't talk such tommyrot. Who are you, any-way?'

The umpire turned out to have a terrifying stammer. His face scarlet with effort and apology, he told the general that he was indeed d . . ., but the word simply would not come.

It was the delay in the verdict which more than anything seemed to enrage the general. 'Look here,' he snorted, 'it's not good enough. Fellow points a gun at me and says bang. May be a bad shot for all I know. Might have come out of the encounter unscathed, what?'

'Would you have preferred me to use ammunition?' I asked.

The general lost his head. 'Who asked your advice?' he blustered. 'Haven't you done enough harm?'

'D . . . ead!' the umpire managed at length.

'I won't accept it. Won't accept it, d'you hear? Not from a mere lieutenant.'

It was the lieutenant's turn to be annoyed. 'I am the acc . . . the . . . oh . . . acc . . .'

'I don't give a damn about all that,' ranted the general. 'I'm off to inspect the forward positions, and I'd like to see the chap who's going to stop me.'

'*Sie sind tod!*' I cried.

The general spun on me, suspicious for the first time. 'What did you say?'

'*Sie sind tod, Herr General!*'

'Are you talking some foreign language, or something?' asked the general, as though he was on the trail of something big.

'*Ich bin Deutscher.*'

'German, eh?' the general asked, his eyes narrowing.

'Acc . . . redited umpire of this exc . . . exc . . . sss,' the lieutenant declared.

Just then, some other Home Guards appeared out of head-quarters.

'I've caught a German prisoner,' cried the general. 'Put him under lock and key,' and then, brushing the umpire aside, he jumped into his staff car, and told the driver to leave the scene of his humiliation as quickly as possible.

The umpire was boiling with frustration.

'I'm s . . . so . . . so . . .' he hissed.

'So am I, sir,' I said as I was led away.

A Home Guard major read all my correspondence, culled from my pockets, and then began a cross-examination.

I refused to answer in any language but German.

The major became very irritated. 'Now look here, I'm going to report you to your unit if you don't pull up your socks and answer a few questions.'

'*Dass ist mir egal,*' I rasped.

'That's your final word?' he asked, evilly.

'*Heil Hitler!*' I shouted.

'That does it.'

They chose to lock me in the armoury.

I seized a Sten gun, broke open the door, upset the staff table, smeared ink on the maps and plans of the local high command, before I was overpowered by a cohort of old gentlemen, to whom I wished no harm, and therefore allowed myself to be locked into a disused scullery. They were all very angry indeed, and I felt that the frontier between fact and fiction had become unclear. One or two of them looked at me as though indeed I were a Nazi.

In the mid-afternoon, the colonel of my battalion arrived. He was a man whose voice rarely rose above a whisper, and whose head emerged from the front of his uniform at such an extravagant angle that from the side one could read the name of his tailor inside the jacket. He had the curious prehistoric look of a bemused turtle, and I always felt that if we ever had to face actual warfare in the company of this gentleman, he might well, in a moment of difficulty, disappear into his uniform until the storm blew over.

'Now what is all this?' he asked me almost inaudibly.

I explained, as so often, my version of the truth.

'I see,' he murmured. 'But was it really necessary to confuse the issue by speaking in German?'

'It's a manner in which the Germans are likely to confuse the issue, sir, if they should ever land in Maidstone,' I suggested.

'See what you mean,' he said, 'although that's an eventuality I consider to be most unlikely, don't you?'

I was a little surprised to be consulted, but decided to suggest that if there was no likelihood of the Germans landing in Maidstone, we were all wasting our time.

'Quite, quite,' he agreed absently, then smiled briefly. 'Full marks.'

On his way out, he hesitated a moment. 'You are one of my men, are you?'

'I'm wearing the uniform, sir,' I pointed out.

'Yes, yes. I just thought you might belong to the Home Guard. But then, of course, there'd be absolutely no point in your talking German.'

Muttering confirmations of his own opinion, he left the room, and secured my release by suggesting the Home Guard should all learn German in order to know how to deal with recalcitrant prisoners if, of course, the Germans ever had the bad taste to come to Maidstone.

Something happened to the British army around this time. While it was loath to abandon the extraordinary abstract attitude of many of its officers, to which it believed it owed many of its successes in history, it was nevertheless exasperated by the endless retreats before Germans and Japanese, who seemed to have got hold of something new by way of battle procedure. The result of these meditations in high places took various forms, all of them immensely unpleasant. It was determined that a new, more aggressive fighting man would arise like a khaki phoenix from the fires of abandoned supplies and gutted citadels. We were made to rush up and down the pebbled beaches barefoot in what were called 'foot-ardenin' hexercises' by the non-commissioned officers who ran by our side, boots on their feet, encouraging us to ignore the pain of jagged stones, broken glass and desiccated seaweed. Then there were the battle courses, usually converted golf-courses, in which the conditions and some of the idiocy of battle were simulated, officers lying in ambush among the bushes with pots of animal blood which they would try to spray you with in order, so they declared, to get a man used to the sight of blood. These traps were quite easy to avoid, since the officers were not very adept at concealment, and had no great faith in the psychological soundness of their task. Machine-guns would blast away over our heads to give us confidence in covering fire, which didn't prevent them from shooting dead a man running near me. Those responsible had negligently mounted their guns on sand, and when they began firing these automatically dug themselves in, with the result that instead of giving us covering fire they were merely shooting through us. This may be another reason why the officers lay low with their pots of blood.

Then there was a new secret weapon called Battle Drill, in

which an infantry unit was sub-divided into platoons, each man having a specific and prescribed duty during an advance on an enemy position. I have no idea what was supposed to happen during a retreat, because we never practised those any more. Anyway, linking the activities of this combat group was a runner, who was supposed to charge over exposed ground with vital messages. My battalion was selected to produce the demonstration squad which would inject the whole South-Eastern Command with this new formula for success. My Battalion Commander selected my Company for the honour of forming this squad. The Company Commander then picked my platoon, and I need hardly add that I found myself in the demonstration squad, not as one of the chess men, but as the connecting runner! Out of the entire South-Eastern Command, they had to pick on me as a runner, with my heredity. Their horribly fallacious theory was that, being an actor, I was trained to commit long and complicated messages to memory. What they failed to realize was that, on eventual arrival at my destination, I was far too out of breath to deliver the message, and that by the time I had recovered my breath, I had forgotten the message.

All over the counties of Surrey, Sussex, Middlesex, and Kent we travelled in lorries in order to demonstrate this new method of defeating the Germans. I must have run hundreds of useless miles carrying information I was unable to deliver. For many years, before the advent of new highways, I was never lost in these counties. I recognized every hedgerow as a refuge where I had panted my lungs out, with the grass going in and out of focus as I stared at it in order to avoid looking at the corporal who cast his shadow over my wheezing form.

'Deliver the fucking message, damn you!'

I recognized every hillock as an obstacle I had had to run across, doubled up, in order to lessen the target. I recognized every ditch as a gaping mouth ready to snatch my ankle in its jaws. Dante had his inferno, I had mine.

There was still one lesson to learn.

When eventually an application arrived to join Carol Reed, in Scotland, in order to write a film about the techniques of Combined Operations, I was marched in to see the colonel. He vaguely recognized me from somewhere, Singapore, Kuala Lumpur, Maidstone ...

'You don't want to leave us, do you?'

'Yes, sir, I do.'

'How very odd.'

He informed me that I could leave the very next day after lunch, and after a morning spent in the rifle butts. I was so intoxicated with relief at being able to leave this Alice-in-Wonderland unit that I shot like a sheriff in a Western, fast and furious and carefree. When they fetched my target, it was revealed that I had shot all ten bullets into the same hole. The centre of the target was just demolished. The colonel affixed the target to his notice-board, my posting was cancelled, and I was sent on a sniper's course. Not only did Great Britain have Battle Drill up its sleeve, it also had a Wyatt Earp. The only trouble, as they were to find out, was that however good a shot I might be, I needed the help of ten men to lift me into a position from where I could wreak havoc. A few days later I left for Scotland after all.

And here is the lesson I learned in the army. If you want to do a thing badly, you have to work as hard at it as though you want to do it well.

– 9 –

Officially I still belonged to my old regiment, but was seconded to the Directorate of Army Psychiatry. It would have taken a lunatic to discern any immediate change in my condition. I travelled up to Glasgow by train, and was put up for the night by an Ordnance Depot in a huge warehouse full almost to the ceiling with mattresses. There was, indeed, just room for a man between the top layer of mattresses and the ceiling. I dreamed of tanks and submarines all night, and had my ration of claustrophobia for life. The next morning, I left for Troon.

It was in the pleasant if rather baleful surroundings of a half-deserted seaside town, with a particularly strident colony of gulls, that I first met Carol Reed and Eric Ambler. Carol was a captain who behaved as though the war was a superb invention of Evelyn Waugh's. He had a tendency to daydream which was most engaging and blissfully unmilitary, and his mind was tremulous with tender mischief. Eric, on the other hand, was a gunnery major who talked fitfully of trajectories and ballistics as though he were the young Napoleon, giving an impression of tetchiness and vanity which was quite illusory, for once circumstances divorced him from his playthings, he mellowed into the most gracious and considerate of men. I was, I admit it, abnormally sensitive to the changes which uniforms seemed to impose on people, because I was privileged to have a snail's eye view of the whole giddy structure. Since I was the only member of the unit who was not an officer, I fell victim to a superannuated

156

makeup man from a small film studio, who was now a lieutenant, and whose battledress sported medals from the 1914 war. This man, perfectly docile in peacetime and an excellent make-up man within the limits of his epoch, insisted on commandeering a military vehicle every Friday, and driving with me to a disused boarding-house, for which he borrowed the keys. There I would wait in the entrance hall until he had set up all his paraphernalia. When he was ready, he would call, like a child during a game of hide and seek. I would knock at the door.

'Come in!' he would command.

I would open the door to see him seated majestically behind a tin box at the head of the dining-table. I would then march up to him, salute, sign for my pay, gather the miserable pittance into my pocket, salute again, and march out. There I would wait once more while he collected his props, and perhaps his thoughts as well, and when he appeared at length, all chipper with a kind of post-orgasmic glow, we would drive back to work in the same commandeered vehicle while he regaled me with tales of great pay-days of the past, in Gallipoli and on the road to Mandalay.

Among Carol's first initiatives was to interview a colonel who had become famous as a fearless leader on various dangerous excursions up sheer cliffs and rocky promontories.

'If I may pose a rather delicate question,' said Carol, oozing tact, 'what would the average casualties be on one of your commando raids?'

'On the contrary,' replied the colonel, 'damn good question. Got to be asked sooner or later.' And he thought for a moment, his white eyelashes like the legs of a centipede against his irises. 'Of course, you have to realize that most of your casualties are not caused by the Hun at all, but by your own covering fire.' The others looked at each other, but after my experiences on the assault-course, I can't say this was much of a revelation. 'Eighty per cent,' said the colonel at length in a reasonable sort of a voice, and added, 'but I don't think we ought to frighten the public, say seventy per cent.'

Before we had achieved very much, the famous raid on Dieppe took place, which occasioned a fundamental revision of all landing procedures, and it was realized that whatever film we managed to produce, it would be out of date long before reaching the screens. We were sent home, but not before I had entered a local talent competition at the local theatre in Troon. My chief rival was an eleven-year-old lad in a kilt who sang 'Annie Laurie' ingeniously and consistently flat. Here was obviously a great future talent for atonal and dodecaphonic scores. His only drawback on this occasion was that he foolishly chose a melody that was known. I scraped home by improvising a Bach cantata, doing all from vocal timbres, and the instruments of the orchestra as well. The first prize was ten shillings, which I accepted gracefully, using a heavy Scottish accent in case it be suspected that my talent was not local. I have always had slight feelings of remorse at having robbed the unmusical child of his ten bob, but my excuse was that not for the first or last time in my life, I was flat broke.

In London, seated with the military psychiatrists, we debated how we could avoid being sent back to our parent units. This threat was especially grave for Carol Reed, who had no parent unit, having been made a captain for this specific duty, so there was no telling where he might not end up. I must say, as an officer he had perhaps even less natural aptitude than I did as a private. He wore his clothes with exemplary elegance, but had an unfortunate tendency, perhaps as a result of having directed one or two historical films, of raising his cap to those who saluted him. I was in mortal fear of being sent back. I could already visualize my old colonel in my mind's eye. 'Ah, there you are! Now where have you come from ... Dar Es Salaam, Solitary Confinement ... Maidstone?' It was desperation which made me eloquent. I suggested a film specifically for those who had just entered the army, a film in which the bridge between civil and military life would be created by means of humour and comprehension.

Since none of the psychiatrists nor Carol Reed had ever been private soldiers, they listened to me with an awesome respect to which I was quite unused. Eric, who had been a gunner, agreed that such a film would serve a purpose in the modern world, in which patriotic duties could no longer afford to seem to be punishments.

On October 6th, 1942, *House of Regrets*, the play which Agate had so praised, opened for a limited season at the Arts Theatre in London. It was beautifully directed by Alec Clunes, and received a press which I have never had since and can never hope to have again. The headline of the *Daily Mail* was bold: 'Best Play of the War.' The press chased me into Hyde Park, and took photos of me hugging Isolde and smiling. Jonathan Cape published the play, so that I could actually see myself in print. The play was dedicated to Herbert Farjeon. I had arrived, and this event was the *coup de grâce* which convinced the military psychiatrists that the recruiting film was worth doing.

For administrative purposes I was now attached to the Army Kinematograph Service in Wembley Park, a unit composed of film-makers posing as soldiers. The quasi-military atmosphere was uncongenial to creativity of any sort, while the fact that we were all artists and technicians in peacetime, linked by certain shared interests and democratic habits, made us rather shabby soldiers. In spite of being allowed to sleep at home, I had to cross the whole of London before dawn every day in order to march to the Express Dairy, knife, fork and spoon in hand, in order to eat breakfast. Then I had to march back and wash up my utensils, after which I was free to cross the whole of London again in order to settle down to work in an annexe of the War Office. Once a week, I had to stand guard all night at Wembley Park in case the Germans tried to capture some of our films.

It was a great improvement on my previous existence, and yet full of administrative silliness which served no purpose other than to prevent the best work from being done. I had, however, grown in cunning. London was a nightmare for private soldiers, since there seemed to be someone to salute every ten yards. Since the only greatcoat to fit me across the shoulders reached almost down to the ground, I wore this even when the weather hardly justified it. I puckered the cloth of my beret by means of affixing a safety-pin to the inside, which sucked my regimental badge into a fold of material. I wore glasses all the time, smoked cigarettes from a long amber holder, and carried an empty briefcase. As a result of this, I no longer saluted anyone, but Poles of all ranks saluted me.

Once, while on forty-eight hours' leave, I did salute a French officer, making an exception to my rule. Since we had no obligation to salute foreign officers, my gesture took him by surprise. He stopped me, and asked in halting English why I had saluted him.

Without really thinking, I replied in French, '*Parce que la France me manque, mon Commandant.*'

The officer immediately broke down in a flood of tears. I was stuck with him for practically the entire length of my leave, going from bar to bar, drinking toasts to eternal friendship. He was in no condition to reveal his identity, and if by chance he did, towards the beginning of the Odyssey, mention his name, I was in no state to remember such a detail. This was the last time I voluntarily saluted an officer in the street while on leave.

Our little film, entitled *The New Lot*, seemed to go extremely well, and it was still being shown to recruits until quite recently. Many celebrated actors gave their services, including the late Robert Donat, who was extremely amusing as a kind of Errol Flynn hero in a film within a film, which our recruits, now trained in modern methods, laughed to scorn, to the embarrassment of the regular patrons of the cinema.

Filippo del Giudice was an extraordinary man, a kind of Diaghilev of the English cinema. He lived beyond his or most people's means in a huge house about thirty miles from London. As an Italian, he had been interned as an alien, and there had laid plans as idealistic as they were crazy for a golden cinematic future. On a practical level he charmed Arthur Rank, a man diametrically opposed to him in spirit and in manners, and

Rank gave him the use of a palatial mansion and the capital to play with.

At first all went well. Noël Coward's celebrated naval epic *In Which We Serve* was the result of Del's initiative, and it was splendidly successful. His secret was simply to go straight to what he called his 'talents', whom he infected not only with his enthusiasm, but whose confidence he inspired, by his outspoken and often bitter reflections about distributors and exhibitors, whom he saw as the moneylenders in the temple of the arts, to be scourged in moral imitation of Jesus Christ. It was so unusual to hear a producer give opulent expression to the secret misgivings of directors and writers that it truly seemed as though a renaissance were upon us, even if one at times suspected that the mantle of the fanatical reformer lay uneasily on the shoulders of this volatile hedonist, with his unending stream of pinchable starlets.

At this point, however, a series of circumstances led to a new and happy situation. First of all, the Army Council, jealous of the success of *In Which We Serve*, searched around for a propaganda film which would do some good to the army, which traditionally enjoyed rather less prestige than the navy, known in England as the 'Senior Service'. Secondly, one of the untarnishable glories of the international screen, Lt-Col. David Niven, was at hand and available, by kind permission of Samuel Goldwyn and his own elevated sense of duty. Thirdly, *The New Lot* was enjoying a success with recruits.

It was decided to expand *The New Lot* into a full-length film which would accommodate David Niven as both star and symbol. It was at this point that the Army Kinematograph Service sent me to an officer selection board. I informed the army psychiatrists to whom I was still reporting during this transitional period. They were extremely put out by my news until they heard that I had been called to an establishment at Watford. All at once their conversation became conspiratorial, and I was asked to 'wander to the further end of the room'. Eventually they invited me to return to within earshot, and gazed at me as the Puritans in that famous picture 'When did you last see your father?'

'You know our method?' asked one, with fearful intensity, the saliva in his pipe making little clicking noises as he tried to force a passage for the smoke.

'I think so, sir.'

'Oh, don't bother about the "sir", for God's sake. Not here.' He laughed, suggesting the office was a haven of superior sensibility. 'At all events,' he went on, seeming to find even simple expressions with some difficulty, or at least after considerable rumination, 'at all events, you are no stranger to our way of thinking.'

'No,' I agreed. They conspired again in whispers, which enabled me to remember all the marvels they had revealed to me. One of these was the danger of showing men about to go into action films of the high seas fleet with heavy guns beginning to train on the camera. It had been observed that men who had been exposed to this kind of newsreel invariably slept the night with their tin-hats over their genitalia, suggesting that a castration complex was the conditioned reflex to having a 15-inch howitzer pointed at them. I had no way of knowing whether such a phenomenon was true or not, but as with nearly every other manifestation of Freudian psychology applied to the events of every day, I found it highly improbable. In any case, it would seem to me to need a man of extraordinary sexual prowess to feel his virility threatened by a battleship. At the risk of laying myself open to suspicions of inadequacy, I would suggest that in my case a battleship would make me feel that my life was threatened rather than my potency, and that had I a nature to be impressed by newsreels, all the tin-hats in the world would still fall short of assuring me of a tranquil night.

My meditations on the often unrecognizable world in which these brilliant men existed was cut short when their leader spoke again.

'Truth to tell,' he said, 'we are not terribly sure of one man

162

out there. Naturally, as an applicant for a commission, you will be interviewed by him. Would it be too much to ask you to hand in a confidential and, needless to say, quite unofficial report on the kind of questions he asks you, the way he phrases them, etcetera, etcetera?'

I told him I would willingly report the facts, and allow him to draw his own conclusions from them.

'Now why do you say that?' he suddenly asked.

'Because the greatest psychiatric literature was written before Freud,' I suggested. 'Shakespeare and Dostoievsky achieved by sheer observation and instinct what no one has been able to achieve since these seas were charted. I will therefore humbly learn my lesson from these two titans, watch my quarry like a hawk, and carry my findings back to you, so that you, with your superior knowledge of navigation in the subconscious, can draw your own conclusions.'

I left them arguing fiercely about Shakespeare, Dostoievsky, Freud, Jung, and their man at Watford.

On arrival at the Gothic establishment in the middle of a great park, we were all given numbers, and told we had no names for the next two or three days. We were put in a classroom to await some elucidation and perhaps an address of welcome by the commanding officer. To while away the time, a sergeant spoke to us. He had curly brown hair and a waxed moustache, and spoke with curious gentility, as though the effete, oblique colloquy of the officers' mess had seeped out and infected his rougher ways with its contagion. Had he not been a sergeant, he could very well have been a butler.

'Good morning, sirs!' he said, and swung on us, 'That took you by surprise, didn't it? You 'adn't thought of that, had ye-e-ew? Well, it's true. Some of ye-e-ew are going to be called "sir" and you'd better fuckin' get used to it.'

All this was said in a tone of menace, as though a commission were a death sentence. Since the C.O. was a long time in coming, the sergeant warmed to his subject, terminating by shouting:

'While in this establishment, you will be treated as though you were officers and gentlemen, whether you are or not, is that clear? You'll undergo a lot of tests, sense of leadership, esprit-de-corps, table manners and the like. I don't hold with these goings on, but then, who am I? A mere sergeant. If I were you, I'd treat the whole thing as a game, and I don't know about you, I play games to *win*!'

His tirade was cut short by the entrance of the Commanding Officer.

'Now, I don't want you to consider any part of your stay here as a game . . .' he began, and behind his back, the sergeant smiled evilly, and winked.

I sat next to an officer at lunch, who told me how much he had enjoyed my play at the Arts. I was loath to answer, since I felt this might be a trap to lure me out of my anonymity and attribute to me qualities of earthly vanity incompatible with officers and gentlemen unless they happened to be called Montgomery.

I told him frankly of my quandary, and how difficult it was for 6411623 to take credit for a play written by Ustinov.

'Oh shit,' said the officer; 'if I'd stuck by the rules of this idiotic establishment, I'd have gone off my rocker years ago. I'm supposed to sit here and observe the manner in which you eat peas. I've given up watching men eat six months ago. I pass them all, on principle.'

I was much heartened to know I had not flunked in table-manners, but I did have problems with the more strenuous tests. After lunch, we were supposed to disappear into a hole in the ground at five-minute intervals, and crawl for a small eternity in pitch darkness until we found a way out. This was, without doubt, a test of a man's nerves, and most unpleasant it was. I was despatched five minutes after the previous man, and advanced slowly on all fours. All sorts of uninvited fantasies invaded the mind, lack of air, being buried alive, what happens if I faint? At long last, I fancied I saw a glow of light in the distance. I stopped crawling for a moment, and reflected with enforced calm. It would be just like the army to place bars across the distant opening, so that a man would have to crawl backwards, searching blindly for the diversion. Anything to make life difficult. Was it not better to search the sides of the tunnel now, before going any further? In fact, my left hand met no resistance. I veered off to the left, haunted by new doubt that perhaps this extension of the tunnel, once again entirely black, was made for unobservant creatures who hadn't seen the light. However, it seemed more likely that the army would penalize the thoughtlessly vigilant rather than the thoughtfully myopic, and I crawled on my way. All at once there was another distant radiance. It was once again just like the army to attempt to break your spirit by making you fall into the same trap twice. This time there was no resistance to my groping hand on the right. For the second time I plunged into the darkness.

All further doubt was dispelled when my head met the earth-caked trousers of the previous aspirant, and my hands fell on to the backs of hobnailed boots. He had, of course, lost time by being lured like a moth by the light, and had had to go backwards, searching for a way out of the trap.

'Once, or twice?' I asked.

'Twice,' he grumbled.

'What prevented you from getting out?'

'Fucking bars, thick as your wrists.'

We both emerged from the final hole. The officer was smiling when he saw my precursor, but his smile faded when he noticed me.

'Who tipped you off?' he enquired.

'No one, sir,' I replied.

'Now look here,' he said dangerously, 'someone is bound to have tipped you off. You couldn't possibly have picked up five minutes on the other man all by yourself. I'll soon find out.'

It was evident that my foresight was going to count against me, and that the other man was more likely to get his commission since he had paid the army the necessary courtesy of falling into its traps. Traps, after all, are made to be fallen into, and any avoidance of them displays an unwillingness to understand the spirit of the service, and may even be interpreted as idleness, or malingering.

The climax of a series of unfortunate episodes such as the one I have described came with the visit to the psychiatrist.

Pictures of a vaguely troubled nature were flashed on to a screen, and we had to write a short story in three minutes based on what we had seen.

One of these drawings was that of a man in tatters letting himself down by rope over some crenellated battlements. It looked very much like one of Goya's 'Desastres de la Guerra'. I therefore wrote a piece cunningly conceived to please a knowledgeable examiner.

'This is perhaps', I wrote, 'a Spanish insurgent contained in the fastness of Zaragoza during the Peninsular War, making good his escape with some vital information from General Palafox to the advancing troops of Sir Arthur Wellesley.'

I thought this fanciful legend to the drawing remarkably astute. Wellesley was not yet Wellington, and the British were advancing, which was calculated to please. My pains were wasted. Once again my judgement was deficient in the mysteries of things English.

I entered the room where the psychiatrist sat in wait for me, a great shaggy man with a mop of muddy white hair, and the kind of lost and found expression of clergymen who go on peace marches. He pretended to be immersed in my writing, then sent the first page over so that it hung upside down over his hand. I recognized my favourite piece. My elegant literary beginning, 'This is perhaps,' had been underlined with no less than three red pencil marks, accompanied by the single word, 'Indecision'.

I felt the blood rush to my cheeks. He had evidently reached a decision about me without as much as raising his eyes from the page. I now repaid the compliment. He gave me a bad report. Back in London, I gave him a worse one. I failed to become an officer. I was told he was removed from his job. So ended the most fruitless of many fruitless days spent under arms.

— May I break in?
— You don't have to ask.
— All this foolishness reminds me of your son coming home from school in tears of rage, and complaining of the unfairness of some schoolmaster or other.
— That was much, much later. My son hasn't been born at this juncture.
— Of course not, but it was in consoling him that you realized for the first time that the most difficult acceptance in life is the realization that there is no arbiter and no appeal. We are condemned to rub shoulders with injustice all our lives, and we are often judged by our acceptance of this fact. The spirit in which we manage it can even be said to be a measure of our maturity.
— I agree, of course, but find it strange that you should bring it up at this particular juncture. Justice had no place in the army. I never expected it, and therefore I was never disappointed by its absence. As for being an officer, I frankly didn't give a damn whether I was one or not.
— I wonder how true that is. You were always fascinated by military history and techniques. I suspect that if they had given you the responsibility you craved, you would have thrown yourself into it wholeheartedly, and would even have been extremely sensitive about the kind of criticism you see fit to hurl at it today.
— Oh, if I had been accepted as a spy that morning in front of Sloane Square Underground Station, I would have seen

to it that I became a very good one, at least while hostilities lasted. That is hardly the point. I am interested in military history and the organization of armies as I am interested in lawn tennis or football or the processes of justice, but the idea of gratuitous death scandalizes me. Let me explain myself. The French are deemed an extremely intelligent, or at the very least, an extremely intellectual people. In Pierre Laval they had a politician who saved millions of French lives by processes which were judged to be below the dignity of France. As a reward he was degradingly prevented from committing suicide, and was led before the firing squad so weakened by st. mach-pumps that he could barely stand. Such a procedure seemed more in keeping with the dignity of France. At the same time, a romantic little mafioso like Napoleon splashed French blood liberally all over the European landscape, assured the unification of Germany by compelling German to fight German, therefore being directly responsible for Prussian sentiments of revenge, 1870, 1914, and 1939, and is worshipped as l'Empereur by a nation of republicans who consider that the gratification of panache, the lump in the warrior's throat, outweighs the millions of dashed hopes, of broken lives, of annihilated talents in the balance of national history. This seems to me and will always seem to me a distortion of the values we are born with.

— Were you not opposed to Laval at the time?

— Exactly as I would have been opposed to Napoleon at the time. I hated the idea of striking bargains with the fascists, especially since I had a pretty good idea of the sinister side of the Nazi adventure, to which the only answer for us was its total destruction, but on the other hand I do not think it commensurate with human dignity for us to lower ourselves to the level of an enemy as though revenge were only possible below the belt. I am not saying for a moment that Laval was right. I am merely saying that he and Pétain between them

168

saved millions of lives, an error for which France could never forgive them.

— It is perhaps a little easier to reach such conclusions in retrospect.

— I thought so at the time. I even wrote a play about it in 1950. In many ways it is the best play I have written, although few people agree with me.

— I remember. But why this sudden outburst? All because I invoked the name of justice?

— What higher name could you invoke, especially at a moment when it was far indeed from my mind? Do you recollect the precise wording of the result of my War Office Selection Board? 'On no account is this man to be put in charge of others.'

— That makes you smile now?

— It made me smile at the time. Doesn't it remind you of something?

— 'He shows great originality, which must be curbed at all cost'?

— Precisely. Our favourite school report. And do you remember being asked the name of the greatest composer who ever lived?

— Remind me . . .

— I put down Bach, and I was told that I had the wrong answer, since Beethoven was the greatest of all composers at that time. I was heard to murmur that to my mind, Mozart was his superior, and was made to write out, one hundred times, Beethoven is the greatest composer who ever lived.

— It's a wonder we can still stand fate knocking at the door after such an unpromising introduction to his genius. And wasn't there another question, in a general knowledge paper? Name one Russian composer?

— Exactly. The correct answer was Tchaikovsky, wasn't it?

— It was indeed.

— What did you put?

— I put Rimsky-Korsakov, and was upbraided before the whole school for showing off.
— I see your point about living with injustice.
— Oh, the beauty of injustice is that it works both ways – without that, it would really take a great deal of getting used to. Let's face it, James Agate and Herbert Farjeon were at least as unjust in our favour as Harold Hobson, Clive Barnes, and Walter Kerr were against us.
— Three against two?
— That's my prejudice at work. It's probably more like forty against forty. But injustice on our level is largely a matter of opinion, while opinion itself is at the mercy of vogue, whim, camp, chi-chi, all the little mannerisms which make of the Gadarene swine a cohesive and reasoned entity, endlessly renewed, and endlessly rushing down the well-worn path, generation after generation.
— Are you hurt by the comments of critics? It sounds as though you are.
— I find them hard to forget. When Walter Kerr virtually accuses me of plagiarizing works I have never seen, I consider it careless of a man of undoubted distinction to hazard such opinions in public, and I have no burning desire to see him again. When Clive Barnes, in trying to say something agreeable about a work of mine he found feeble, reverts to paying a curious compliment about my earliest play, remembering it as having had a 'fleeting honesty', whatever that may mean, I become a little irritated when I find out that he made this Olympian judgement when he was fifteen and a half years old. He frowned when I brought this to his attention during an unsolicited encounter at a New York social gathering. 'I always thought we were contemporaries,' he said. I urged him to look himself up in Information Please Almanack for all our sakes, not least his own.
— In other words, you are hurt by what seem to you careless comments of those who should know better?

— Hurt! What does hurt mean? We survive, don't we? Whereas injustice is something we not only have to live with if we are lucky, but which can kill us if we are not. How can one compare a damp little squib from a critic to the kind of injustice we see all around us? I wouldn't dream of ever being other than slightly cold towards those who, to my mind, have behaved in an unpleasant manner towards me, and I wouldn't even have thought these matters up at all if this hadn't been *my* autobiography, and if I hadn't been put up to it by you.

— Just as well to get it out of your system.

— I'm not even sure of that, but how can one compare the imperceptible scratches on our hide with the terrible 'moments of truth' in which men have been destroyed by the law at the expense of justice?

— *The Moment of Truth* was the name of your play about Pétain and Laval.

— It was the title chosen because the producers feared the original one, *King Lear's Photographer*, would sound facetious. On second thoughts, *The Moment of Truth*, a title of magnificent pretension taken from the bullfight, where the bull is ceremonially put to the sword at the signal of the president of a court, is perhaps more far-reaching and significant. My play was not only about Pétain and Laval. There are other King Lears on record: Hindenburg, Badoglio, Franco. It was the tragedy of a man who outlives his life, if I may coin a phrase, and of another man who pragmatically exploits the reputation of this living legend. I believe that injustice is tolerable up to a point in the heat of war, or of revolution. It is for that reason that I could never be a conscientious objector. I find it impossible to claim for myself a particular delicacy of spirit when there is chaos all around me. At the same time, I regard injustice, or even the risk of injustice, perpetrated in the august precincts of a court of law, with calm consideration and time for reflection, utterly repellent.

— What made you write your play?

— I think it was the sight of Pétain, sitting expressionless and silent in the courtroom, beyond thought, beyond reaction, merely the catalyst for the high-flown oratory of lawyers, which branded my mind. On and on went his life in his wind-swept island prison, forgotten except by some of the most intransigent and retrogressive of his supporters, silent now because the altar of patriotism had been redecorated with other symbols.

— You are very tough, you who are usually so bland . . .

— I am very tough, especially with those I love. I love the French. I have spent a long time in their midst. I believe that one admires people, collectively or individually, for their virtues, but that one loves people for their faults, if such love is true.

— Of all nations, the French seem to me the most vindictive, and the most able to carry their quarrels into the beyond, after death has put a period to their tumultuous eloquence. Ancient hatreds are nurtured like precious flowers in a garden, and diatribes about half-forgotten and even historical contentions have all the freshness of a burning topicality.

But these characteristics do not for a moment make them especially prone to injustice, far from it. They merely give French injustice a particular colour compared to the multitude of other injustices. Look at poor, dumb, parachuting, ill-informed Rudolf Hess all alone in Spandau prison in his early eighties. Even Louis XVI was never all alone in Versailles. And all this because the 'Great Patriotic War' has so scarred the Russian sense of compassion that they must needs force their victim to pretend to drink the bitter dregs of defeat long after the cup is empty.

And what of the trials of Bentley and of Evans, to mention only two very doubtful cases before bewigged and robed British judges, traditionally so liberal in their dispensation of benefits of the doubt? Their wisdom and moderation did not prevent them from perpetrating several proven miscarriages of justice, and a host of cases in which doubt has only received its benefit after hanging.

Finally for the sake of argument, although there can never be a finality in the infinite annals of injustice, what about Chessman, executed nearly twenty years after his crime, after every avenue of delay and appeal had been used up in the legal system the most prodigal in safeguards against abuse? When Chessman eventually died, he was a different man from the one who had been foolish in his youth. He was eloquent and creative.

Apologists for the American legal system will say that the delay in execution was Chessman's own fault. If he had not conducted his own defence with such astuteness, he could have been put to death earlier. In reply to this atrocious argument, I would merely say that the sentence is not really one of death, for man has no control over what occurs after life. In this sense, it is a careless and pretentious misnomer. In fact, it is a sentence to spend the last days of life as unpleasantly as possible, and over unpleasantness of this sort man's control is only too hideously obvious.

— Have you any proof of this?

— Certainly. If it were really a sentence of death, why remove shoelaces, neckties and belts from the prisoner? Suicide is a do-it-yourself, labour-saving form of death, which should meet with the approval of society if such were really the sentence. But no, the prisoner must live out his time and suffer all the hideous little rituals invented by man for his own degradation, the last wishes, the menu of the ultimate meal, the final cigarette (now no longer particularly dangerous for the health), the embarrassed murmuring of the priest. A President of France once commuted a death sentence on a criminal whose appointment with the guillotine had been delayed for three weeks by appeals and doubts. He understood that after six weeks life in the shadow of death becomes inhuman and self-defeating. Seen in this light, the eighteen-year-vigil of Caryl Chessman is not only barbaric, but does no credit whatsoever to the hundreds of wise people who contributed towards this unequal battle.

— And would you say that the army first made you conscious of your feelings about these aspects of life?

— National Service is the only dictatorship of the spirit permitted in a democratic society. The navy has its own particular traditions, the air force is by definition more modern and more technical. At the time I was in it, the army was the least exclusive of the three, a kind of nightmare school for backward adults, in which degrees could be achieved in monstrous disciplines. I can tell you frankly that I hated it like poison, and would not have missed it for the world.

— Why?

— I said before that for some temperaments, a bad education is the best. The army was deplorable as a finishing school, and therefore I will for ever be grateful for all it taught me.

— Isn't there a risk that your attitude leads you to be unpleasantly negligent about all those – among them, some good friends of yours – who lost their lives?

— Oh, come on. I have told you how scandalized I am by death.

— By individual death, by calculated death, yes you have. But how about the others, the six million Jews, the twenty million Russians, the uncounted, uncountable others?

— They induce a melancholy in anyone of the remotest sensitivity, but they are not only uncounted but incalculable. We cannot comprehend, as we cannot weep for the thousands who die in traffic. Life was cheap in the Middle Ages. It has become cheaper since. It is only in specific battles for specific lives that our culture is put to the test, and with it our humanity.

— Could it be that you are a pessimist, after only fifty-five years of precious life?

— Precious only to you and me. Cheap as any other on the open market. A pessimist? Not at all. I am an optimist, unrepentant and militant. After all, in order not to be a fool an optimist must know how sad a place the world can be. It is only the pessimist who finds this out anew every day.

— Are we advancing at all?

— We have fought two wars to end war. In 1976, the nations of this world set aside the same amount of money for its starving children as they lavished on armaments every two hours. Can any right-minded man afford to be a pessimist? That was a luxury for easier days.

I joined Col. Niven, Capt. Reed and Major Ambler in an office at the Ritz Hotel. The film, now blessed by the army, was to be produced by Two Cities Films (the Two Cities being, no doubt, London and Rome), of which Filippo del Giudice was the guiding light.

My status was still rather obscure. It was easy to gather a handful of officers together arbitrarily, for the pursuit of a particular end. To add a private to this assembly was virtually impossible. There had been no reason for such an anomaly at Waterloo; there was no reason for it now. Not much had changed in military thinking since then. The only conceivable reason for a private soldier to have any prolonged contact with an officer was if he were appointed that officer's servant, or batman. I consequently became David Niven's batman, with one set of barked instructions to keep his boots and belt polished at all times, and with another set of whispered ones to help produce a film as good in its way as *The New Lot*.

Our work in a room at the Ritz Hotel had some advantages as far as I was concerned. By the intervention of David Niven, I was excused from crossing London in the dawn's early light for the purpose of marching to breakfast. Another was a pass, conceived by David, which announced to the prying eye of the Military Police that, 'This man may go anywhere, and do anything at his discretion in the course of his duty.' (An M.P. who stopped me in front of the Hippodrome Theatre, and demanded to see my pass, read it. His cruel mouth dropped open, and he asked me, "Ow d'you wangle that?' I told him that such passes were extremely rare, but that they came with 'David Niven's autograph, an' all'. He sent me on my way with an obscenity of such surpassing vulgarity that even the permissiveness of the day does not allow me to quote it, but it did adequately dramatize the degree of his envy.)

There was, from my point of view, one drawback in working at the Ritz. All my distinguished colleagues had made a certain capital before the war, and therefore had a little to fall back on. I had had no time for this. Consequently they rang room-service as we worked away at the script, and absently ordered rounds of drinks. My embarrassment increased with each glass because of my utter inability to reciprocate. I calculated that on those rare occasions when I did call the waiter, and order a round with what I imagined was the same nonchalance as they, it cost me ten days' pay. This could quite clearly not go on.

I had at home one single article of value, which I had bought in a moment of folly. It was a nude by Derain. I now solemnly took it to a dealer, who told me it wasn't a very good nude and that it wasn't a very good Derain, and who bought it for £60. With this, I reckoned to be able to keep up with my officers in hospitality for a couple of months at least.

Many years after the war, in Hollywood, David Niven invited me to dinner. There, on the wall, I was staggered to see my Derain. I asked him where he got it.

'Dear chum,' he replied, 'it's perhaps the best bargain of my life. D'you remember when we were all working at the Ritz . . .?'

I felt the colour drain from my cheeks.

'. . . Well, I bought it from a dealer for £65.'

Earlier, while still in the infantry, I had been commissioned by a small London gallery to write a piece for a catalogue about human physiognomy, which was to accompany an exhibition of portraits. The fee was £5. When I turned up with my article, written by the light of a failing torch on the barrack-room floor, the owner of the gallery told me he could no longer afford £5, and that he was going out of business. Seeing my evident distress, he said the best he could do was to give me a picture out of stock, and call it a day. He gave me a framed picture which I didn't even deign to look at, such was my anger. It was only in 1965, when I built a chalet in Switzerland, that I looked through all my neglected belongings to take stock of what I possessed. I found this picture again, and looked at it for the first time. It is a large water-colour by Kokoschka.

As I said before, half the time injustice is on your side. My heart goes out to the two dealers, who were the ones who really suffered in both instances.

The film progressed, and we were accorded military advisers who had a high enough rank to acquire facilities for us, but who were not urgently needed in the war effort. These specifications limited us to officers temporarily in limbo because they had had rows with Montgomery. There was quite a pool of these. The first one inspired immediate confidence. He had a neat black moustache and earnest brown eyes, and carried a leather attaché-case which I imagined to be full of secret documents. When eventually he opened it, it was revealed to be full to the brim of pipe tobacco. In other words, he filled his pipe directly from the attaché-case. He apologized because he had been away from the day-to-day business of soldiering for quite a time.

'One officer,' said Eric Ambler, referring to the script, 'marches his men along a defile waiting to attack the enemy. What would he do when he comes within the sudden sound of gunfire?'

The adviser's eyes narrowed as he lit his pipe in order to concentrate better.

'What would he do ... what would he do ...' he kept murmuring. 'Christ, it's so long since I ... hm ... officer ... defile ... enemy ... gunfire ... what would he do ...'

At length, when the meditation had extended itself to embarrassing lengths, I broke in nervously. 'Would he halt them?' I asked.

His face brightened. 'That's it! Of course! What else could he do? Halt them,' he said. While Eric and I exchanged glances, the officer, his confidence now restored, asked, 'Next question?'

Eventually shooting began in Denham Studios, and with it, the exciting news that we would do our locations in North Africa. Once again, the problem arose as to what to do with me. As a private on a troop-ship, I would be isolated from my collaborators, and the same might well be true in Africa. This time, the project had advanced sufficiently for me to be made a temporary civilian, so that I could at least deal with the military advisers on equal terms. The good news was charmingly broken to David Niven by a friendly general, who was also a movie-buff, 'Tell Ustinov he can reach for his bowler hat.'

The journey to North Africa was uneventful, if one can call frequent submarine alarms and mountainous seas uneventful. We were aboard a luxury liner, *The Monarch of Bermuda*, together with Canadian, British and New Zealand troops, and a single Italian officer, the first we had seen on our side, foolishly ostracized by many allied officers, but befriended by an English nurse in what was to become a touching shipboard romance.

Some years after the war, during my first and only visit to a certain London restaurant, I saw them again at a distant table. Curiously enough, after all that time, I recognized them instantly. They were engaged in a sombre and difficult discussion. He had been weeping. I risked going up to them. They were now married, she was pregnant, and he had been told that his permit to stay in the United Kingdom could not be renewed owing to the fact that he had no employment. I asked him what his profession had been before the war. He told me he had been an announcer on Rome radio. I called a friend in the Italian section of the B.B.C., only to discover that they had just lost one of their announcers, with the result that the shipboard Romeo went to the B.B.C., and I am told eventually rose to dizzy heights within that hierarchy.

As an ancient boy scout, I can say that this is one of the very few neat and tidy good deeds I can come up with in my favour at the pearly gates.

Also aboard were a handful of American sportsmen, on their way to entertain American troops with illustrated films of their exploits. Among the group was Jack Sharkey, an ex-heavyweight champion of the world. He was an engaging if monosyllabic character who drank rather heavily one night when the seas were particularly high, with the result that he was obsessed with dreams of bygone glory, and staggered into the large state-room in which I was trying desperately to control my queasiness, looking for a fight. I was right on the level of his haggard eye, and tried to make myself small and insignificant.

In the bunk above me lay Bob Fellowes, an officer attached to us, who had lost a leg by standing on a land mine, and who was not to survive his injury for long. He had just received the latest artificial limb from the United States, and he now began easing it out of his trouser-leg. When Mr Sharkey had already loomed into the immediate foreground, Bob held his leg above his head, and said in the voice of a strict governess: 'Mr Sharkey, if you don't leave us alone, I'm going to kick you.' Sharkey must have seen, as in a haze, a man holding his own leg above his head in a menacing gesture, without realizing that it was artificial. A khaki sock and a hand-made brogue shoe were still attached to it. At all events, he let out a howl as though in the presence of the supernatural, and staggered melodramatically out into the passageway.

My only other memory of this troubled voyage was the inevitable ship's concert, in which I was constrained to do my party turns, but the star of which was undoubtedly a Maori unit who performed a war dance. At the end of the show, the entertainment officer, an elderly major with sandy hair and a monocle, proposed a vote of thanks for all those who had contributed to the gala, 'Most especially,' he went on, 'the group of talented aboriginals.'

The well of insensitivity is indeed bottomless.

In Algiers we acquired another temporarily rejected colonel to help us, this one with a predilection for sitting on his shooting-stick indoors, at the expense of carpets.

Naturally, being cooped up in England for the duration had given me a somewhat parochial viewpoint of the war. Now we began to have our vision broadened, forcibly. Shooting in Philippeville before a fine stucco house, I noticed the curtains rustling. Someone was observing us. After a while, an Arab girl dressed as a European maid, with white lace cap and apron, ran out towards us and curtseyed. Her master had been watching the shooting, and invited Carol Reed and myself in for a brandy after lunch. We accepted.

He was sitting at the end of a long table, eating an orange. His napkin was tucked into the top of his sports shirt. He was a man in his fifties, bald and portly, with sad, unscrupulous blue eyes. His wife sat not at the other end of the long table, but by his side.

Ah, he complained, in a flat voice, what a tiresome war it was, and what a cruel destiny to have been born on the wrong side of the Mediterranean. The Arabs, he said confidentially, were dirty and unreliable. We wandered out into the pool area, where he offered us cigars. What would we prefer, Uppmann, Hoyo de Monterey, Punch, Romeo y Julieta, Henry Clay? He had them all. And as for a brandy, did we fancy Martell, Remy Martin, Hine, Courvoisier? He had had the presence of mind to lay in a stock. He beckoned to the deck-chairs while the chlorinated water sent its little shivering reflections on to the parasols. Yes, he repeated, the Arabs were dirty and unreliable, and he chose to say it as the Arab maid was serving us. We puffed our cigars and swilled our cognac round slowly in our balloon glasses.

He was, it transpired, a wholesale wood merchant. He would have given anything to transplant his house to Cannes or to San Remo – his family had come from the luxuriant region between the two, this French *piednoir* of Italian origin – but one must be realistic, over on the other, civilized bank of the Mediterranean, there were neither the business opportunities nor the cheap labour. There were small mercies in abundance, and one must be grateful for them. More brandy? Only yesterday, for instance, he had returned from Algiers after having concluded yet another large and lucrative contract with the Allied High Command.

'A contract?' I asked. 'What for?'

'Coffins,' he replied.

Episodes like this help explain subsequent history. Naturally, being in the hands of the military is not the ideal way to visit foreign countries, but sometimes poetic images are enhanced by the abnormality of the situation. The casbahs of Bizerta, for instance, in which the inhabitants seemed to have been evacuated at a moment's notice. Coffee cups, some with coffee still in them, stood on the little Moorish tables, as though a latter-day Pompeii had been the victim of a false alarm. Elsewhere, we were blowing up buildings for the benefit of a film, in which I was also playing the part of an Italian innkeeper. American sappers were joyously doing the damage, and when in their cups, played practical jokes on each other with booby-traps and dynamite.

Our colonel was absolutely impervious to what his hosts were up to as he sat impassively on his shooting-stick in the living-room, puffing at flat Turkish cigarettes flown out specially for him by Fribourg and Treyer, London's most exclusive tobacconist. He demonstrated once again those qualities of sangfroid and steadfastness which had won him the highest medals at Salerno. A huge explosion rent the air, bringing half the ceiling down on him. He did not move an inch. He just sat there, ridges of cream-coloured dust on the brim of his cap and the top of his whiskers, and carefully examined his cigarette, which he had only just lit.

'Ruined my confounded weed,' he grumbled. The American engineers, sobered by the miscalculation in their practical joke, gazed at him as though he were some kind of Machiavellian spoilsport.

One day, Carol Reed was directing a scene with Stanley

With Tamara
and Isolde

Tamara in
*The Unknown Soldier
and his Wife*

Liselotte Beethoven-Fink

Lola Montès; with Max Ophüls

Models by Mary Nicoll in the foyer of Wyndham's Theatre
during the run of *The Love of Four Colonels*

Discussions about Nero's mother with Mervyn Leroy

Romanoff and Juliet
'Harry Truman knew perfectly well that what you call criticism is
engendered by respect and affection, not by feelings of aversion.' In the
background, Bess Truman and Suzanne

Advice from a great actor, Sir Ralph Richardson

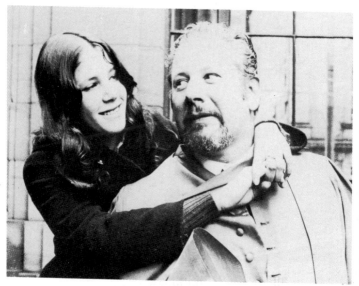

Advice from my daughter Pavla
when I was Rector of Dundee University

A choice of mounts

Hotel Sahara (Tower Film Productions)

The Sundowners (Warner Bros)

Viva Max
(Mark Carliner Productions)

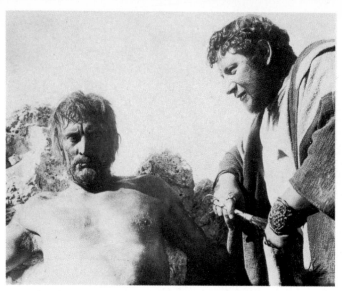

A script conference with Kirk Douglas: *Spartacus* (Universal)

Romanoff and Juliet
(Universal)
President of my
own country at last

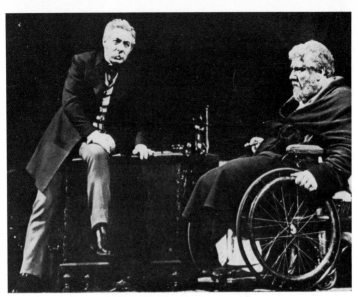

A *Photo Finish* with Paul Rogers

Beau Brummell (MGM)
with Rosemary Harris, Peter Ustinov and Elizabeth Taylor

U Thant outlines his problems

More problems for UNICEF

Holloway and some other actors playing a game of darts in my café. He asked me to bustle around in the background, talking Arabic to the extras. I told him that Arabic was one of the enormous quantity of languages I didn't know. He told me to make Arab noises. 'It's almost out of earshot,' he said. 'Who's to know?'

I did as I was told, and all went well until take four, when without warning, all the extras rose and left. 'Cut,' said Carol. 'What's wrong?'

They seemed to be on strike, although the reasons for their industrial action were, to say the least, obscure. Eventually it was explained as intermediaries argued with the extras. Apparently, in improvising my Arabic, I had appeared to refer to them as tortoise droppings. I swore to them that nothing had been further from my mind. After all, why should a restaurateur call his clients tortoise droppings while he is taking their orders?

'We thought you didn't speak our language until you called us that unmentionable name,' said the henchman, his eyes flashing with fury. 'Now we know you do!'

Apparently it was not the fact that I had inadvertently referred to them as droppings which was offensive, it was the size of the droppings which counted. Camel droppings, or better, lion droppings, would be deemed almost flattering, as far as insults can be flattering. Flea droppings would have occasioned assault with the cutlery. Tortoise droppings were just on the borderline between assault and strike action, and they had taken a clement view of my lapse.

Two hours later, shooting resumed. I steered clear of the tables of the troublemakers, and stuck to Italian.

All too soon, the great breath of fresh air was over, and we were back in England, our job finished. *The Way Ahead* opened on the morning of the invasion, and was a great success. Flushed with my contribution to this triumph, I was called back into the army. Whereas it was admitted that the Germans now had their hands too full to bother much about Wembley, there were perhaps fears that the Japanese might parachute Kamikaze editors into the outskirts of London in order to disrupt our training films. Whatever the truth about this, Wembley had become far more military with the passing of an overt military threat.

Now it was hard to believe that the place had anything to do with a craft, let alone an art. A new and extremely busy sergeant-major had been installed in order to whip the establishment into shape, with the result that it was difficult for it to fulfil its primary function, the production of training films, even though, in compensation, brasses gleamed brightly and spoken instructions were now shouted.

I remember the projection of a training film about how tanks should use smoke, towards which I had made some minuscule contribution. A celebrated general came to see the result of our work, and all the officers, the ex-production managers, second-assistants and clapper-boys jockeyed for position to receive the congratulations of the gilt-edged pundit. As the lights went up, the general patently ignored the gallant assembly, opened the door of the projection booth, and said to the private in charge, who didn't even have time to hide his comic-book: 'Damn good show. Keep up the good work,' and strode away unaccompanied to his staff car.

It was not I who began to crumble in this fruitless atmosphere, but my stomach. Despite the fact that I was ostensibly doing my duty by being in uniform, I have never in my life had such feelings of being absolutely useless as I had during my four and a half years in the service. At the same time, I am by no means ungrateful, since it did enable me to work with highly disciplined and talented creators such as Carol Reed, Eric Ambler and David Niven, and to form friendships which have lasted throughout my life. Nevertheless, the shock of being consulted by high-ranking officers and psychiatrists one moment and being berated the next for having boots in which some oafish corporal could not see an entirely faithful reproduction of his face began to tell on my constitution. I suffered from cramps, which may well have been psychosomatic, but the word was not yet in common use. I was sent to a military hospital for observation.

My observer was a charming Sinhalese (or is it now Sri Lankese?) doctor with a Portuguese name, who had a greater sensibility than usual towards the vagaries of the spirit under martial law. It was established that my gall-bladder was emptying too slowly, and that the origin of my complaint was surely nervous. I was consequently ordered a complete rest in a wing of the hospital which overlooked the playground of a lunatic asylum. Through the window I could see, at all hours of the day and night, elderly ladies looking distressingly like those in Thurber drawings running about, hooting like peacocks, and lifting their shifts over their heads. It was as though these delightful caricatures had suddenly broken away from their master's pen, and turned sinister.

Since my complaint had been put down to nerves, I was eventually sent to a man called a Personnel Selection Officer, who was in fact a kind of lay psychiatrist with the function of avoiding what were, in the jargon of the day, known as square pegs in round holes. All was to be done to find me employment compatible with my inclinations. That was the theory. The practice, as so often, was rather different. The man was Scottish, with the rather unusual physical features of a coal-black moustache and a snow-white crew-cut. He looked like Groucho Marx in his heyday in a very bad print, but he was less engaging, less comic, and finally, far less human.

He said he had examined my case, and asked me how much I earned in civvy street.

I told him that since I was self-employed, my earnings would fluctuate.

He patiently renewed his question, as though dealing with some dim-witted colonial.

'It's not too difficult to understand,' he crooned in his lilting Scots accent. 'I merely wished to know your weekly income in time of peace.'

I told him I had understood his question, and would make every effort to make the answer as simple.

'Since I am an actor and a writer, I have no regular employment. I very often make nothing in a week – ' I attempted a laugh, in which he failed to join. 'When I do make something, it is of a variable or inconsistent nature.'

He closed his eyes as though summoning hidden reserves of patience, and breathed deeply.

'I don't know why you are making this so difficult,' he murmured in a clenched voice. 'I merely asked you the extent of your pay cheque at the end of every week.'

'And that is precisely the question to which I cannot give you an accurate answer,' I replied between my gritted teeth. 'You must have heard of an actor having a bad year. Well, a bad year is made up of a preponderance of bad weeks over good weeks. By the same token, a good year is made up of a preponderance of good weeks over bad weeks. It surely stands to reason that it is impossible to give a mean ratio of good and bad weeks because I haven't been going that long.'

He sighed, and looked up at the ceiling as though something of rare interest were going on up there. I declined to follow his gaze, since I knew perfectly well that nothing at all was going on up there.

'Let me phrase my question differently,' he said at length. 'If we were at peace this week, how much money would you have made?'

At this juncture, I had a brainwave.

'If you wish, sir, I can tell you how much money I have made this week.'

He shut his eyes and broke a pencil.

'I know how much money you have made this week,' he moaned, as though tears were not far off. 'You are a private soldier in His Majesty's Armed Forces. I *know* how much money you have made this week!'

'But you do not, sir,' I insisted. My fourth play *The Banbury Nose* had opened in Edinburgh, starring Roger Livesey and Ursula Jeans. The notices were very promising, and I had just received a royalty cheque. I consulted a bit of paper. 'Last week, I made eighty pounds seventeen shillings and fourpence, not counting my private's pay.'

He banged his fist on the table, and sprang to his feet.

'You're lying!' he yelled.

I explained the facts of the case, hoping that the mention of Edinburgh might soothe his anger. He was probably a Glaswegian, for my information did nothing but stiffen his intractability.

'Right,' he said, fixing me darkly across the table, on which lay one of those simple-minded games which children of six play with ease, but over which the hesitations of grown men are supposed to betray their strengths and failings. 'Right, these are my findings. You are clearly psychologically unsuited to film writing, therefore I am sending you as a clerk-storeman to the Royal Army Ordnance depot in Donington Park, where your duties will be to grade underwear in sizes – '

I neither listened nor heard any more. For once in my life, I surrendered to an outburst of temper. All my frustrations with the idiocy and the uncertainty of this cringing existence overflowed into a transcendent rage. I picked up the game, and dashed it to the ground. The Scotsman, alarmed, backed to the door and called for help. I was seized by a couple of Military Policemen, and rushed to see the resident psychiatrist, who turned out to be a female colonel with flashes on her shoulders carrying the surprising word 'Bermuda'.

Asked about my reactions to the Personnel Selection Officer's decision, I pointed out that it was hardly his province to say that I was psychologically unfit for film-writing when a film I had helped to write was on general release to extravagant critical acclaim. I went on to speak sentimentally about the happy times I had spent working for the Directorate of Army Psychiatry, times that were no more now that I was destined to grade underwear so that the Japanese could be brought to their knees more effectively.

She was sensitive to my sarcasm, and laughed merrily as though the absurdity of my situation brought her a certain relief from routine. She ordered me a cup of tea, and told me not to worry. I would be transferred in a week or so to a branch of the army specializing in entertainment. I went back to my hospital room unaccompanied by the Military Police, and gazed at the mentally ill.

A man dressed in a morning coat was being upbraided by a grey-haired woman in a shift.

'Harold, you always come and see me in your working clothes!' she howled.

There were, as ever, far worse predicaments than mine.

I was still at the Military Hospital when *The Banbury Nose* opened in London at Wyndham's Theatre. My second play, a one-acter, the only one of the genre I have ever written, opened successfully at the Arts Theatre in 1942 in a double-bill with *The Playboy of the Western World*, and my third, *Blow Your Own Trumpet*, put on by the Old Vic in 1943, was an unqualified disaster. Of rhapsodic construction, somewhat reminiscent of Saroyan, it seemed far too wayward for the very critics who had so spoiled me initially, and the play ran for thirteen performances.

Now I had written another tragi-comedy, this one running backwards from the nineteen-forties via the nineteen-twenties to the turn of the century. The ironic content was given a sharp dramatic relief by this construction, since the characters were all old and bitter at the beginning and young and full of hope at the end.

Bill Linnit, the impresario, wished me to attend the dress-rehearsal in order to effect last-minute changes should these be necessary, and rang the Commandant of the hospital. The latter, a colonel, was quite agreeable to my going, but let drop a huge hint that he, and more especially his wife, were very keen on the theatre, and that their hostage would be more readily released at the price of two good stalls. A bargain was struck, and I travelled to London.

The first night was a qualified success, and I was forced to accept several curtain-calls along with the cast. This was the first of my plays to run over a hundred performances and James Agate in his notice referred to me as 'the greatest master of stage-craft at present working in the British Theatre'. Here was another example of injustice working in my favour. A balance was struck when, on returning to the Military Hospital, I found myself on a charge for having taken my curtain-calls in uniform, wearing suede shoes.

Before any penalty could be exacted for this unthinkable affront to military protocol, I was hurried out of the hospital by the psychiatrists, and sent to an Army entertainment unit. First I had to return to my parent establishment, the Army Kinematograph Service, where my reception was cool, to say the least. The new sergeant major made some caustic remarks about my being a — 'nut-case', his unblinking eyes boring into what he imagined to be my vulnerability. As he helped load a mountain of kit on to my back, tightening straps unbearably to contain me like a corset, his parting shot was, 'And I can tell you, young man, that *whoever* your next sar'nt-major turns out to be, you will remember me as *mild*, as *helpful*, and the soul of *kindness*, is that *clear*?'

These words were, by their very nature, snarled. I arrived at my new destination, an early Victorian house in Grosvenor Square, and faced my new sergeant-major. He smiled at me, and said, 'Let me help you out of all this *hideous* equipment.' In his way, he was quite as emphatic as his counterpart in Wembley.

He was, in normal times, a celebrated wigmaker, a career he pursues profitably and brilliantly to this day. I was sent to Salisbury, where I directed *The Rivals* by Sheridan. Dame Edith Evans, as a gesture of customary generosity towards the war effort, played Mrs Malaprop for the first time in her long and glorious career, while I attempted the role of Sir Anthony Absolute. We had a happy mixture of civilian and military actors, and as an unexpected bonus, eight members of the Berlin Philharmonic Orchestra, under their leader, Lance-Corporal Professor Doktor Reinhard Strietzel, and seven members of the Vienna Philharmonic, under their leader Private Professor

Doktor Rudolf Stiasny, all now members of the Pioneer Corps, a section of the British army organized as a reserve of foreign talents, eager to do their 'bit' against Hitler.

Rehearsals had their ups and downs. The orchestra seemed divided against itself, the first violin and conductor, Professor Strietzel, seeming to be at loggerheads with the first cello, Professor Stiasny, which culminated in an ugly scene, a storm, as it were, in a schnapps glass, during which Lance-Corporal Strietzel threatened to put Professor Stiasny under close arrest. He pointed to the single stripe on his arm with the tip of his bow, calling out in a thick German accent – 'You know vat zis means?'

The conflict was complicated by the intervention of Edith Evans, who reminded us all that it was a play with music, not an opera with dialogue. Immediately the musical contention between Austria and the Reich was forgotten. All fifteen bickering musicians were united against the muse of drama, or more accurately, against Edith Evans. As they filed out of the rehearsal hall to make way for the mummers, Professor Strietzel, carrying his violin case as though it contained a machine-gun, looked straight at poor Edith, and said with a wealth of sinister meaning, 'I don't know . . . how all zis . . . shall end!'

The play, performed in garrison theatres in very flimsy yet evocative sets, assuring a rapid continuity of action, opened in Salisbury, and was an instant success. One distinguished admiral was even compelled to admit to Edith Evans, 'By Jove, I'm embarrassed to say that this is the first play by Shakespeare I've seen since Richard of Bordeaux!'

One drawback of these garrison theatres was that there was no method of concealing the orchestra. Its members sat on the same level as the audience. It was merely the actors who were elevated. I noticed on the first night that the orchestra made use of a miniature chessboard in order to while away the time during the histrionics, and often musicians crept forward like troops in a dugout to make some snide move. As far as I could understand it was a permanent championship, Berlin versus Vienna.

I hoped and prayed that Edith Evans wouldn't notice what was going on, but on the fourth night, during a brilliant tirade, she stopped dead. One eye had alighted on the tiny chessboard just as an Austrian viola player had spotted a crack in the enemy defence, and was creeping forward on all fours to deliver the *coup de grâce*.

She faltered, fumbled, and then, with superb dramatic instinct, she looked at me and said, in a tone of pained surprise, 'What did you say?'

Determined not to be placed on the defensive, I invented a little Sheridan: 'Madam, though the humours of Bath be but a diversion to our contumely, I will not presume on your generosity to the extent of belittling those very qualities which, while they do us but scant justice before the evil tongues of the town, nevertheless becalm the odious, and bring success to fools.'

Neither I nor the audience knew what on earth I was talking about, but I said it, or something like it, with immense conviction, with the result that our exit was rewarded by a burst of spontaneous applause.

Poor Edith was livid, and kept referring to the chess playing as a 'Gilbertian situation'. After the show, I accosted Professor Strietzel. To soften the blow somewhat (for after all, he *was* a lance-corporal, and I had seen how hostile he had become towards poor Private Stiasny) I told him he had never played better than on that night.

His face lit up.

'You are a *real* musician,' he counter-flattered, 'tonight, for ze *först* time, ze Boccherini was good, alzo I still have trouble mit ze Mozart und ze Dittersdorf.'

'Yes,' I replied reasonably, 'but even there, I noticed a distinct improvement.'

'Even there, even there!' he agreed.

'There's only one thing . . . one criticism.'

'Ach!' His face darkened once again in anticipation of some searing words of truth.

'The game of chess,' I said.

He bridled like a frisky horse. 'Are you serious?' he asked quietly.

'I'm afraid so. There has to be an end to it. It is frightfully distracting for the actors. We can see your every move down there, and – '

'It distracts you?' he enquired, all innocence and soft surprise.

'Yes,' I said.

'No!' he roared. 'You are too fine an artist to be distracted. It's zis voman!'

'Now come on!' I snapped, simulating crossness. 'She's a most distinguished actress and a wonderful person – '

'It's not as zough it vas a big chessboard,' he shouted, and then his voice became dramatically diminutive. 'It vas a little chessboard.' His two index-fingers reduced its imaginary size to about one inch square.

'The smaller the chessboard the greater the distance you have to travel to make a move, and the greater the distraction for us,' I declared.

He knew a checkmate when he saw it, and retired from the scene of battle.

The next night, Edith found it hard to concentrate, which was unlike her, being a creature of a ferocious inner discipline, and usually impervious to external influence. As soon as I hobbled on the stage in the guise of my gouty paterfamilias, I saw what was happening.

The orchestra, deprived of its chessboard, had now arranged the lights from its music-stands so that its members were lit from beneath, and they now followed Edith's every move in this ghostly light, looking for all the world like war-criminals following the arguments of their advocate with misgiving and resignation.

Once again, at the end of the performance, I was compelled to accost Professor Strietzel.

'Tonight,' I said sternly, 'it was not so good.'

He was in surly temper.

'Once again,' he grumbled, 'you give proof of your musicianship. Stiasny is like a mule so stubborn. The Boccherini vas one Funeral March, not one minuet. A disgrace. The Mozart vas a little better, and the Dittersdorf superb. The rest – '

'I have a criticism.'

'Please.' He smiled like a head-waiter confronted with a fly in the mayonnaise.

'Why do you follow Edith Evans with your eyes in a manner calculated to disturb any performer, any artist?'

What was left of his smile faded, and he became controlledly rational.

'First, it vas the chessboard. Correct me if I am wrong. Chess ve shouldn't play . . .'

'That is correct.'

'So ve leave the chessboard at home. Vot else can ve do? Ve follow the play. Ve look at the voman.'

Suddenly the constriction of his voice and the coolness of his presentation of the facts deserted him. He shouted volcanically: 'You think it gives us *pleasure* to vatch zis voman? Ve, who have seen Paula Wessely at her height!'

I tried to top him in bluster, but he lowered his voice to a kind of lugubrious mutter, at the same time looking into the distance to lend a cosmic significance to his words.

'You know, ven ve left Germany, mit concentration-camps and persecution, ve thought ve would come to a land vere ve could breathe – '

Here he gave an ingenious impression of a plant opening its petals to the sun, but he quickly shrivelled. 'But no,' he said brokenly, 'it's all ze same . . . persecution . . . prison bars . . .'

I was outraged. I told him angrily that I saw no connection between myself and a Gauleiter.

'Not you, dear friend – '

Nor did I think that any more ludicrous comparison could be

made than one equating a dear, human, and profoundly religious creature like Edith Evans with Heinrich Himmler.

He nodded in a way which suggested that everyone is entitled to his own opinion, no one more so than he who has suffered a deprivation of liberty to play chess in an orchestra pit.

The next night Edith was brilliant. The only trouble was the almost entire absence of laughs. I made my entrance, and, inspired by the zest and brio of Edith Evans, I acted as well as I knew how, in complete and utter silence. It was acutely depressing. Not even the presence of three generals in the front row could justify the extraordinary dullness of the audience.

When I had a free moment, I rushed to the back of the auditorium in order to unravel the mystery. I did not have far to seek. The musicians had now reversed their positions, and sat facing the audience, their heads just visible above the rail of the orchestra pit. Lit from beneath, like mournful skittles waiting for the usual knocks of fate, they dampened the spirits of the onlookers.

Edith was very upset by the deterioration in the audience's quality, and left the stage with the unspoken conviction that she was face to face with *force-majeure*. I found no words to express my horror at such diabolical ingenuity. I just shook a negative head at Professor Strietzel, who smiled imperceptibly and shrugged a fatalistic shoulder.

The rest of the run was most successful, and for the record, I must add that the chess-games on the miniature board were resumed, and Edith never seemed to notice them any more. By the last performance, the Austrians were leading the Germans by twenty-four matches to twenty-one, with nineteen matches drawn.

I was faced by the prospect of being sent to the Far East, playing a comic bishop reduced to his underwear in a well-known farce, the rights of which were owned by an officer of the unit. This was certainly one way of increasing his pocket money, and I only mention it because when an application to join SHAEF saved me from this destiny, he roundly accused me of a lack of patriotism.

Another officer of even higher rank called me to his office and told me to lock the door behind me. He talked awkwardly about the uncertainties of life now that the war was coming to an end, and commended me on *The Banbury Nose*, which he said he had enjoyed. Then he tried to sell me his wristwatch.

SHAEF, the Allied Supreme Headquarters, wished an official film to be made about the war in the West. It had assembled Carol Reed and myself representing the British side, Garson Kanin, the poet Harry Brown, and the screen-writer Guy Trosper from the United States, and Claude Dauphin from France. The music was to be written by Mark Blitzstein, then in the American army.

The scheme of the film was ambitious, in that Harry Brown was to write lyrical bridges in blank verse to the various episodes, which were to be constructed as they came in from the material of courageous frontline cameramen. It was often my duty to go to the seat of the military censorship in Davies Street, near Claridge's Hotel, and watch these films as they arrived. Often this work was quite boring, more especially since a Dutch censor might ask for certain shots to be cut owing to the fact that a physical landmark might give away the Allied dispositions, or his Belgian counterpart might decide that a church steeple or belfry was easy to recognize, and that therefore it was unwise to let the film of a battle in such a locality out before the place was well behind our lines. In such cases, everything stopped while the incisions were made. My work was to earmark certain highly dramatic or evocative sections for use by us.

One day of heat, without any warning whatsoever, Hermann Goering appeared on our screen. There had been no mention whatsoever of his capture, no hint even. He was, to our astonishment, surrounded by American officers who were posing with him for pictures, smiling, patting his back in friendly fashion, demanding autographs on behalf of small relatives, who would live close to history from that day on, and offering to initiate him in the mysterious rites of chewing-gum. Goering looked sallow and thinner than I had imagined, quite apart from being distinctly nervous. Having been informed about the Allied war aims, he certainly had every right to his nervousness.

This began to wear off, however, under the relentless impact of these big puppies, leaping all over him and licking his face. By the time the lights went up in the auditorium, he was as relaxed and playful as any of his captors, and we spectators could only look at each other in petrified amazement. Later that day, so I gathered subsequently, General Eisenhower saw the film, and in an uncharacteristic rage sent every recognizable officer home to less exacting duties. The next time we saw Goering, he was having his belt forcibly and unceremoniously removed by a U.S. top sergeant. I shall always remember the pain on his face at this brusque behaviour, which so contrasted with the earlier delights of captivity. I never thought I would feel a pang of sorrow for the man.

The second document which will always live with me was of a graver and more terrible character, the entry of British troops into Belsen concentration camp. A sergeant came out of the gates, and even on the black and white screen, his face had gained an expression over which he had no control. It was of extraordinary complexity, at once earnest, furious, resolved and glacial. His men had fallen out by the roadside. They were smoking and chatting among themselves. He shouted an order. They were not too quick in obeying him. He shouted again. Needless to say there was no sound on any of this film. It was all pantomime, which often made it seem exceptionally graphic in that the onlooker's imagination was stimulated to fill in the gaps.

The troops seemed puzzled as the sergeant gave the order to slow march. They could hardly believe the order, because they could see no necessity for such solemnity. Once again, it was repeated.

The long line of soldiers marched slowly through the gates into the stench, and came face to face with the obscene evidence of genocide, the mountains of bones, linked by a webbing of flesh; the expressionless eyes of the fittest, the survivors; the miserable human garbage scattered on the soil. One after the other, individual soldiers fell out, vomiting helplessly on all fours. The sergeant could threaten and bluster, it made no difference. The shock had felled these men with a blow to the stomach, and there was nothing discipline could do. Suddenly one soldier went beserk. He broke ranks for no visible reason. Eyes wild, he ran, and the camera followed him.

On a step sat a derelict German soldier, an over-age man in a huge greatcoat and a muffler. The flaps of his forage-cap had fallen over his ears, and he looked like an exhausted gun-dog as he sat staring at nothing. The British soldier ran up to him, let his rifle drop to the ground, picked up his victim by the collar of his vast coat, and began kicking and hitting him without mercy. The sergeant arrived at the double, and struggled with his man. The German dropped into precisely the same position he had occupied before. On his face there was now something horribly like gratitude.

This irresistible assault on our sense of normality was, happily, matched by a counterpoint of slapstick worthy of Laurel and Hardy. There was the formal surrender of Field-Marshal Milch to a youthful British general, in which the field-marshal, true to protocol, saluted by bringing his baton up to his cap, and then formally handed it over. The British general took the baton, weighed it for a moment, and smacked it down hard on the field-marshal's head, sending him down for the count. It was all so surprising, and so unexpected that it released an explosion of laughter from the censors, quickly controlled as they realized the embarrassing consequences of such an act. Since I was more bound by the rules of comedy than by the terms of the Geneva convention, I have always marvelled at the pure untrammelled comic technique of that particular general.

Filippo del Giudice, who had always befriended me, now thought the time had come for me to write and direct a film of my own. Since I was twenty-four years of age, it struck me that the time had, indeed, come. The Air Ministry, by now eager to have a film of their own about the discovery of radar, had approached del Giudice, known as Del by friends and enemies alike, guaranteeing full co-operation for such a project. Del, in his turn, decided to confide in me, and asked the spokesman of the Air Ministry, an ebullient gentleman by name Sir Robert Renwick, to apply for me to be attached to the air force pending demobilization.

I was flattered and delighted, and as so often, foolishly free of qualms about the magnitude or the difficulty of the project. Sir Robert Renwick liked to do things by telephone, and went his bustling way organizing the assistance which would be given me when I visited Malvern, the semi-secret government scientific research establishment.

He telephoned me, and said, more or less – 'Now look here, Ustinov, I've laid everything on. You are to be treated as a V.I.P. and nothing will be held back. Feel free to ask what questions you will, and if there's any holding back, I want to know about it. We want a good film, an informative film, a commercial film, a little laughter, a little pathos, a lot of hard facts and rip-roaring adventure. Because that's what it is, you know. Adventure. Unadulterated bloody adventure. No fiction can stand up to it. I'm sending a staff car to fetch you at O nine hundred hours tomorrow morning, as ever is. Look out for a mud-coloured Humber, with R.A.F. markings, and – oh, Ustinov, since this is a somewhat formal visit, I should wear uniform.'

'But, sir . . .' I pleaded urgently.

'Call me Bob,' he snapped, and hung up.

Just after nine o'clock, a mud-coloured Humber limousine drove into the mews in which we lived. I stood there, once again carrying all my equipment on my back, and holding a rifle.

An R.A.F. sergeant was at the wheel. He whistled for me to come towards him, and cast a critical eye over my appearance.

'D'you know where No. 34 is then?' he asked.

'Yes,' I replied, 'it's my house, over there. Since you are a little late, I thought I'd save time by waiting for you in the street.'

Privates can be cruel too, given half a chance.

We drove in utter silence. Two Military Policemen on motor-cycles nearly fell off their mounts when they saw us pass. They turned round, caught up with us, and gave me a cautious once-over. I nodded gracefully to them, and made a gesture with my hand, regal in its economy. They gave up the chase out of prudence, and the last I saw of them, they were discussing the matter by the roadside.

I had been told to report to the officer's mess in Malvern, where I was greeted by an elderly squadron-leader, the soul of kindness.

'Hello, Laddie,' he cried, in his singsong voice, 'and what can we do for you?'

'I believe there is a room booked here in my name, sir.'

'Oh, I'm afraid that's impossible, son,' he said, with genuine regret. 'This is the Officer's Mess, savvy? Anyway, full marks for trying.'

'I'm here on official business – '

'Now look here, boyo – ' a sterner note could be heard under the banter – 'there is a camp towards the Welsh border. It's only about twelve miles away. Why don't you hog a lift – some kind soul will be bound to take a soldier, what? Then you can conduct your official business from there. Now, hop it!'

'My business is with Bob Renwick.'

The squadron-leader fell back a pace, and paled.

'Sir Robert? Sir Robert Renwick. You've absolutely no right to call him Bob.'

'He asked me to call him Bob.'

'That's no reason . . .'

'And what is more,' I said, 'I don't need to hog a lift. If I have any reason to go to the Welsh border, I have my staff car here.'

The squadron-leader looked as though he were going to faint. Always a believer of striking while the iron's hot, I leaned out of the door, and called, 'Oh, Sergeant! Driver, here a moment please.'

The driver, in deepest sympathy with the squadron-leader, told his side of the story. Together, they scanned a reservations book. At first they could not find my name, but suddenly they looked up from the pages as though some new act of God had struck. Bob Renwick had done his work so thoroughly that I had been given a suite usually reserved for air-marshals and over.

My battledress was pressed by female corporals, tea was brought with embarrassing frequency, and even my rifle was dusted. My first duty was to go on a tour of inspection of the unit in the company of Air-Chief-Marshal Sir Charles Portal and Air-Vice-Marshal Sir Victor Tait, Director-General of Signals. I was not introduced to the two high-ranking officers until the whole ghastly joke was over, and with true British timidity they could not bring themselves to ask the identity of the sadsack bobbing in their wake.

Whenever they stopped to ask questions, I stopped also. After all, I couldn't very well overtake them. Thus I frequently found myself standing negligently before some colonel or group-captain, staring at his buttons, and glancing down at his shoes. I could hardly ask him the kind of questions he would ask me under similar circumstances, so I remained silent, trying not to make the silence seem insulting. Whenever some expert explained technicalities in answer to questions from the two airmarshals, I leaned forward and nodded sagely, and whenever the airmarshals glanced nervously back at me, I seemed to be digesting this knowledge while making rapid mental calculations.

Eventually Bob Renwick joined us for yet another tea, and thought the whole thing an enormous joke. 'Why didn't you tell me you were only a private?' he laughed, and characteristically gave me no time to reply.

The so-called Boffins, or scientists, lent themselves to dramatic interpretation with extraordinary unconscious felicity. The first one I met had cut himself shaving at least as doggedly as old Mr Gibbs in my youth, and most of the fly-buttons of his corduroy trousers were open or missing.

'I want you to clear your mind of the old cliché about the absent-minded professor,' he said; 'all that is just so much . . .'

Here, for some reason, he could find no end to his sentence, so just left it in the air, and went on to speak of other things.

Another one invited me to dinner. Many of them were surprised by this invitation, since my host had a reputation for stinginess, and had apparently never extended his hospitality to any of his colleagues. Accompanying the dinner was water, not of the greatest vintage. It was old lecturer's water, with tiny gondolas of dust clearly visible to the naked eye. The sight and taste of this unexpected nectar has absolutely effaced from my memory the meal itself, although I do remember that it was not even tempting by regimental standards.

After dinner, I was tactless enough to offer my host a Havana cigar. My father had brought some from Portugal, and they were a little powerful for me at the time. He regarded it with incredulity, almost as though I had stabbed him in the back. He didn't trust my offer; he made a gesture to take it, then withdrew his hand, and searched my face.

'Oh, no . . . may I really . . . no, indeed I shouldn't . . . what? I can't believe it. No, it's your last. No. D'you really mean it?' His hand trembled a little as he lit it, and allowed the half-forgotten vapours of untroubled civilization to invade his oral cavities. His eyes closed in ecstasy. Then he suddenly woke out of his voluptuous daydream as though some urgent social necessity were claiming his attention. He looked furtively round his room in order to find some riposte to this normal generosity which had so scurrilously invaded the stagnancy of his instincts. Suddenly he brightened.

'I tell you what . . .' he cried, and rushed to a drawer of his desk. 'Barley-sugar!'

He produced a paper bag in which some barley-sugar had been hibernating. It had by now congealed into a tortuous mass, which clung to the interior of the paper bag, and threatened to rip it to pieces if attacked in its lair.

I struggled for a while with the contents of the proffered bag, while he tried to hold it as still as possible. As the unequal struggle grew embarrassing, he was evidently suffering a frightful indecision, as though his avarice was being put to some unusual and terrible test. At last the bubble of his thoughts burst.

'Oh never mind,' he blurted recklessly. 'Take two bits.'

I completed the script of *School for Secrets* while still technically in the army, and was not released from its grudging grasp until I was actually shooting the film on the floor, when we had to stop production for a day at considerable expense in order to allow me to be formally discharged and to receive a civilian suit.

— May I say something?

— You don't have to ask.

— You enjoy yourself a great deal at the army's expense, and evidently this exercise of yours finds some favour, since you are often asked on the television to tell some story or other from your military experiences.

— What are you driving at?

— No need to be irritated. I am merely suggesting that you know perfectly well that without the army – or rather without armies in general, there would have been no possibility of defeating Hitler, and –

— I obviously know that as well as anyone else. I trust you are not trying a thoroughly reprehensible manœuvre, hoping to make me recant like a faint-hearted heretic before the true faith of regimental tradition?

— That would be useless. You forget, I hated the army too. I hated the reduction of my potential to practically zero.

— Then why, for Heaven's sake . . .?

— I want you to give the correct impression of your protest against the great waste. It is not something frivolous or facile, but a deep-rooted well-argued revulsion. It is not merely light-hearted mischief, but a scream of horror.

— There you are wrong. I have neither the temperament nor the build for screams of horror. I am resigned to the fact that anything profoundly felt by me takes on the mantle of light-hearted mischief just because it emanates from the heart of a jocular rotundity. Appearances cannot alter an intrinsic content, however. To defeat Hitler, the countries of the so-called free world had to play the same time-dishonoured game as he, each falling back on traditions of comportment which history had rendered solemn to some, ridiculous to others.

There is no profession in which the books are easier to cook than the military. Generals are capable of mistakes so gross that they would lose their jobs in any other walk of life, but since the losses are not so much financial as merely human, they are either given posts of more responsibility or else left where they are. There is hardly a battle in the entire history of conflict that was fairly and squarely won. They were nearly all lost, and it was invariably the loser who realized it first, retiring from the field to the intense surprise and often disbelief of the victor. Inefficiency on the scale of warfare would be impermissible in any field in which the prosperity of shareholders was involved, while the wastefulness of battle is comparable only to the arbitrary exchange of wealth in a casino.

Mark you, I am not speaking of war alone, with all its mindless horrors, but of peace. In the interests of defence, all advanced nations have the capacity of destruction out of all proportion to the requirements of legitimate self-protection. The super-powers have the privilege of being able to destroy our planet several times in rapid succession, and yet there are still those who try to score political points by declaring that one or other of them is lagging dangerously behind the other in its potential for obliteration. It is not melancholy that such arguments should be advanced seriously. The world has never been short of idiots, however hard the times. What is melancholy is that such arguments should be listened to, and acted upon, as though they made the remotest sense.

The cost of this gargantuan and useless arsenal is such that thousands upon thousands die every year because there is not enough left in the physical and moral treasury to bring the most elementary succour to those in need. That is to say that if the great countries would be content with a twofold or at most threefold destruction of the globe as a valid deterrent, the problems of famine and disease would be easily solved, but no, there is evidently no security in logic, but only in absurdity.

Thus thousands die, not because of the cannon's roar, but because of the cannon's existence. Armaments today take their toll of life even without a shot being fired.

— Yes, today, today. You are expressing your views today, now that you work intermittently for UNICEF and UNESCO, but when did you first begin to think of such monstrous paradoxes?

— Oh, that's easy to answer. While standing stiffly to attention, staring at nothing with the intensity of a zombie, awaiting the next primaeval howl from a Neanderthal man with three stripes on his shoulder. And perhaps, partially, even earlier, while lying among the damp ferns of Richmond Park with my rattle, pretending to be a machine-gun company. I never had a greater impression of wasting my time and indeed my country's time than I did in the army. As I have already said, I loathed every moment of it, and I would not have missed it for the world.

— 12 —

On July 25th, 1945, our daughter Tamara was born at the Woolavington wing of the Middlesex Hospital in London. She is now a creature of grace and charm, with an expression ever youthful and delicate. Then she was entirely bald, a physical feature she retained for an alarming length of time, and her face had about it much of the secrecy and doggedness of a Soviet field-marshal. As I looked at her, trying to kindle feelings of paternity which are entirely intellectual with such tiny children, she stared straight back at me with surprisingly steady blue eyes as though awaiting a complete confession.

My confusion at this inquisitorial gaze was checked by the remark of a swarthy gentleman next to me, who was gazing for the first time at his daughter, in the next slot on the hors-d'oeuvre tray. His girl had a full head of black hair and carried an expression of irritation on her small features, as though she couldn't get her castanets to click. 'They're all much of a muchness, aren't they?' he said, heaving with fraternity.

We moved from our mews house, a small, rather ramshackle bohemian pad, into a most uncharacteristic apartment full of amenities but without any character whatever. After the long enforced absences of the war and the independent development of two creatures who had entered marriage at the age of nineteen, there was nothing more calculated to put a strain on a fragile relationship than this enormous abode, which could in fairness and without political bias be termed bourgeois.

I was kept very busy directing my first film, which did not make me the most communicative of husbands. Having been involved in forms of propaganda, and having observed Carol Reed at work, I was fairly well equipped to deal with a semi-documentary subject of this nature, and I was at home with the more or less academic camera techniques of the time. As soon as I was shot of the army, I applied for the release of my favourite corporal, Michael Anderson, today a renowned director.

Our paths have crossed with entertaining frequency throughout our careers, and we could not have met under more fortunate circumstances than in the topsy-turvy world of the Army Kinematograph Service. As yesterday's make-up artists and assistant production managers pointed to the pips and crowns on their epaulettes, and sent us out on menial errands, our eyes met in constant disbelief that a change of circumstances could make men of doubtful fibre take advantage of their temporary condition of marginal superiority in such a shoddy fashion.

Now Mickey joined me as a first assistant, but from the beginning he was much more than that, a mentor, a collaborator, and a friend. We were fortunate in obtaining the services of Ralph Richardson for the lead. He was then playing Falstaff at the Old Vic, and in the finest fettle.

There is always something engagingly lunatic about Ralph, a Quixotic quality, although his windmills are ditches and his faithful nag a powerful motor-cycle. He is always magnificently surprised to see you, his eyes rounder than two perfect circles, his eyebrows raised to somewhere near his hair-line. Then, with a little negative wobble of the head, he elocutes his delight at this perfectly foreseeable encounter in a language at once full of filigree and backbone.

I hope I am not giving away any military secrets when I reveal that owing to his predilection for destroying motor-cycles and, rumour had it, aeroplanes, the Fleet Air Arm was quite glad to let him go to the Old Vic, where the damage he could do was limited by the architecture. I equally hope that I am not revealing any Hippocratic secrets by disclosing that his running love affair with machines had cost him several teeth, and that by 1945 there was a complicated system of bridgework lodged in that noble mouth, which was a tribute to the unrelenting march of dental science.

On the third day of shooting he appeared on the set in high good humour, half Falstaff and half himself, bellowing his delight at being alive, but whistling like a kettle on certain sibilants, a sound which he evidently attributed to someone other than himself, since he kept looking around him to find its origin. It was clear that he had left the bridgework at home. Mickey and I exchanged a furtive look, and we controlled our mutual tendency to giggle.

'Why can't we shoot?' asked Ralph, with a piercing whistle, by now riled by the delay.

While Mickey slipped off to call Ralph's home, I panicked, a director of twenty-four faced with one of the greatest actors of the age.

'The camera is broken,' I said foolishly.

Unfortunately Ralph is not only fascinated by speed and its consequences, but also by fiddling with wreckage in order to resuscitate it. He now approached the camera to see if he could mend it.

'I hear the camera is broken,' he said to Jack Hildyard, the cameraman.

'No,' replied Jack, reasonably, who had heard none of this.

'What sauce!' cried Ralph, with another blast on the whistle, which made Jack Hildyard flinch.

'Why did you tell me the camera was broken? It isn't,' he went on, looking me in the eye.

'It's my inexperience, Ralph,' I pleaded. 'It's the sound-mixing machine.'

'The sound-mixing machine!' roared Ralph, with two separate and well-defined blasts, which caused the sound-mixer to turn all the knobs on his machine urgently to zero.

Ralph crossed over to him. 'I hear the sound-mixing machine is out of commission,' he said, with a particularly penetrating whistle on the last word.

'Yes. Yes, it is,' the sound-man confirmed, intelligently.

Just then Mickey returned.

'Your house wants to talk to you on the phone, Mr Richardson,' he said.

'Oh no,' Ralph replied, rather petulantly, 'I want to work. I don't want to speak to home.'

'It may be urgent,' I suggested.

'No,' he said flatly.

'Since we can't shoot in any case . . .' I said.

'Confound it. All this is quite insufferable,' he declared, with one final blast as he went to take the call.

He reappeared a moment later, walking a little unsteadily, his hand to his brow.

'What is it?' I asked, worried.

'It's nothing. Nothing. A migraine. Comes over me suddenly. The consequence of – oh, but why should I bore you with that? I have some powders – a prescription, you understand . . . like a fool, I left them at home . . . they'll bring them out here . . . straightaway, straightaway . . . perhaps if I could lie down a moment . . .'

Mickey walked him gravely to his room as he seemed to sway under the influence of some latent tropical disease from the time he crashed into a palm tree, the whole incident made more menacing by its understatement. The whistles were by now no more than the sighing of the wind in a leaf-less tree.

Twenty minutes later a Bentley drove up to the studio gates, and a small packet was delivered for Mr Ralph Richardson.

Ten minutes after that Ralph reappeared, once again in high spirits.

'I feel much better now. *Mens Sana In Corpore Sano*,' he announced. All that Latin and not a trace of a sibilant whistle.

The sound-man turned the knobs on his console back to normal, and we did a good day's work.

The film was a great success, which led people to believe that I was an up-and-coming director. Only I knew that my ambition did not really lie in that direction. I was too wedded to the word by habit and by inclination to allow a purely visual imagination to develop. Nevertheless, the temptations were great.

Before doing another film, I appeared for a limited season in Rodney Ackland's version of *Crime and Punishment*. It was an enormous production with upward of forty actors either waiting to make entrances or exits, and it starred John Gielgud and Edith Evans. Anthony Quayle was our director, and I was engaged to play Porfiry Petrovitch, the police chief who tracks down Raskolnikov relentlessly. It was a formidable challenge for a young actor to play a man of sixty (much more difficult than seventy or eighty), and most interesting to be involved with another of our leading actors so soon after the film with Ralph.

John Gielgud was certainly the idol of the drama students of my generation, and his single-mindedness has been constant even when challenged in the mentality of superficial assessors by the meteoric energies of Laurence Olivier. It is, of course, vain to talk of who is and who is not the greatest actor. There is simply no such thing as a greatest actor, or painter, or composer (in spite of what I was taught in my prep school about Beethoven).

The great become assets on an artistic Stock Exchange of their times, or if they are lucky, of all times. They may go up or down a few points as fashion plays its tricks, but they do not predominate, or sink very low; they are merely interdependent in the panorama of their epoch, stones in the mosaic, each contributing his own colour, her own patina.

I do not think that Raskolnikov was Gielgud's greatest role. His tremulous voice, so exquisite an instrument in illuminating classical texts with clarity and passion, seemed to me a little highly strung for the sly down-to-earth subtleties of Dostoievsky; in fact, it made it extremely difficult for me to play at cat and mouse.

With such a declamatory rodent I had to be a more than normally somnolent feline. My instincts were to arrest him as soon as I set eyes on him, so apparent was his guilt. I only performed the rest of it because the text was written, but by the end of the evening, I had no very high regard for myself as a sleuth.

Never mind, it was an intensely rewarding experience, since I began to know and understand John Gielgud as one of the kindest and most profoundly considerate of men, virtues which are too often a positive disadvantage among the insensitive, for whom '*monstres sacrés*' are by definition more *monstre* than *sacré*.

Innumerable stories exist about the comic vanity and acidulated repartee of actors, from Sarah Bernhardt to Sacha Guitry, from Mrs Patrick Campbell to Noël Coward. No such stories exist about John Gielgud, not only because they could not exist, but because, in any case, they would be entirely eclipsed by his fame as a master of the *faux-pas*. All of these, true or apocryphal, are part of the public record, and sometimes, I dare say, the apocryphal ones ring truest of all, which is a measure of how John Gielgud's minor talent has captured the imagination as an affectionate adjunct to the major talent we all respect.

I once saw him on a local late-night television interview in Saint Louis, Missouri. He was busy playing *The Ages of Man*, his one-man show, in half a ball-park, and now he was being interviewed by a long-winded intellectual.

'One final question,' the interviewer said. 'Sir . . . Sir Gielgud . . . did you . . . oh, you must have had . . . we all did . . . at the start of your very wonderful . . . very wonderful and very meaningful . . . let me put it this way . . . did you have someone . . . a man . . . or . . . or indeed, a woman . . . at whom you could now point a finger and say . . . Yes! . . . This person helped me when I . . .'

By now John understood what was being asked of him, and he prepared to answer, disguising his dislikes of all that is pretentious by a perfect courtesy.

'Yes, I think there was somebody who taught me a great

deal at my dramatic school, and I certainly am grateful to him for his kindness and consideration toward me. His name was Claude Rains.'

And then, as an afterthought, he added – 'I don't know what happened to him. I think he failed, and went to America.'

I regard this as the jewel of my collection, since I must have been one of the only ones to hear it, and am probably the only one to remember it.

Much later, when John was directing a play of mine, *Halfway up the Tree*, at the Queen's Theatre, I remonstrated with him about a certain scene during rehearsal.

'John,' I said firmly, 'I just don't think that scene is going to work unless that young woman is *much, much* more aggressive.'

John replied by thinking aloud. 'Perhaps I should have allowed her to wear her hat after all . . .'

This gift for blurting out a train of thought without a capacity for censorship can lead either to the celebrated lapses, or else to fragments of inspired surrealism, moments at which one is permitted a glimpse into the sorcerer's workshop.

He has always had the gift of a ready tear, and his sensitivity is as evident as his sensibility. After one last night in Manchester, I saw a small pink and white suitcase at the stage door. Since I had a complicated make-up, I always left the theatre long after John, and I realized at once that he had forgotten the suitcase. I took it with me to the Midland Hotel, and found him dining alone. I told him I had it, and his face transformed itself into a grimace of gratitude, eyes deflected somewhere above my head and sideways, a vein zig-zagging its way up his temple like a mountain highway, mouth forced into a strained smile.

'Won't you join me?' he asked.

I did, for a while, but was tempted, once he had finished, to join another table where Max Bacon, a celebrated Jewish comic, was regaling members of our cast with the riches of his repertoire. I told John I wouldn't be long, and that I would deliver the suitcase to his room in a little while.

Unfortunately it was only around three in the morning that Max Bacon got round to his first story again, and the second house began. It was only when I was on the way to my room that I remembered the suitcase. Despite the lateness of the hour, I determined to try and deliver it. When I reached John's room, I knocked with the greatest discretion. A voice both clear and brilliant rang out, 'Come in!'

The door was on the latch. Because of the timbre of his voice I did not enter the room so much as make an entrance into it. He was lying on his bed as though posing for a sacred picture by El Greco, naked and immobile. He put an end to my confusion by another ringing phrase, this time with a dying cadence and a throb of bitterness. 'My pyjamas are in that bag,' he cried, and immediately his eyes grew moist.

I was glad I hadn't waited until the morning to deliver the suitcase. Such prudence would have occasioned the longest stage pause in history.

John Gielgud is so contorted with shyness at first meetings that he makes a normally shy person like myself feel brash, and even boorish. And yet, despite this gossamer delicacy, there are the heights to rise to before an anonymous public, and an ego, totally invisible in the drawing-room, imperceptibly takes over. As the curtain fell on the first act of *Crime and Punishment* during the first performance, he suddenly trumpeted a message to us all. 'If there are going to have to be all these people in the wings, they *must look at me*!'

He found it impossible to play to backs turned in discretion, in order not to break his concentration. To hell with the concentration, once there were people he was hungry for faces!

My domestic life was falling into nerveless and dispassionate ways, in spite of the delightful cavorting of Tamara. It was clear that it could not last. There were arguments. These were never rows but rather wearisome exercises in self-justification which never stuck to any point for very long, but dragged across a whole landscape of differences along prescribed furrows. A kind of tedium enveloped us, made worse by the heedless happiness of our daughter.

All this was the fault of no one, only perhaps that of circumstances. During the heroic days of war, our way of life was everybody's way of life, but now, with the coming of peace I was testing my ability to be myself to the full, making up for lost time, whereas Isolde, more mystical and abstract by nature, seemed to me to be removed from my realities in a numb withdrawal.

The withdrawal was perhaps not quite as numb as it seemed to me, since I noticed the frequent presence of a young fellow at home with a pleasantly pugnacious face. It was a little surprising that I was never introduced to him, but since I am a great believer in personal liberty, and I think there are few characters sillier than suspicious husbands, I never asked who he was. I was informed soon enough, however, when Isolde announced that she wished to marry him.

I asked her to reconsider her decision. Her mind, she said, was made up. She was hankering for a steady, undramatic life, removed from the mainstream, a life constant in climate, without stress. She slid silently out of my life, and I hardly more noisily out of hers. My regret was for Tamara, although the positive nature of her disposition boded well for her capacity for survival. All the same, if there is anything I detest in life, it is irresponsibility. I have a puritanical revulsion for the kind of self-indulgence which creates life and then abandons it to fend for itself.

The end of our marriage seemed to me curiously tepid. It was all very English and very reasonable, with the added spice of that ludicrous charade of sending a detective to a prescribed room in a transient hotel where Isolde would be discovered playing cards with a hired adulterer. It all worked like a spell, without a trace of collusion, and soon I was ready for the Law Courts. One morning my solicitor called me to tell me to hurry up, the hearing was at eleven o'clock, and the Judge was Mr Justice Tudor-Rees.

I sat in my bath with a copy of *Who's Who* on my wet knees. I looked up Mr Justice Tudor-Rees just to know what I was up against. His credentials seemed overwhelming for a mere divorce, but I did happen to notice that his wife's maiden-name was Dorothy Sidebotham, a distinguished name in the northern countryside which is hard to forget.

I reached the Law Courts as the previous divorce was in progress. A pathetic woman faced the judge, wearing a black straw hat adorned with plastic cherries. She smiled doggedly, as though she had been told to create a good impression.

'It was while your husband was away on his battle-cruiser that you invited the Pole in question, Jerzy . . .' and here the barrister struggled unavailingly with one of the more complicated Polish surnames, eventually giving up and looking appealingly at the Judge. 'There is a Pole in question, m'Lud.'

The Judge, scribbling away, looked up briefly and nodded. '. . . You invited the Pole in question to your rented apartment in Lee-upon-the-Solent . . .'

The barrister nodded at his client, who hissed her assent.

'And it was there, in the living-room, on Friday the Fourth, that, upon the sofa, connection took place,' roared the barrister, in a huge voice, and nodded.

I reflected that I had never heard the act of adultery described more sleazily than in a law court, beneath the Lion and the Unicorn.

Once more, the wretched woman, with rouge on her cheeks like a doll, nodded back and hissed.

'Would you kindly ask your client to speak up,' asked the Judge suddenly. 'I have not yet heard one word of her evidence, and I am not inclined to give judgement in a case I cannot hear.'

'I must crave your Lordship's indulgence,' yelled the barrister, 'but, as I think I have explained, my client is deaf.'

'Yes, but I'm not,' said the Judge, 'and I don't see why I should be submitted to this kind of thing.'

So saying, he deferred the hearing until such a time as the wretched woman could throw a clearer light on the facts of her Polish connection.

I was frankly horrified at the callousness of the procedure, a horror which dissipated into alarm when I found I was next on the agenda.

My lawyer, a Member of Parliament from Ulster, asked me a series of predictable questions, which I answered in an overproduced theatrical voice, so eager was I not to be misunderstood. I was given technical custody of Tamara, although this right was waived owing to the child's age. All seemed to be going swimmingly in this hypocritical ritual, when the Judge suddenly fixed me with an eye both awake and aware.

'Why?' he asked, without continuing. Emergency was written all over my lawyer's face.

'Why?' repeated the Judge again. 'Why did you give your daughter the eccentric name of Tamara?'

'I don't consider the name at all eccentric,' I replied, not without haughtiness.

The Judge flushed with irritation.

'In all my experience,' he remarked, 'it is among the most eccentric names which have come to my notice.'

'You must realize, m'Lud, that my surname is Russian,' I said. 'It would be ridiculous were I to call my daughter, say, Dorothy.'

He looked up in surprise, forgetting for a moment to frighten me. 'Dorothy's a perfectly good name,' he said.

'In certain circumstances, m'Lud, it cannot be bettered. Not, however, in mine.'

A mischievous smile played about his mouth for a moment. I saw an anecdote forming in his mind. On arriving home that night, he was going to say – 'Oh, incidentally, Dorothy my dear. You'll never guess. I had that actor-fellow Ustinov in Court today, and d'you know what happened . . .?'

Thanks to *Who's Who*, I was through the minefield. I left Court a free man, with all that entails, now once more open to burdensome temptations and the unnecessary exhaustion of uncertainty.

My father wasn't in terribly good form either, living alone in a service flat in London while my mother lived in Gloucestershire. It was never clear whether they had separated or not, but he was very active in his bachelor pad cooking meals of extraordinary richness which he shared with those who admired him and whose livers could stand the assault of cream and tarragon.

At the theatre I shared my dressing-room with an improbable character called Campbell Cotts, whose real name was Sir Campbell Mitchell-Cotts, Baronet. He was a big man, tall and fat, with a low, pomaded hairline, brown eyes at once cool, arrogant and childish, and a mouth twitching incessantly in a kind of sensuous assessment of nothing in particular. He had fallen into the acting profession by mistake, and his comportment on the stage was identical with his comportment anywhere else. His conversation was bewildering to say the least, since when you laughed at what seemed vaguely amusing, he appeared hurt, and when you listened with careful attention to what was solemn, he appeared equally hurt.

One evening he declared that, although not a Catholic (pronounced Cartholic), he had presented Brompton Oratory (pronounced Brumpton Uratory) with a considerable sum as a penance for having wet his bed. My nascent smile was nipped in the bud by his fixed, fanatical stare and his munching. I tried outstaring him, and he turned away, flushed with annoyance.

My father, now in the full glow of his Englishness, found Campbell absolutely irresistible. He must have sensed in such a man a little fallout from the intransigent majesty of Empire. At all events, he begged me to invite him to lunch, which I did.

They spent their time criticizing my choice of wines, and exchanging obscure anecdotes about the lowest of deeds in the highest of circles. I said not a word, having no word to say. Eventually, as they swilled the brandy around their balloon glasses, Campbell, flushed with wine and good fellowship, slapped my father affectionately on the knee with his free hand, and, as he began to light his Havana, asked the rhetorical question, 'What are we, my dear friend, but a couple of old poachers in the hedgerows of society?'

Klop looked at me in some alarm. He had never seen himself as a poacher, nor did he understand to what part of society the hedgerows referred. I could not help him. He seemed crestfallen, as though his inherent foreignness had been discovered owing to the neglect of some finer point, whereas Campbell, rosy and pouting, sat staring at the ceiling with an aura of self-satisfaction, savouring both the cognac and his remark to the full.

13

After *The Banbury Nose*, and during the last days of servitude in the army, I slaved away at my fifth play, a curiosity which had not much chance of commercial success at the time. It was called *The Tragedy of Good Intentions*, and was a story of the First Crusade, in which I was aided by the *Cambridge Mediaeval History*. It was the first of my plays for which research was necessary, and I stretched a fictitious tale on the framework of an authentic historical reality. It was performed by the Old Vic at the Liverpool Playhouse in 1945, and attracted not much attention.

The conviction was growing in me that, whereas Shakespeare was admittedly the greatest of our playwrights, there was a general recognition of the fact that Sir Arthur Pinero was the best of them. To attempt any kind of an emulation of Shakespeare was, of course, foolhardy on a purely artistic level, but quite apart from that, it was also regarded as a form of heresy, an act of shocking self-confidence, whereas an emulation of Pinero was eminently acceptable. Shaw was regarded as a prattling interloper, tolerated because of his gift of laughter and joy which made his iconoclasm irresistible, but he was certainly to be no beacon suitable for a young author at sea.

Had England had the equivalent of those University Chairs for Play-writing which to this day colour minor American criticism, Pinero would have been the supreme example of dramatic carpentry for the fledglings to follow, and lose their gifts. The theory which is all too often advanced by the pundits is that there are thousands of wrong ways to write a play, and only one right way. It is nearer the truth to say that, even if there are thousands of wrong ways to write a play, there are hundreds of right ways, on condition that the personality of the writer is allowed to be an ingredient in the result. None of the important dramatists of the century followed the rules laid down by experts. Chekhov would have been told that he lacked action, O'Neill that he must cut, Ionesco that he must clarify, Brecht that he must impose practical limits on his vision.

In other words, the Academy is, as ever, the temple of mediocrity, and the ideals it imposes are strictly useful only for those with nothing to say.

With my sixth play, I decided to toy with the criteria imposed by my critics, by writing for once a realistic play in an abundantly realistic set (the rain fell in buckets, literally, in the third act). The theme was mildly provocative at the time. A clash between two clergymen, the one a good man but a third-rate cleric, the other a man of doubtful quality but an excellent cleric. The catalyst, the wife of one and the sister of the other, was Gladys Cooper, who made the part very much her own, even supplying many of the lines, which varied from night to night.

In spite of these frequent surprises and anomalies, she gave a performance of extraordinary power as a woman frustrated by the vacillations of a husband addicted to goodness. There has rarely been an actress who exuded more animal health, even in old age, or who was more fatally attractive, her deep and lovely voice cajoling or cruel, or both at once.

The play, entitled *The Indifferent Shepherd*, was not a great success, although it had a satisfactory run at the Criterion. It was as though the critics resented the fact that I had, in some measure, heeded their advice. This was encouraging.

Another play followed at the 1949 Edinburgh Festival, called *The Man in the Raincoat*. It was written in one long act, artificially split in order to accommodate drinking habits. It was played by Mary Ellis and George Coulouris, who disliked each other so heartily during rehearsals that there was nothing left over for the performance. Alan Wheatley was the third member of the cast, Percy Cartwright the fourth, and neither of them disliked anybody.

I directed the play myself. Since its theme of a miscarriage of justice was very close to my heart, I evidently thought higher of it than did the public, and it had no subsequent career, except in Oslo where it did very well under the charming title of *Mannen i Regnfrakken*.

I was by now inured to being an *enfant terrible*, although I felt I had been one for rather too long. My second film, *Vice-Versa*, based on the admirable book by F. Anstey, was according to many ahead of its time. With Roger Livesey in the role of the negligent, hypocritical Victorian father who tells his snivelling son about to return to a hideous seat of learning after the holidays, that schooldays are the happiest days of any man's life, only to find himself transmogrified into his son's body, the film seemed to me to have a good chance of success. For the boy, I engaged a young and extremely precocious fellow called Anthony Newley, for the terrifying headmaster, Dr Grimstone, an unknown actor who had fought in the Spanish Civil War on the side of unpopular legitimacy and been a collaborator of my father's in the early days at the Reuter's building in Blackfriars, James Robertson Justice, and for his daughter, a sweet little English rosebud, Petula Clark.

Had the film been made by Disney, it would have had fewer rough edges. What am I saying? – No rough edges. But it would have been less ambitious even on the humble level of a farce, and there was one sequence especially close to my questing heart which I still consider among my happier inspirations.

That exquisite actor Robert Edison, playing the romantic sportsmaster with no interest in sports, sat reading a book of poems while twenty-two boys ran riot in a roughhouse of a game of football. Suddenly he looked up. Horrors! The mortar-board of Dr Grimstone was travelling like a pirate ship on the skyline of a privet-hedge, coming his way. In a flash, he was on his feet, exhorting the boys to renewed efforts. The only trouble was, the ball had become mislaid during their extracurricular activities.

The boys entered into the spirit of the emergency, and played as they had never played before, dribbling, heading, shooting, saving goals all with an imaginary ball. The headmaster observed the scene with evident pleasure, his eye moving sideways, upwards, downwards. Only after a considerable time did a doubt begin to cloud that imperious, bearded face, until it had hardened into a hideous conviction.

'Where is the ball?' he thundered.

'That's funny,' said Robert Edison, looking around himself and tapping his pockets absently.

Perhaps a degree of surrealism was too abstract for the tastes of the time, but it was one of those films which acquire a handful of fanatical addicts at once, who only serve to annoy those closed to its little mysteries even further.

The same became true in 1949 for my third film, *Private Angelo*, based on the charming book by Eric Linklater about an Italian private, forever in search of the 'Dono de Corraggio', the gift of courage, which is eventually imposed on him by adverse circumstances. It must be said that it was a book hardly calculated to please the Italians, since it was based on prejudices about their warlike qualities which were distinctly paternalistic. The Italians have always seemed to me to be almost over-endowed with courage expressed in the form of personal panache, or recklessness. They are nonpareil in the production of Condottiere, poisoners, boxers, racing-drivers, stuntmen, popes angelic and diabolic, gangsters, and unflinching martyrs. Place all these disparate elements in a trench, however, and cover them with the same drab uniform and a coat of mud, give them an officer or two they don't necessarily respect, and of course their splendid qualities of individual radiance are tarnished. They prefer not to die under anonymous, or worse, under stupid circumstances.

The proof of this is the outraged Italian private who leapt on

223

to the parapet in the last days of the war, during a violent German bombardment.

'Mascalzoni,' he cried, 'don't you know there are people here?' only to fall under a hail of bullets.

No sane man can discern a lack of resolution here. He had merely had the sorry genius to find a way to die intelligently and nobly in a situation which was neither intelligent nor noble.

There was, however, not much room for considerations of this nature in a book which was almost pastoral in nature, and which derived its poetry from a sort of serene oversimplification of the grave events it grazed on its journey.

I played Private Angelo myself, in retrospect rather too placid for the conventional view of an Italian, and rather too fair also for that unobservant multitude which considers all Italians to be swarthy. My father, in the film, by indiscretion rather than by marriage, the Count Piccologrande, was played by Godfrey Tearle, that most aristocratic of actors, imbued with a certain distant loneliness, like a St Bernard with an empty cask of brandy. I always wished to invade his solitude, and yet respected it too much to do so. Charming, elegant, yet with the massive vocal possibilities, the diaphragm, which belonged to a previous generation of classical actors, he performed every role with extraordinary dignity, which was also his greatest limitation.

I once saw him play a dishonest judge, and believed it not at all. He did all he could to look dishonest as he was exposed by the police, but all he succeeded in doing was to appear anxious, and once the handcuffs were clamped on him, he immediately looked innocent, and the perfectly polite men from Scotland Yard seemed like brutes.

And yet, when he played the Italian Count, resilient in misfortune, looking up at the Roman balcony where American generals were posing for American cameramen, British generals for British cameramen, and a solitary French general for a solitary French cameraman, his face assumed the features of age-old disenchantment as he intoned softly: 'Ah, Angelo, what have we learned? A different text for every school-book, a different inscription on every tomb. Nothing. We have learned nothing . . .' and his fine face was lost in the carnival of popular rejoicing at the coming of peace.

I used no music in this film, shot largely in the Tuscan village of Trequanda. At least, the music was not written specially for it, as was the habit in those days, but supplied by the village orchestra, the Società Filodrammatica e Sportiva di Trequanda. The local conductor, an imperious old gentleman with a limp, conducted, among other numbers, the 'Miserere' from *Il Trovatore* and the 'Marcia dei Bersaglieri', and he was as exacting with his ensemble as any great conductor, and twice as unpleasant towards recalcitrant musicians. The moderating influence of the trades unions had not yet penetrated here, and he was not beyond making personal reflections which would have occasioned walk-outs anywhere else.

When he transported the orchestra to Rome for the recording sessions, it was rumoured that this great maestro, whose crumpled nose was crowded with constellations of blackheads, so that at times it appeared like a weathered miniature score, had no use for or knowledge of the sanitary amenities placed at his disposal, and that consequently his presence in the four-star hotel was tantamount to locking a puppy in one of the better rooms.

Nevertheless, he arrived in the recording-room as sure of his destiny as ever, clutching a black leather baton-case. When he opened it, he withdrew from it an olive branch with which he proceeded to conduct with a precision and a sense of tempo I have never come across even in professional film musicians. Told that the 'Miserere' lasted two seconds too long, he immediately, without reference to metronome or stop-watch, produced a 'Miserere' exactly two seconds shorter. There was no symbolism attached to his use of an olive branch, however. To achieve his uncanny results, he was just as unpleasant with his orchestra as ever.

The recording-session, planned for three days, was over in just over half a day thanks to the extraordinary ability of this instinctive musician, which was just as well, since it limited the damage to his palatial room.

I spoke previously of the moderating influence of trades unions. I referred, of course, merely to the verbal decorum upon which they insist, quite rightly, but not to the pressures they exert which are too often self-defeating. No one in his right mind could possibly deny the existence of the original grievances which compelled the workers to organize themselves. It was an automatic outcome of industrial revolutions everywhere. And yet, in every human endeavour it is success which is the challenge to the highest of aspirations even more than failure.

While directing *School for Secrets* I had committed the tactical error of offering my film unit a cold lunch out of my slender resources. It was a particularly scorching day on the Thames, and a fashionable riverside hotel was the site of my confusion. Cold salmon and strawberries and cream were eaten with pleasure, hock was drunk. Afterwards a shop steward rose and proposed a graceful vote of thanks to me for my generosity and brotherly sentiments, at the same time reminding me officially that I owed them for the hot lunch they had been deprived of. His statement was greeted with prolonged applause as the hock glasses were raised to drink my health.

Once again, in Italy, everything stopped at certain statutory hours for the taking of tea, even though the temperature was well over 100° Fahrenheit, and cold drinks were available at all times. The Italian crew looked at us in amazement. They were stripped to the waist to a man, and wore their political convictions on their heads in the form of paper hats made of *Unità*, the Communist newspaper.

At first the British crew remonstrated with me to try to force the Italians to stop for tea also. Nothing would induce the Italians to do so. The British searched their moral armoury for sanctions. I reminded them that we were in Italy, and there was no way in which Italians could be forced to drink tea on their own soil. The

British became sullen, as people do when they feel they are up against unfair opposition. Eventually a delegation came to see me. They would forgo their tea so long as it appeared in the books that they had had it. Apparently the whole thing would be difficult to explain in a draughty office in London. The arteries of liberty had hardened already; the careless dictatorship of privilege had been replaced by the careful dictatorship of regulations. Disobedience was the only escape road for men of good will.

The last problems I had were during the filming of *Billy Budd*, many years later. The shop steward was a small rakish individual whose dearest wish was evidently to grow a moustache like Clark Gable's to finish off his pleasantly disreputable appearance, but this was a wish unreasonably withheld by nature. Not a hair would grow on his upper lip. Undismayed, he made good nature's lapse with a mauve eyebrow pencil. Unfortunately, however, he was short-sighted, yet too vain to wear glasses, so that his moustache was very rarely even remotely symmetrical.

We were in Spain, at sea off the coast near Alicante, rolling about on an eighteenth-century man-of-war, commanded in the film by me, and when filming ceased, by Captain Alan Villiers, who spent his time howling archaic commands to the winds, interspersed with expletives in no recognizable language. It stands to reason that, on such a boat, the toilet arrangements were necessarily almost as primitive as they had been in Nelson's day, and this found no favour with the unions.

The shop steward warned me once or twice, and then one fine morning he came to announce a strike. I knew he was upset by the fact that his moustache was particularly carelessly drawn, as though his mind had wandered over knottier problems before the bathroom mirror.

'It's no good,' he said. 'You wouldn't heed my warning, and there it is, strike action. I did my best. I'm known as a governor's man – it's no good for my reputation within the movement. Never mind. I stuck my neck out, but it's no good. It's the Spanish boys, you know. They are the straw that broke the camel's back, in a manner of speaking, if you follow. We got definitive news only this morning that three of them reported sick with crabs.'

Fortunately for me, the last part of this was being overheard by the delegate of the Spanish union, which was, of course, no union at all in our sense, but a kind of concession in the direction of modernity made by authority of General Franco. This man now flared up with an indignation both righteous and magniloquent. 'It is a lie to say that three of our men ha' gone sick wi' crabs,' he shouted. 'It is an insult to the Spanish labour force, to the quality of Spanish artisans, and it betrays an unfriendly attitude whi' I resent deeply.'

The British shop steward became conciliatory, and eventually the Spaniard calmed down, owing more to the limits of his vocabulary in English than for any other reason. Once a degree of peace had been restored, he explained that the truth was that three of the Spanish crew had reported sick with gonorrhoea.

'Ah, that's different,' agreed the British shop steward. 'That's a question of diet, isn't it?'

Thanks to a certain weakness in the British shop steward's diagnostic sense, the ship sailed again with its ancient toilets, and a full crew.

In case it be thought that I am opposed to unions, I hasten to say that I am a member of fourteen of them, which is outrageously expensive, but the reward is that I have never been on strike, simply because it has never happened that all fourteen have come out at the same time.

Also, at their best, they can even be instruments of enlightenment. When we worked at Trequanda, the unions decided there also that the toilets were inadequate to meet the high standards set for the reception of British waste matter, and so we built a couple of conveniences at the side of a sandy area used by the local sportsmen for a variety of games.

When we left Trequanda, we formally presented the toilets to the commune, and they were unveiled officially in their civic form by the priest in the course of a simple ceremony, during which he prayed Almighty God to render our labours fertile. I visited Trequanda quite recently, and the toilets are still there, doorless, rusting, and with cracked ceramics, yet stubbornly resisting the passage of time and vandals, still managing to proclaim their purpose to all who pass. Just as the vestiges of Roman sanitation are still found in England, fragments of mosaic, steam pipes, dim outlines of baths, so, thanks to the unions, remnants of British plumbing are still found in Tuscany, their origins gradually lost in mystery as the relentless march of time clouds the truth in theory and speculation. What will the archaeologists of the future make of those tiny chips of porcelain found in a Tuscan wasteland, which, when pieced together, make up the following hieroglyph, 'Thomas Crapper and Son, King's Road, London S.W.3'?

Among the actors in the film were two of my particular favourites in that galaxy of distinguished performers England never ceases to turn out, Robin Bailey, one of the greatest comic technicians I have ever worked with, not as well known as he deserves, and Peter Jones, with whom I evolved a comic series for the B.B.C., which preceded the Goon Show and was like chamber music to the orchestral follies which were to follow. Pat Dixon produced these programmes, and our guardian angels and consistent inspirers were Denis Norden and Frank Muir, masters of the ridiculous.

Peter and I invented a couple of characters out of the folklore of London, Morris and Dudley Grosvenor, low characters with high ambitions, as their name suggests. They spoke in the lisping accent of London's East End, and had endless wife trouble with their platinum-haired companions, as they did with the wretched character called simply 'The Boy' who was sent out on dangerous and sometimes criminal errands, in which he consistently failed. These programmes were improvised within a certain framework, and often they reached satisfactory heights of comic melancholy.

Foolishly asking 'How's Zelda?' on one occasion, I received the following exercise in gloom from Peter Jones.

'Zelda? I'll tell you this much, Mowwie, if every evening after work you are hit on the head with a beer bottle with monotonous wegularity, mawwiage soon loses its magic.'

Our satire delved into all fields of fiction as well. In our Coronation number, we produced a series of famous lines from the obscure moments of history, such as 'Give me ten Grenadiers, and I will give you Harwich,' and 'What? There are no flags left? Strap *me* to the flagpole!'

It was light-hearted and quietly wicked, and people seemed to like it.

Robin Bailey, Peter Jones and I, accompanied by Brenda Bruce, and Molly Urquhart, also performed a play of Eric Linklater's entitled *Love in Albania*. We started it at the Bath Festival, and made a success of it at the St James's Theatre in London. It was again an affectionate kind of literary comedy, and I played one of the more simple-minded purveyors of America's cosmic message, a military policeman of Albanian origin searching Europe for his long-lost partisan daughter, 'Wounded in the Bosoom for democracy.' Peter Jones was a stuttering, exasperated intellectual, and Robin Bailey a suburban husband faced with these lunatic intruders.

It was far-fetched and preposterous, but the situations were such as to keep the audience in stitches, which was a hazard for all three of us, since we are all dangerously addicted to helpless laughter on occasion, and we are in distinguished company, for John Gielgud too is as fragile in this respect as anyone I have ever played with.

Once the pause imposed by the audience was just too long, and Peter Jones and I were off. We turned our backs to the audience, but it was of no avail. The audience that night had the same dangerous characteristic, and now they began to laugh as heartily as we for as little reason. It became an almost sinister form of mass hysteria, like a dance marathon. To make matters worse, we had an excellent stage-manager, who was a pillar of the Boy Scout movement in his moments of leisure. His head suddenly appeared in the fireplace, upside down behind the false logs, the fire reflected in his glasses.

'Pull yourselves together!' he snarled.

Thanks to him, we were both now well beyond the point of no return. Only exhaustion enabled us to continue to the end of the play when the worst was over.

I adapted a play during this period, the only one in my career. It was by Ingmar Bergman, then known as a promising playwright rather than as a film director of immense distinction. He had written a film for Alf Sjöberg, entitled *Frenzy* in England and *Torment* in America, a strange piece about the perils of young love in Swedish schools, a triangle composed of a youthful street-walker, a schoolboy, and a sadistic schoolmaster. It was absorbing, as a film, perhaps because the background of Swedish scholastic life had to be accepted as genuine by those unacquainted with its traditions, whereas in London, the schoolboys, who included Denholm Elliott and Alan Badel, seemed strangely old for such a school, and the terror imparted by the odious schoolmaster, played by me in rimless glasses, was somewhat damped by having to speak in English. The experience was a curious one, in that it made me realize the enormous value of incomprehensibility in certain works of art, both plastic and dramatic. In removing the exoticism from the text by making it understandable, we had also dispensed with a certain mystery which gave the work its quality, or illusion of quality, there was no knowing which. Perhaps all we had done was to discover the Achilles heel behind that stout woollen Swedish look. Or perhaps subtitles, habitually accused of inadequacy, are merely the sentinels which guard a work's secrets, or its lack of them? Dispense with a foreign language, and you are suddenly a conjuror without a mirror.

Frenzy made for a passable evening of tension, largely owing to the exquisite Joan Greenwood, whose gritty voice suggested the erosion of innocence by the sad necessities of a flagrantly empty life, but the niceties and above all the nastiness of Scandinavian pedagogy escaped most of the men in the cast, as Mr Chips might well have left them even colder than usual in Uppsala.

— One moment.

— Yes?

— You seem somehow to be rushing through these years. Your narrative is formless compared to the careful reconstruction of your early years.

— That is perhaps because I am, in retrospect, less interested in them than in the years of my relative helplessness, where I could chart a progression from obstacle to obstacle, where I had my parents to complement, to accommodate, to consider. Now I was alone, after the failure of a marriage. More than alone, I was adrift, making up for a time which had never been lost, but merely neglected because of ignorance, a lack of curiosity, a certain complacency. Despite the rigours of the British taxes, I had the illusion of a certain transitory wealth for the first time in my life. I bought weird motor-cars which spent a great deal of time lifeless by the roadside, with me, as often as not, rain-sodden, trying to make sense of the engines. Among these monsters was a Hispano-Suiza Boulogne with only three seats and the flag of a defunct yacht-club on the doors. It had come to England mysteriously at the time of Dunkirk, and had spent the intervening years abandoned on a dock, where the cylinder block had cracked. I drove this vast machine of 1927 with all the assurance of a Michael Arlen rake, and I have been told by reliable witnesses that I was even more sinister at the wheel of my Mercedes-Benz 'S'-wagen, a supercharged two-seater, like a propelling pencil on four huge wheels, linked by cable brakes, about as unsafe a vehicle as it was possible to conceive, especially as it was capable of Valkyrie-rides at over 100 m.p.h., with supercharger howling. I often exceeded this speed on the way to the studio. The car is now safe in the geriatric ward of Lord Montagu's Motor Museum at Beaulieu.

— You complain of your solitude, and yet you seem to have enjoyed yourself inordinately.

— There are always elements in solitude which are distinctly enjoyable, but they are not usually elements which wear well in retrospect. They are selfish and purposeless. They are ephemeral, often destructive. I flitted from affaire to affaire as I flitted from car to car. By this I don't mean I was deliberately inconstant, but rather that I was in active search for the fulfilment of marriage, and that there was a certain desperation in this. I think, you see, that there has always been an atavistic undertow dragging me towards the image of the patriarch I was meant to be by nature and by tradition, but at the same time there was a tumultuous impatience about my work and my life which made me avid in the exploitation of my own you .a.

— You were pleasure bent?

— Perhaps, but I gave myself no pleasure. As you know, I am by temperament responsible, and I had no patience for the person I was. The characteristics of an ageing *enfant terrible* gave me no more solace than it did my critics. Oh, I never stopped learning. I learned what it was to be lovesick, to wait in endless agony for telephone calls which rarely came, and when they came, how suddenly the mood of desperation would change to one of elation. I learned what it was like to be callous, out of sheer mental fatigue, a sense of self-preservation. I learned that women seemed all the same when things went wrong, all different when things went well.

— Do you really think that is true?

— No longer, because I no longer have to. The relationships between the sexes are so inextricably fouled up by wits, cynics, wiseacres, philosophers, psychologists, psychiatrists and finally Women's Lib, that it takes the best part of a lifetime to find out that the general has no bearing whatever on the particular. Those who maintain the link exists are like explorers who lose heart in the face of a natural barrier, and never penetrate into the hinterland where people are people, and not merely slaves to physical apparatus which have slanted minds into channels dictated by convention. You are silent. Why?

— I just fear you may be a little square for your age.

— It is out of fear of what is known as squareness that we rarely say what we really think or feel. After all, what is profundity but a convoluted way of expressing the obvious, in which the matter is disguised by the manner to the satisfaction of intellectuals? It is no error that 'To be or not to be, that is the question' is an essay in profundity which has become the property of all, even if the vast majority have not the faintest notion of how the speech continues. And yet, what the hell does it mean? It is merely a key to what follows, which is unknown to most people, and yet it is accepted as the acme of human vision by those who have never bothered to examine it or to open the door to which it is the key. 'The evil that men do lives after them', 'Uneasy lies the head that wears a crown', 'To be or not to be': Shakespeare, thank God, was not afraid of squareness.

— He wouldn't have known what squareness was.

— Exactly. It takes a long time to struggle through to your own being, to uproot all the weeds of a certain kind of education, of a certain kind of locker-room scepticism which evolves as the barnacles of other people's experiences and of other people's prejudices begin to stick to you and imperceptibly hamper your progress.

— You learned that then?

— I have never ceased learning, and I am convinced that it is of primordial importance to learn more every year than the year before. After all, what is education but a process by which a person begins to learn how to learn?

— And, perhaps, a process by which a person begins the long journey of discovery of himself?

— Precisely. People know themselves when they are children, and then everything is done to integrate them into society as what is pretentiously and erroneously termed 'useful members'. It is here that they lose themselves, sometimes irrevocably, in a prison of convention, where individual thought is replaced by conditioned reflexes imposed by a sense of propriety and its attendant hypocrisy. The roots of racialism, for example, are planted deep in this fallow soil. Anti-Semitism is one of its bitter fruits, and the excesses of those who hate Arabs with imagined or pseudo-historical acerbity are just as ugly and just as sterile. Old men of quality are those who have fought their way very successfully to a rediscovery of themselves in spite of every temptation, and it is no wonder they tend to befriend children. They have common ground, themselves, the ones not yet lost, the others rediscovered.

— Would you say that because of your meticulous ear and gift for imitation, you were very prone to the unconscious influence of others?

— I would, yes. My plays were eclectic at this time, with an almost ferocious rejection of any kind of obvious influence. I was utterly determined to be myself without as yet a very clear conception of who I was. I was, if you like, escaping from the pigeon-hole with the same application that others preferred to use on concentrating on personal attitudes. This made for obscurity and disturbed people. Hence the *enfant*, hence the *terrible*.

— May I suggest that it was perhaps more difficult for you than it was for others?

— You may, of course. Although you must know I hate the idea that anything was more difficult for me than for others.

— You are just averse to self-pity, but I do feel that it was difficult with a background as diffuse as yours with bloodstreams gallivanting to all points of the compass and an empathy with widely divergent attitudes, Russian at one moment, English the next, then French, and Italian, and God knows what. You must, at times, have felt a pang of envy at those younger dramatists who wrote with the uncomplicated anguish of personal experience about boarding-houses in Nottingham or rented rooms in Croydon. Their authenticity was never in doubt, and their passions rang true.

— Envy? I honestly doubt it. Where can you go after a boarding-house in Nottingham except to another boarding-house in Nottingham? And nothing is as deeply felt as the first literary explosion. After that, art and artifice take over. Success there may be, and astuteness, but the freshness of the first plunge into public consciousness is gone for ever. That is a destiny common to us all.

— Ibsen did well enough with his fjord-side houses, as did Chekhov with his slatted mansions. They never left their Nottinghams, their Croydons.

— Did they not? Chekhov's next play, had he lived, would have been a symbolical drama about a bird-woman in the Arctic regions. I am convinced it would have been a disaster, since his enormous talent did not stretch to such *fin-de-siècle* extroversions. In *The Seagull* he already dabbled in such a theme, and I believe that the play within a play purportedly written by the emotional young poet Konstantin was, in fact, conceived in the utmost earnestness by Chekhov, in order to test a more lyrical style on his audience. With his sophisticated and self-mocking demureness, it was disguised as the immature outpouring of a youthful talent, but it was, I feel sure, a prototype of what was to come if the audience listened in silence. As for Ibsen, his last play, *When We Dead Awaken*, is almost entirely incomprehensible, and ends with an avalanche. All who slept in Nottingham or Croydon, Smolensk or Bergen do their best to escape. I needed a special kind of launching pad to crystallize whatever talent I have, and admittedly it was less easy to find than was Nottingham to the talented local boy . . . But I did not despair.

— Would you say these were unhappy years?
— To live for the moment has its thrills, but the moments have a habit of accumulating and creating time. I drove myself hard, as though life were really as short as it seemed. I remember my adventures with a mixture of amusement and pain, in the hope that I created more amusement than pain in others, but there is no accounting the degree of love invested when one's own sentiments are confused by old-fashioned ideas of permanence, mingled with a latent misgiving which was ever-present. I lived in a charming flat on the Thames Embankment, helped by my then secretary who found it for me. She is now a busy and successful writer of detective stories under her married name of Patricia Moyes, and I like to think that she discovered her ability while heroically dealing with the many problems of my own creation.
— What finally brought this period of public apprenticeship to a close?
— A chiding voice calling out of the Heavens 'Whither goest Thou?'
— Quo Vadis?
— Exactly. And the chiding voice was that of the venerable lion of Metro-Goldwyn-Mayer.

14

An exciting proposition came my way when I was twenty-eight years old. M.G.M. were going to remake *Quo Vadis*, and I was a candidate for the role of Nero. Arthur Hornblow was to be the producer, and I was tested by John Huston. I threw everything I knew into this test, and to my surprise John Huston did little to restrain me, encouraging me in confidential whispers to be even madder. Apparently the test was a success, but then the huge machine came to a halt, and the project was postponed for a year.

At the end of the year, the producer was Sam Zimbalist and the director Mervyn Leroy. They also approved my test, but warned me in a wire that I might be found to be a little young for the part. I cabled back that if they postponed again I might be too old, since Nero died at thirty-one. A second cable from them read 'Historical Research Has Proved You Correct Stop The Part Is Yours'.

To celebrate I purchased the first new car in my life, a rather ugly post-war Delage convertible in cream with a cherry-red top which it took three men to open and many more to shut, and cherry-red upholstery which indelibly stained the clothing of all who sat on it. I determined to drive round Spain on the way to Rome, where the film was to be shot. I broke down in Granada, Seville, Barcelona, Madrid, Badajoz, Jerez de la Frontera, Lorca, Perpignan, Narbonne, Cannes, San Remo, and at the gates of Rome, where a ball-race broke in a wheel, causing it to overheat.

When the car was raised, I saw a stamping on the underside of the chassis dating it October 1938. The ugly body had been added in 1949 to a chassis which had survived the Occupation in some shed, and now it had been sold to a patsy as a brand-new car. I only bought it in order to replace a second-hand one, also built in 1938, which was one of the most agreeable cars I ever owned, and reliable to boot.

Rome was in the throes of Holy Year, and bursting with pilgrims. It was also one of the hottest summers on record. I met Mervyn Leroy for the first time some hours before we began to shoot. He is an affectionate man of less than average height and of slight build. His blue eyes are friendly, although he has a vocational addiction to shouting, which is the right of any army commander, and, I was quick to discover, the production of an American epic is the nearest peacetime equivalent of a military operation, with time as the enemy.

I spoke to him with unaccustomed earnestness about my role, and asked him if he had any observations to make.

'Nero? Son of a bitch,' he declared.

I was inclined to agree with him.

'You know what he did to his mother?' he suddenly said, with decent Jewish concern, as though there was something one ought to do about it.

I replied that, yes, I did know what he did to his mother.

'Son of a bitch,' repeated Mervyn, almost angry.

I nodded my head. So far we saw eye to eye. 'But is there any specific aspect of the man you wish me to bring out?' I asked.

To my surprise, Mervyn replied by doing a tap-dance routine.

I applauded, and he beamed with pleasure.

'I used to be a hoofer,' he said.

I said, truthfully, that I didn't know that.

There was a long pause while I wondered uncomfortably if by some hideous chance he expected Nero to tap-dance.

'Nero,' said Mervyn.

I pricked up my ears.

239

'The way I see him . . .'

'Yes?'

'He's a guy plays with himself nights.'

At the time I thought it a preposterous assessment, but a little later I was not so sure. It was a profundity at its most workaday level, and it led me to the eventual conviction that no nation can make Roman pictures as well as the Americans.

The Romans were pragmatic, a people of relaxed power with *nouveau-riche* lapses of taste. They too believed in the beneficence of atrium living, in pampering the body with steam and the laying on of heavy hands after the excesses of a four-star cuisine. They too believed in dressing for comfort, and the intrigues in their senate matched anything in Washington, while their total belief in Roman know-how led to a few ugly surprises, as did the total belief in American know-how in Vietnam. They too garnished their official walls with flags and eagles, and eventually the Roman way of life was all-important, being practised even when the later Emperors were of Iberian or Dalmatian origin; it mattered little, what mattered was a family feeling, a *modus vivendi* which was sometimes gracious, sometimes coarse, sometimes civilized and sometimes violent and cruel, and yet, ever, unmistakably, Roman.

The inevitable vulgarities of the script contributed as much to its authenticity as its rare felicities. I felt then as I feel today, in spite of the carping of critical voices, that *Quo Vadis*, good or bad according to taste, was an extraordinarily authentic film, and the nonsense Nero was sometimes made to speak was very much like the nonsense Nero probably did speak.

So gargantuan was the production that I was sent to the Rome Opera House for three singing lessons, in the belief that such a crash course might make of me another Mario Lanza as I sang my lament to the burning city.

I arrived at the Opera one morning in an atmosphere of high tension. Apparently *Samson and Delilah* had just been hissed the night before, and I was taken to be the new Samson from Paris.

I pointed out that I would consider the part after I had had my lessons, but not before. It was on this abrasive and highly operatic note that I was ushered into the presence of my professor.

He confessed to me after dismissing a distraught soprano who had just waded through the mad scene from *Lucia de Lammermoor* that in agreeing to teach me how to sing in three lessons, he was motivated by financial considerations. I reassured him that such considerations had not been absent from my mind when accepting to play the part of Nero. We drank a toast to M.G.M. only with our eyes, and he confessed that his task was hopeless. Three years, perhaps, he said, but three lessons . . .

He sat down disconsolately at a piano which was as out of tune in its way as the late departed soprano had been in hers. It twanged like a guitar on some notes, like a banjo on others, and other yellowed notes produced no sound at all. Almost at once the score, by the Hungarian composer Miklos Rozsa, proved rather too advanced for the professor, who was accustomed to the predictable patterns of Donizetti and Verdi. He berated the music for its inordinate number of flats, and delivered to me the pith of his first year's course in a single lesson.

'Always, as I tell Gobbi, always breathe with the forehead,' he declared.

I wrinkled my brow as though it contained a small pulse. He was enchanted. Never, he informed me, had any pupil been quicker on the uptake.

At the start of the second lesson, he asked me what I remembered of the first lesson.

'Breathe with the –?' he asked.

'Forehead,' I replied.

'Bravo!' he cried. 'What a memory! Really fantastic.' Now followed the second lesson, containing all I would learn in the second year, in concentrated form. 'As I tell Gobbi, think with the diaphragm,' he said.

I adopted a distinctly constipated look, which seemed to me the faithful outward proof that my diaphragm was wrapped in thought. I set the pulse going in my forehead at the same time.

'My God, it's fantastic, fantastic! One at a time, yes, perhaps, but both together, so soon! Fantastic! What a talent!'

Before the third and final lesson, he decided on the usual refresher.

'Da Capo,' he said. 'Breathe with the –?'

'Forehead.'

'Bravo! Think with the –?'

'Diaphragm.'

'Bravissimo!'

And here followed the third and most difficult lesson.

'As I say to Gobbi, always, in all circumstances, sing . . . with the *eye*!'

I came away as enriched musically as the professor had been enriched financially, and whereas those who saw the film might not have guessed that I was thinking with my diaphragm or indeed breathing with my forehead, I fear it was painfully obvious that I was singing with my eye.

The heat was absolutely tremendous. Among the senators surrounding me on that hallowed balcony from which we were supposed to watch Rome in flames, there were some eminent English actors, among them Nicholas Hannen and D. A. Clarke-Smith. To add to the heat of the sun, braziers were burning all around us, shedding black ash on our togas, and the lights bored into us from above. A gallant lady harpist from the American Academy in Rome sat, drenched in perspiration, on a podium, waiting to accompany my hand movements on the lyre with her daintier sounds. Mervyn Leroy was shouting orders and counter-orders from a crane, and thin green rivers began snaking their way down my face from my laurel-wreath, which was made of inferior metal, and emanated a horrible ferrous odour. It was utter misery in this creative cauldron, and I feared for the health of the older actors as their nostrils grew black with dust from the braziers, and their lungs began heaving in their boiling chests.

A miniature of Rome caught fire to add to the inferno, and a back-projection screen came alive with visual pyrotechnics behind us. At last we were ready to shoot. I recalled the words of my crazed song, 'O Lambent Flames, O Force Divine', and cleared what throat I could still sense.

Just then Mervyn cried, 'Let me down! Let me down, for Christ's sake, will you?'

A sense of exasperated anti-climax set in as Mervyn disappeared from sight. Then the balcony began to shake, indicating someone was scaling it. Mervyn's head appeared over the battlements, cigar gripped between his teeth, his eyes confident and understanding like those of a manager telling a half-dead boxer that he's leading on points, and he summoned me to within confidential distance.

Waving his Havana at the burning city, he said quietly, 'Don't forget, you're responsible for all this.' Mervyn was never a director to leave anything to chance.

The third in the triumvirate of inseparable English actors was Felix Aylmer. They were inseparable only because of *The Times*, and more particularly of its crossword puzzle. Whichever of them was called latest would stop on the way to the studio and buy three copies of the airmail edition. They would sit on the set, their glasses on their noses, and solve its riddles.

It didn't take long to notice a curious atmosphere among them, however. Felix Aylmer and D. A. Clarke-Smith would only communicate with one another through Nicholas Hannen. This fact gave rise to odd dialogue like

CLARKE-SMITH: Revulsion.

AYLMER: Ask him where?

HANNEN: Where?

CLARKE-SMITH: Sixteen across.

AYLMER: Too many letters, tell him.

CLARKE-SMITH: Tell him I already know.

HANNEN: He already knows, he says.

Intrigued by the absurdity of this dialogue, reminiscent of

Eugène Ionesco in his English mood, I asked Nicholas Hannen to explain it. He revealed that the two had not spoken since 1924, when Clarke-Smith's wife had left him after a nocturnal argument, and had taken sanctuary at Felix Aylmer's cottage. Hot on her heels, Clarke-Smith banged on Aylmer's door. The two men in pyjamas and dressing-gowns faced each other.

'I have reason to believe my wife is here,' cried Clarke-Smith.

'She's in the spare room, D.A. Let's be reasonable and talk about this in the morning, after a good night's rest.'

Those were the last words they had exchanged until 'Revulsion', 'Ask him where?'

Occasionally they were summoned to work, and they tucked their copies of *The Times* into their togas. Unfortunately D. A. Clark-Smith was afflicted with a hacking cough, which he successfully suppressed, thereby only making the air-mail edition of *The Times* noisier as it was buffeted against his heaving chest, making a sound of someone stamping on a pile of autumn leaves. Immediately the sound-man looked up at the eaves.

'Goddam birds nesting up there,' he said.

Shooting was frequently held up while technicians attempted to winkle out the imaginary intruders. When nothing was found, they searched for rats, for ticking pipes, for mirages.

I would never give away my friends and their humble enjoyments. After twenty-six years of silence, they deserved a little consideration.

There were, of course, absurdities galore, as there could scarcely fail to be in a production of such magnitude: the fighting bull enclosed in a freight car of the Portuguese State Railways, and lured out into a corral designed for horses by the ten-gallon-hatted experts, against the considered advice of a diminutive Portuguese bullfighter, with the result that at the height of the luncheon break, an angry bull ambled into the Commissary, having butted his way to an easy freedom. Then there was the animal which Buddy Baer as Ursus was supposed to wrestle, and kill by breaking its neck. Out of prudence, the idea of a bull as specified in the book was rejected, especially after the company's previous experience with this animal. Consequently a chloroformed cow was selected, placed in such a way that the udders were invisible. Unfortunately every time that Buddy Baer twisted its neck, this had the effect of bringing the poor animal to, and every time he stood in triumph with his foot on its carcass, the cow looked up at him and mooed pathetically. And let me not forget Mervyn's inspired instruction to a couple of mountainous wrestlers, one Italian, one Turkish, who were supposed to kill each other with savage grunts and groans for my pleasure as I nibbled at larks and fondled my favourites: 'Action! And make every word count!'

I returned to London brimful of new experiences, feeling that I had widened my horizons irrevocably. In any case, no one who spends close to five months in Rome, that glut of over-ripe peaches in a dish of hills, can ever be quite the same. The emphasis on sin, perhaps inevitable in a place so overtly dedicated to the material majesty of God, and in which the spiritual majesty has to be taken for granted by those less than entirely gullible, gives one a feeling of turpitude and languor. The climate, the sleepy days and wide-awake nights, add to this sentiment of nervous exacerbation and squalid temptation, and one turns away from the city with a kind of weary revulsion, only to be impatient for one's return.

London seemed ordered and proper after Rome. The thefts were methodical, the burglaries routine, with nothing left to brilliant inspirations of the moment. Cops and robbers, like people in the street, moved at a regulation clip, without surprises. There was no darting out of archways, no driving up on the pavement, no midnight bathing and glamorous suicides in the Serpentine, no traces of heroin among the abandoned clothes, no scandal implicating the scions of ancient houses in decay.

And yet, I could work in London, whereas in Rome it had become utterly impossible. Refreshed by my absence, and by my enforced abstinence, I began to develop an idea in which the four powers were compelled to administer the Palace of the Sleeping Beauty by means of a commission. Out of this grew a play called *The Love of Four Colonels* which was constructed almost musically in a theme, variations, and a final fugue.

The four colonels, British, American, French, and Russian, were utterly realistic in the first act, disgruntled men with longings and aspirations beyond their grasp, beyond their means. A wicked fairy comes to tempt them. The Russian fires at him, he scratches his belly, complains of the bullet's itch, the Russian faints. A good fairy arrives to maintain the age-old balance.

In the second act, they move to the enchanted Palace, which has resisted the horrors of war wrapped in its impenetrable foliage. Each colonel is automatically in love with the Sleeping Beauty, and acts his passion with her in the form of a play within a play, according to his tastes and his nostalgia. The mild and monosyllabic Briton becomes a turbulent romantic in a scene of unrestrained Elizabethan lechery; the Frenchman, more true to himself, changes least to become a petit marquis of the seventeenth century, all bawdy asides laced with vinegar; the Russian, gruff and bear-like, becomes a nostalgic Czarist officer with epaulettes, cradling himself on a Chekhovian swing while he knits a jumper; the American, pill-taking and gaseous, turns into a saccharine fighting father, the founder of 'Girls' Town', converting evil-doers to the true faith with a straight left.

In spite of the encouragement of the wicked fairy, and thanks to the intervention of the good fairy, they all fail to seduce the Beauty. Then, by magic, they perceive their wives who have arrived at headquarters to visit their husbands, and the awful reality is revealed to them as the wives speak of them unrestrainedly. Two of them, the romantics, the Frenchman and the American decide to stay on in the endless pursuit of their ideal, forever destined to fail. The Englishman and the Russian decide to return to reality out of differing senses of obligation, where a pursuit of ideals has ended long ago and can never torture them again.

The play opened at Wyndham's Theatre, London, on May 23rd, 1951, and was my first great success. For me, it marked a coming of age. From now on I might be *terrible*, but the *enfant* was gone forever.

The play was performed in New York by Rex Harrison and Lilli Palmer, directed by Rex Harrison, in sets by Rolf Gerard. Although it did not last nearly as long as it did in London, it won the Critics Award for the Best Foreign Play of 1953. In Paris it ran for about six years at the little Théâtre Fontaine, and has been revived twice since. In Germany, the meeting place of the control commission was dubbed the 'Palace of the Sleeping Beauty' by sections of the press.

Meanwhile *Quo Vadis* appeared, and I was nominated for an Oscar as best supporting actor. The wind was in my sails. I moved from Chelsea Embankment to a house in King's Road which belonged to the Church Commissioners, and boasted a plaque informing the passer-by that Ellen Terry had lived there. Actually the house, a lovely and rather reticent building dating from 1702, should have displayed another plaque, for I discovered that the composer Dr Arne had lived there also and in fact, had written 'Rule, Britannia' while in residence. I played the work in many versions and at various volumes, but I was unable to evoke any reaction from the doctor's ghost.

The house had an enormous studio in lieu of a garden, and I spent most of my time in there with my books, my records and the few works of art I was beginning to accumulate. My mother, who had done the costumes for *Vice-Versa* and *Private Angelo*, often stayed with me, while my father still occupied his bachelor apartment round the corner. It was a curious arrangement, but I asked no questions, especially since they saw much more of each other now than during my mother's fairly long sojourn in Gloucestershire.

After a time, they announced that they had found a flat not far away, and I was delighted that time had seemed to heal what wounds there were. Like everyone else, I had made myself into a company, which was believed to be the only way at the time to ride out the storm of nightmarish taxation, made worse by a system which made you the caretaker for money which you had earned, but which wasn't yours to spend. This, I will be told, is normal in the tax-structures of free countries, and yet there were few free countries at the time where you were supposed to hold on to up to 95 per cent of your earnings until asked to surrender it like a good fellow for the government to misspend, because it had more experience than you in the matter.

At all events, despite a fairly frugal existence, my tax affairs were pronounced to be in a sorry state. This discovery came about owing to the death of my tax accountant, who was revealed by his successor to have been somewhat unimaginative in the handling of my affairs. Taking into consideration the almost medical code of honour which prevents accountants from talking ill of their peers, one can well guess what word he might have employed if he had not limited himself to unimaginative. All of which raises a very serious point. How does a person like myself distinguish a good tax adviser from a less than good one? Usually, alas, by whether he is agreeable to be with or not, and whereas this may be a social criterion, it is worse than useless with tax advisers. For instance, the unimaginative, deceased one was a very agreeable man indeed, and to cloud the issue even further, so is the imaginative, alive one. This makes nonsense of a nascent theory that probably a corrosive unpleasant individual tends to inspire confidence in a layman, since taxes are, by their very nature, corrosive and unpleasant inventions. But then, in any case, how would a layman arrive at a definition of a good tax adviser? Probably by considering him good when he takes the same amount in salary as he saves you in taxes. A bad tax adviser is clearly one who takes more in salary than he saves you in taxes. What both good and bad advisers take in time is simply unassessable.

When Henry Wallace, then a Presidential candidate, recklessly proclaimed this to be 'The Century of the Common Man', he was as wide of the mark as only an ambitious politician can be. This is still, and will be to its bitter end, the Century of the Middle Man. In the United States, life-style leader at this time, it is advisable to retain a lawyer long before any litigation, as well as an agent to keep your name in the forefront of employers' minds. Then, possibly owing to the population explosion and the need to create jobs, the business manager is created, along with the public relations man. All these people watch each other like hawks on your behalf, but since they are also bound by the highest moral principles, they never warn you in time when things begin to go wrong, since on no account can they permit themselves to be critical of one another. And so, any reasonably good-natured performer sooner or later treats these outsiders as personal friends, and no longer cares if they are good at their job or not. The fact that they are tax-deductible seems to be sufficient to carry them in overlapping advisory capacities through life.

So it was that my new tax adviser, while tut-tutting a great deal as he deciphered the 'unimaginative' mess of his predecessor, asked me, in the light of the deplorable state of my finances, what kind of car I drove.

'Aston Martin,' I replied.

'Oh God,' moaned my tax-man. 'Must you?'

I answered with some liveliness. I told him London was full of even more expensive cars, Rolls-Royces and Bentleys. Who bought them? It couldn't all be inherited money. Or was it merely that these proud owners had had more imaginative advice?

He grunted in a non-committal way, as though overflowing with bitter secrets.

'All right,' he said, 'what other car have you?'

'I have no other car,' I answered.

'Oh good God,' cried the tax-man, now really upset.

My first economy measure in the reconstruction of my parlous finances was, therefore, to go out and purchase a Standard Eight which I didn't need, as a personal car, so that I could put the Aston Martin down to business. I began to learn the nature of the cloud-cuckoo atmosphere in which we were beginning to live, and the gratuities as well as the price of freedom.

One of the directors of my company was my literary agent, an Australian called Alroy Treeby; another was my cousin, Julius Caesar Edwardes, who ended up at B.P. as Director of Public Relations, and my father, who sat there making notes of what was being said, clearing his throat on occasion as though about to speak, but nothing ever materialized, and putting the minutes into a leather portfolio when it was over. I don't think poor Klop had the remotest understanding of what was going on, but once he was on the board of a company for the first and last time of his life, he made the best of a job beyond his comprehension by looking distinguished and even, at times, shrewd. I felt sorry for him because, although I kept myself out of the phone book for obvious reasons, he put himself into it. He was the only Ustinov in the London book, and received a great many enquiries for me. The extent of these enquiries seemed like an endless reminder that I had not turned out the failure of his prophecy but he never complained and attempted to take all the messages with the thoroughness of a company director, only the theatrical firm of Linnit and Dunfee being consistently beyond his grasp, since he used to inform me with the utmost seriousness that Dunnit and Fifi had called. His quiet efforts on my behalf, his unequal and yet uncomplaining struggle with the complications of a life very different from his own, made me feel like the father, him seem like the son.

He retained his dignity in all this, perhaps because, now more than ever, he was eager not to be seen to be 'letting the side down'.

It was nevertheless my father who first tired of the vanities of town life, and hankered for the country. This desire was peculiar and uncharacteristic. Of all the people I have ever known, he was the most blatantly urban in character. Not that he would ever have been a boulevardier, even had the affluence of his youth made such a desire possible. He preferred narrower streets, and the freedom to wander, unobserved. He liked to browse in shops, buy herbs at greengrocers for his cooking. He liked hailing taxis, and using the telephone. I just could not reconcile the abandonment of all this with his real predilections, unless this emigration to a voluntary exile had about it an abandonment of life itself, a relinquishing of his command over the better things of existence. Why? Because living would merely be an echo of what his had been. He saw no sense of achievement in longevity and old men who asked you to guess their ages with a challenging twinkle seemed to him grotesque. Before he began his long, and by all appearances, voluntary decline, he still had one or two missions abroad on behalf of his wartime employers. Consequently my mother went to the country first, in order to settle them in. Lonely and frightened in the Cotswolds after London, she asked me for a dog – once again a most uncharacteristic request.

I bought a Golden Retriever puppy somewhere in Knights-bridge, and took it to the theatre with me, where its whimpering could be heard on the stage. I named it Colonel, out of deference to its contribution to my play.

The next day I was visited by a rather masculine lady in tweeds, wearing a pork-pie hat and a tie. She wished to deliver the pedigree, and asked me if I had yet selected a name for the dog. I said rather sheepishly that I was going to call it Colonel.

'Oh, what a rattling good notion,' replied the lady, transferring her weight nervously from foot to foot. 'The little beggar was sired by Squadron-Leader.'

I delivered him to my mother the very next Sunday, and he immediately began chewing everything in sight, carpets, shoes, canvases, and even my mother.

I had no occasion to visit my parents until some time later, by when my father had taken his retirement. I arrived unannounced, and to my surprise found that I had broken into a large cocktail party. What was even stranger than the type of reception my parents were giving was the type of guests they had invited. All the men were elderly, and wore moustaches, either great untidy red entanglements hanging over their mouths like rusting barbed-wire, or else tidy little clipped things, like a third eye-brow, or white tufts blocking the nostrils, snowballs at the moment of impact. The majority of them had ice-blue eyes, and the wives looked exactly as you would expect, wizened yet friendly, plagued with discreet nervous tics, and speaking much louder than necessary in jagged uppercrust cadences.

Not long after my arrival, they began to leave in pairs, effusive in their thanks. When the last couple had gone, I asked my father what on earth had prompted such a gathering, He looked at me resentfully, and told me it was my fault, 'yours and your mother's'.

My mother had evidently been far too busy painting, and had not made any effort to train the dog, who was now much larger, less prone to chew, but absolutely undisciplined. Klop, on his return to England, had decided to take the dog in hand, a duty which gave some point to daily exercise he had been condemned to by the doctor, and so he would go out with it for walks.

Naturally in passing through villages, the distractions for a canine nostril grew in variety, and the dog would go streaking off in obedience to some uncontrolled instinct, my father shouting in the distance, 'Colonel! Colonel!'

Inevitably the door of a cottage would open, a gentleman in tweeds would appear, and say, 'Yes? Did I hear my name?'

The encounter would result in some good-natured laughter and an invitation to have a drink.

My father tried to alter his itinerary in order to avoid villages where known colonels lived, but there were more of them than he had reckoned with, and the day inevitably arrived when he ran out of villages. Now, with Colonel as disobedient as ever, he was repaying all those other colonels who had answered his call with greater alacrity, by plying them with pink gin and whisky.

'Why does your mother need a dog? And why did you give him the idiotic name of Colonel?' asked my father as he started washing-up the glasses.

'I could have called him Vicar,' I said as I began drying them.

For two long years *The Love of Four Colonels* continued, exhausting and exhilarating, and it could have gone on considerably longer than its well over 800 performances. During that time I spent some weekends seeing it in other countries, in Germany, Denmark, Holland and Italy. My private life was less erratic than before, but no more settled for that. Although I began to suspect that I was not made for marriage, I knew perfectly well that I was not made for celibacy either. Nor did I care for my profession to the exclusion of all else. I was, in other words, all eggs and precious little basket. And, curiously enough, when all is well these anomalies are far more apparent than when adversity strikes. You look around you at the growing edifice of your life, and admit to yourself that it is beautiful, but beautiful to what purpose? What and who is it for? Solitude is a necessary ingredient in the act of creation, but loneliness is very different – not loneliness while alone, but loneliness in public places, in the midst of gaiety and joy.

My heart did leap once, on the tennis court of all places. I played badly since I kept my eye on my partner instead of on the ball. She was a French girl with an amusing face and a lively temperament, called Hélène. Our mutual attraction was immediate, and we enjoyed one another's company. Then she disappeared to France, leaving me the telephone number of her grandfather, at whose house she lived. He was a Marquis, and his butler sounded like something even higher. The *cordon sanitaire* round my delightful partner was dignified and hermetic. There was nothing I could do.

A little while later, while browsing in Mr Moroni's newspaper shop in Soho, I saw the photograph of a strikingly beautiful girl on the cover of a pulp magazine. There was a story about her in it, with a teasing phrase under her picture, *'J'adore les contes de fées'* (I love fairy-stories). Pretending it was for a non-existent cook, I bought it along with all the other foreign magazines I took regularly. I carried it to the theatre.

Three days later, my French agent André Bernheim appeared in my dressing-room after the performance, accompanied by the very girl on the cover of the magazine. Her name was Suzanne Cloutier, and she was a young French-Canadian actress who had played Desdemona in Orson Welles's film of *Othello*. She was now in England to act in a film of Herbert Wilcox's called *Derby Day*, and André Bernheim asked if I would kindly look after her when he had gone. She spotted the magazine on my dressing-table, and I truthfully told her the circumstances of its purchase. Such providential acts can sometimes rush one into an impression that destiny was at work.

She told me she was on the run from Orson Welles, that his representatives were searching high and low for her to implement a contract for which she had not been paid. Her work in Wilcox's film must therefore be considered clandestine in the extreme. An executive from Paramount Pictures, with whom she had a long-term agreement, and I set her up in a remote but comfortable hotel, and an improbable detective story began, at the culmination of which we ran straight into Orson Welles in a fashionable restaurant.

He was perfectly charming, surprised to see her, and asked kindly how she was. The small talk bore no trace of malice nor of any desire to implement a contract, and all Suzanne's efforts to appear frightened could not turn Orson into the Svengali he patently had no ambition to be.

A little later, while dancing – yes, I had been dragooned into this unsuitable pastime – she told me her mother was a German Jewess called Braun and that her father was descended from an Indian Chief with a name I cannot today recall, but that, apart from that, she was British and defiantly French, and as such had been denied the privilege of learning her own language, which she

254

spoke perfectly, by the villainous Anglo-Canadian authorities. All this was said with utter conviction, and even if I found most of it hard to swallow, these tales had an undeniable comic charm, in which the fact that she seemed to take them so seriously was not a minor ingredient.

People were enchanted by her freshness, her extraordinary capacity for invention and her acumen in pursuing her ends, and I must admit, I was among them. And even if one never quite knew when to reach for a pinch of salt, she had said it herself. She loved fairy-stories – *J'adore les contes de fées*'.

15

Suzanne's first marriage had never been consummated. This is no reflection whatsoever on her husband, an eminent doctor, for when he looked around after the wedding reception, Suzanne had gone. Their married bliss had lasted the best part of half a day, and now his bride was on her way to New York to become a Powers Model. She had, she told me, undergone all the pomp and splendour of a military wedding (for her husband was then still in the army, and his father was a general), simply in order to give her parents pleasure. It never seemed to occur to her to equate their happiness with their dismay at her disappearance, a fact which I found troubling to say the least.

In this perplexity I made a happy choice of legal adviser in Dr Elio Nissim, an Italian Jew who was the logical choice to represent the Vatican at the See of Canterbury, a tribute to the intelligence of the Catholics and the sensibility of the Protestants.

Nissim managed to arrange a divorce under a law pertaining to wives abandoned in Europe by G.I.s, which was brilliant by any standards even if this particular case could hardly pretend to be a prototype for such a situation.

There were more surprises on the way, however. Suzanne's parents had instigated legal proceedings within the Catholic church to have the marriage annulled, a procedure of immense complication. The decision was eventually handed down many years later, and the news was broken to Suzanne by Monseigneur

Leger, the Cardinal Archbishop of Montreal, during a midnight phone call.

I sought to burp our son, who was teething and shouting his head off, and to divert our daughter, who had been deprived of her sleep, and who was therefore shouting back, while Suzanne, making desperate signs at me to keep the children quiet, was in the process of learning that Mother Church had accorded her request for an annulment on the grounds of non-consummation. She expressed her gratitude in a voice of pristine wonder that such marvels could come to pass, interspersed with assurances that they didn't have a crossed line.

'*C'est curieux,*' the Archbishop said, '*je pense entendre des enfants pleurer.*'

'*C'est peut-être l'Atlantique, Monseigneur,*' Suzanne suggested reverently.

Elio Nissim is an extraordinary man, tiny, with a shrill voice, and an eggshell pallor, an advocate of the highest order who eventually gave up the law, I suspect because he was too good at it. His disgust with the fallibility of men and the self-imposed misery of the human condition made him abandon the career he had mastered with such gentle eloquence and lacerating skill. He was incapable of bitterness, and so he preferred the clean air of the pasture to the heat and odours of the kitchen.

Harry Truman, another small man of brisk brilliance, once said about politics, 'If you can't stand the heat, get out of the kitchen.'

For certain temperaments, it is not the heat but the smell which drives them out.

During the run of *The Love of Four Colonels*, Bill Linnit had presented a serious play of mine, *The Moment of Truth*, at the Adelphi Theatre on November 21st, 1951. It starred Eric Portman and that fine émigré actor Charles Goldmer, the first playing a kind of free paraphrase on both Marshal Pétain and King Lear, whereas the latter played a variant on Laval, the man who is a villain, doing a great deal of good in the course of his villainy, and who knows he will have to pay the price. It did not run long, but I consider it one of my good plays. The press was indifferent, except for the *New York Herald Tribune's* Paris edition, which carried a superb notice. This could unfortunately give us but little commercial help, and yet a notice like this gives a dramatist the requisite hope under any kind of adversity.

Another play, *No Sign of the Dove*, for which my mother did the sets, was set in a large country house, and its theme was ambitious despite the angular conventions of a vaudeville. It began on the ground floor, among the guests of a pretentious literary house-party, a flatulent German philosopher, a poetess, her novelist brother, a sycophant and his wife, prepared for a weekend of intellectual delights. Meanwhile the floods are rising. The second act took place on the first floor, among the bedrooms. Partners changed, and a couple of private detectives attempted to keep abreast of events. Only an old man, the father of the house, and a small waif are busy building an ark in a room, refusing all contact with the other guests. The floods have filled the ground floor. The last act is on the roof. The waters rise, and it becomes clear that it is the second coming of the Flood. The curtain falls as the detectives organize community singing to keep the spirits up.

The booing from the gallery began just forty-five seconds after the curtain rose. It was well organized and thorough. Scouts must have seen the play in the provinces, and their smoke-signals were observed from afar by those self-appointed arbiters of public taste who used to shout their frustrations from the dark anonymity of the gallery.

I am not defending the play. If it can't do it for itself, it deserves no help, and nor do I. It may indeed have been too continental in flavour for these insular roisterers, its style may have been too deliberate, its edge too sharp (or too blunt), its message too tragic (or too unjustified), but whatever the truth, the fact that the second night audience clapped fast and furiously meant nothing. It was already too late to save the play, and it is possible that the applause was not entirely a mitigation of its qualities, but a generous vote of confidence in me, a balm after the scourge.

Whatever the truth, I suffered a numb feeling of disgust, and then, almost immediately, a sudden upsurge of confidence, a kind of controlled rage with the outward aspect of insolent serenity. This was, after all, no more than the childish initiation into some scholastic lodge, the ritual all new boys must go through if they wish to earn the respect of their fellows. The great virtue of disaster is that it gives a man the possibility of demonstrating his fibre before so many people.

I did what I had to, wrote an article for the *Daily Express* on what it was like to be booed, and forgot the theatre for a while. I played the part of George IV in my second American film, *Beau Brummell*, at the M.G.M. Studios in London, co-starring with Elizabeth Taylor and Stewart Granger. It was selected later as the Royal Command Film because the committee in charge of such events decided that nothing interested royalty more than royalty. It was only when Robert Morley as George III attempted to strangle me, a most realistic performance, that suddenly a hideous doubt sprang up in the minds of those responsible that the sight of one of the Queen's not too distant ancestors attempting to strangle another one in a fit of insanity was perhaps not the happiest of diversions for Her Majesty, and the press the next day bubbled with that particular form of pious hypocrisy which has marked all recent British scandals, large or small.

We left for Hollywood immediately after our marriage. I had been contracted to play in the film *The Egyptian*, and I was looking forward to acting with Marlon Brando, who was one of its stars along with Victor Mature, Jean Simmons, Michael Wilding, and other famous names. I had already appeared in a view of ancient Rome seen through Polish eyes in *Quo Vadis*, by Sienkiewicz, and now I was about to indulge in a view of ancient Egypt as conceived by a Finn, Waltari. In a sense, Rome is already a part of the modern world, whereas the spirit of ancient Egypt is still wrapped in the secrecy of sphinxes and the smiles of cats which make the enigma of the Mona Lisa seem commonplace.

Unfortunately this relative difficulty of discerning a palpable artistic personality for Egypt outside the stilted murals and the pyramids compels designers to go to *Aïda* for inspiration. And this film was no exception. The sheer size of the décor dwarfed everything that stood before it, men, ideas, intelligence itself.

The only element in this elaborate cocktail half as mysterious as ancient Egypt was the director, Michael Curtiz, a tall and upright Hungarian who had come to Hollywood so long ago that he gazed over the palm trees and stucco castellations of its civilization with the eye of a blind, all-seeing prophet of its faith. He had never learned American, let alone English, and he had forgotten his Hungarian, which left him in a limbo of his own, both entertaining and wild. His eyes had no visible pupils; they must have been the size of pin-points, and the irises were of the brightest blue, the blue of innocence.

I was presented to him on arrival, and he greeted me with the complicated grace of an Imperial corps-commander welcoming a new lieutenant hot from Budapest. The next day I was presented to him again, with precisely the same result. He had evidently forgotten me in the interim. I reckoned I was introduced to him at least ten times during the first week, each time for the first time. After that a kind of shadow passed across his face, as though he was trying to place me.

I came down on to the floor for my début to find him filming a tavern scene. Jean Simmons was sweeping the floor with a large besom broom. Victor Mature was very angry about something or other in Ancient Thebes, and he dashed a papier-mâché goblet to the ground.

'No lips of mine shall ever touch this chalice!' he cried out.

In the centre of the stage sat my stand-in, dressed identically to me, chewing gum and looking round with a very contemporary kind of detachment. I touched Mike Curtiz's arm. He bridled in irritation, then stared at me, trying to place me.

'Cut,' he cried. 'Vie you not on set?'

'Nobody called me,' I said.

'God damn, dat no excuse.'

Angrily, I took the place of my stand-in.

'Vie you not bring my attention?' he shouted at the stand-in.

'I tried to, sir,' shrugged the stand-in.

'We all did!' cried Jean Simmons.

'That's right,' confirmed Victor Mature.

'Ven nobody have interest film in heart, vil suffer only vun ting, film,' grumbled Curtiz.

Of course, by now, Marlon Brando was no longer part of the cast. He had taken one look at the final script, and become victim of a rare illness, from which he made a miraculous recovery once shooting had begun on his replacement.

Communications with Mike Curtiz were extraordinarily difficult. He seemed to understand absolutely nothing I said, while agreeing with it all and doing just the opposite. There was only one slender ray of hope. In a moment of rare repose, he suddenly spoke, apropos of nothing.

'Vienna,' he said, with a fatalistic chuckle, 'I remember ven I vos barefoot boy in Vienna mit my broder, selling in the theatre sveets und magazine-programmes. Life!' His eyes looked heavenward a moment in smiling recognition of his fortune, and he retired once again into his more impenetrable abstractions.

It so happened that I had just received a letter from the 'Theatre in der Josefstadt' in Vienna, on appropriately heraldic and evocative note-paper. They were about to perform *The Love of Four Colonels* and asked for certain precisions. It was a letter so technical it could mean nothing to anybody but myself, but I thought the letterhead itself might lure the nostalgic Curtiz further out of his lair, and expose him to human contact by way of his reminiscences.

The next day, after briefly reminding him who I was, I said,

'Mike, you remember yesterday – '

'Of course I remember yesterday,' he interrupted as though I had insulted his powers of retention. I refused to be side-tracked.

'You told us of your boyhood in Vienna.'

'Dat vos not yesterday,' he cried, 'a long time ago!'

His expression became suddenly serene.

'Vienna,' he said, with a fatalistic chuckle, 'I remember ven I vos barefoot boy in Vienna mit my broder, selling in the teatre sveets und magazine-programmes. Life!' His eyes looked heavenward a moment in smiling recognition of his fortune, and before he could retire once again into his more impenetrable abstractions, I nipped in with my letter.

He took it, and to my dismay did not so much as glance at the letterhead, but went straight on to the letter as though it were intended for him.

'We're ready, Mike,' said the cameraman.

'Mein God, vot manners,' cried Curtiz, 'to interrüpt van man ven his is reading vun letter!'

The cameraman went away in disgust, and Mike Curtiz returned to his incomprehensible reading matter. Then, to my horror, he stuffed it into his pocket, and prepared to direct.

My chief concern was how to recuperate it, and I waited till the end of the day. I cornered him as he was about to leave the set.

'Mike,' I said, 'could I have my letter, please?'

'No,' he replied gently, on a tone of high morality, 'I am not de kind director write letter actors. I know it exist director too scared actors, so dey write letter instead to say vot tink. I not such. If I tink stink, I say. If I think voonderful, I say. Alvays I say. No letter. Alvays say.'

I gritted my teeth.

'Mike,' I said, 'you have a letter *belonging to me*.'

'I no mail-man,' he retorted heatedly. 'Ven is letter for you, it vil be post-office, mit your name on, not mine name on.'

'Mike,' I screamed, 'you have a letter belonging to me from *Vienna*!'

'Vienna,' he said, with a fatalistic chuckle, 'I remember ven I vos barefoot boy in Vienna mit my broder – '

Before he had finished the sentence, I dug into his pocket and removed my letter. He noticed nothing. I made no further attempt to reach a more accessible unity. We were both better off this way.

Curiously enough, he was much more perceptive than he seemed to be, even though extremely absent-minded. Rumour had it that he had injured himself badly not long ago by stepping out of his Cadillac while it was in motion to commit a new idea to paper. Needless to say, he was driving himself.

At the end of *The Egyptian*, which was a film I never saw since I found it so profoundly silly while I was making it, Mike Curtiz asked me to do another film, with Humphrey Bogart, Aldo Ray, Basil Rathbone and Joan Bennett, called *We're No Angels*, based on a charming French play by Albert Husson, *La Cuisine des Anges*.

It suited our purpose admirably to stay in Hollywood a little longer, since Suzanne was reaching the term of her pregnancy, and she could not travel any more. She had been to a celebrated pediatrician whose only interest seemed to be the extent of my salary, since, he explained, he took one-tenth of it, which was deductible in my case. I began to have nightmares about being chided by the tax-man for not having had twins, so that one of them could be put down to business, and leave the other for pleasure.

The pediatrician seemed unable to understand that, being British and resident in Britain, I only had very limited pocket money to spend on luxuries like childbirth, and eventually we found a Canadian doctor who was going to Europe on holiday and was consequently willing to be paid in sterling.

These were not easy times in Hollywood. Some American friends I had made in England, notably Adrian Scott, had virtually

263

disappeared, and asking after them seemed as dangerous as any request for the whereabouts of distinguished colleagues in a dictatorship. The lamentable Senator Joseph McCarthy was on the rampage with his prolonged drumhead court-martial, occupying everyone's attention on television and disseminating a reprehensible panic among those one had thought to be made of sterner stuff, while leading good-natured fools to utter portentous and ignorant pronouncements about the nature of communism and democracy.

McCarthy was investigating the infiltration of subversive ideas into the U.S. Army, and what he succeeded in illustrating was what I have referred to elsewhere as the lack of moral courage in people of admirable physical courage. To watch one brave bemedalled façade after another collapse under the specious pummelling of this sinister clown was more than one's sense of workaday decency could stand. It therefore came as a great relief to me to be invited to do a fifteen-minute recording for the B.B.C. on the sole subject of the Army-McCarthy hearings. I still do not believe that the B.B.C., in their cloistered island freedom, realized the local hazards of what they were asking me to do. They could not know, in the quiet rooms of Broadcasting House, that people actually cowered when the subject of McCarthy was brought up, and cast a hasty eye round the assembly to assess the nature and position of other guests. It was like one of Hollywood's own films about Nazi Germany.

I went along to Don Lee Mutual, Channel 5, and a bored technician asked me who my piece was for, C.B.C.? No, I said, B.B.C.

'What the hell's that?' he asked, marking the as-yet empty reel with the initials.

'British Broadcasting Corporation.'

'British!' He pulled a long face, as though surprised that we had already managed to give up the tom-tom on the hilltop beacon as a means of communication.

I sat down and read my piece, from which I take the liberty of quoting –

'To the outside observer there is nothing particularly striking about the Senator – there is no fire, no perceptible fanaticism, and curiously no oratorical powers. Words come more easily to him than sentences, which is normal; but even words fall grudgingly from his lips – his eyes, meanwhile having all the dispassionate intensity of a lion who is having his own private troubles gnawing a juiceless knuckle. His voice is plaintive by nature, and trembles obediently when a particularly emotional tone is ordered by the brain. On other occasions, it tries the elusive intonations of sarcasm, sounding much like a car with a dying battery, and even attempts the major key of jocularity when bonhomie is called for, but it is a sad laugh, and one which does not invite participation.

'It is as though he had cheated the physical restrictions placed on him by nature, and had trained the very shortcomings of his equipment into weapons. His own evident lack of wit makes him impervious to the wit of others: his own inability to listen makes him immune to argument; his own tortuous train of thought wears down the opposition; his crawling reflexes, his unnaturally slow and often muddled delivery force quicker minds to function at a disadvantage below their normal speeds. And yet, cumbersome as is the Senator in action, his changes of direction, like those of the charging rhinoceros, are often executed with alarming ease. A mind trained in all the arts of tactical expediency urges the ponderous machinery on its provocative way.

'Whenever he is compelled to admit that he doesn't know, he does so with an inflection suggesting that it isn't worth knowing. Whenever he says he does know, he does so with an inflection suggesting that others don't – and won't. This then is the outward face of the man who has heard voices telling him to go and root out Communists – and this is the face of a man who recognizes his potential enemy in everyone he meets. Like a water-diviner, he treads the desert with a home-made rod, and

265

shouts his triumph with every flicker of the instrument, leaving hard-working professional men to scratch the soil for evidence.

'No one who has enjoyed an argument, no one who has entertained a challenging doubt, no one who relishes an unfettered view of history and of the current scene, could possibly be a communist. But anti-communism is no creed – democracy is no creed – it is a vehicle for the enjoyment of freedom, for the ventilation of thought, for the exercise of mutual respect, even in opposition. This is the heritage which has given debate its laws. This is the heritage which is traditionally so near the heart of this immense republic, and for which so many of her sons have died.

'When anti-communism attempts to become a creed, it fights with the arms of its enemy, and like its enemy, it breeds injustice, fear, corruption. It casts away the true platform of democracy, and destroys the sense of moral superiority without which no ethical struggle is ever won.

'This majestic land, these United States, know by instinct – in fact they have often taught us from more venerable parts – that democracy can never be a prison – it is a room with the windows open.'

When I raised my eyes off my paper, I saw that whereas there had been one bored technician at the outset, the control-room now looked like a tankful of trout in a restaurant, full of surprised and hypnotized faces glued to the glass. All that was missing were the bubbles.

As I left, there was a chorus of questions. 'Hey, did you really mean that? D'you work for a group? Wow, when's this going out? Are they willing to accept this kind of thing in England?'

There must have been one of them who was eager for a fast buck, because a report appeared in one of the less responsible gossip columns adding all manner of red frills to what I had said, presumably in the interests of freedom of the press. The Studio was extremely worried, and asked me to lie low and avoid questions, which was an indication of the wretched atmosphere at the time. They even asked me not to come down to lunch while Hedda Hopper was there. Since time has not been generous with her memory, I had better remind some of the younger readers, and even, thank heavens, some of the older ones, that Hedda Hopper, in her time a useful starlet, became in her dotage a feared columnist whose virtue was that she said what she thought, and whose vice was that what she thought didn't amount to much.

As it turned out, the request for me not to confront her was occasioned not only by my utterances, but by a conviction she held that 'he was so great in *Quo Vadis*, he has to be a fag, and you know what I feel about fags!' Needless to say, I had my meal in the restaurant as usual.

Our daughter Pavla was born at St John's Hospital in Santa Monica on June 2nd, 1954, at 3.33 in the afternoon. That evening I was invited to the Bogarts, and arrived late, having spent the day at the hospital. Bogie was mixing drinks in a bar on the way to the living-room.

'Well?' he said, his eyes anxious.

'It's a girl. Both doing well,' I replied.

His face, so human and involuntarily kind, turned into the disenchanted mask he was known by.

'What's the matter?' I asked, not without a grain of irony. 'You disapprove?'

'No, no,' he muttered. 'Congratulations, and all that usual crap. I can just hear in my head the noise those women in the living-room are going to make when you tell them.' And, holding a tray of drinks, he did a wonderfully overdrawn imitation of a roomful of women greeting the news of a childbirth. 'Aaaoow – '

We went into the living-room together. Bogie said he had an announcement to make, and spoke in the dead tones of a ringside announcer. 'Peter's just become the proud father of a baby girl. Both mother and child are doing well.'

'Aaaaooow – '

Bogie gave me the filthiest of his enviable repertoire of filthy looks, while he dispensed his martinis. I recognized that his imitation was not overdrawn at all.

When I had finished the film we decided, in spite of the presence of a new-born child, to return to England slowly, by way of Mexico, Cuba, Haiti and Jamaica. There we caught a French ship, the Antilles, which stopped at Guadeloupe, Martinique, Port-of-Spain, La Guaira, and Vigo on its way to Plymouth.

Hollywood had been exciting, despite a permanent financial stringency. We were young and adventurous, and life in our tiny apartment on Wilshire Boulevard was full of incident, most of it pleasant. Our neighbour was Frank Sinatra, then still a hermit saddened by his worship of Ava Gardner. Morning, noon, and night he sang. I had been writing *Romanoff and Juliet*, and whereas I had been impervious to the German bombs, I frankly found it difficult to concentrate with this insidious serenade going on, hardly deadened by the cardboard wall.

When I mentioned this to my wife, I was lectured. 'There is a man who really works at his craft, always honing his instrument in search of the ultimate perfection, driving himself relentlessly towards the pinnacle of his profession. Whereas you – '

Just then the needle stuck in the groove. They were records. All the wall eliminated was the orchestral accompaniment.

Once, when visiting him, the inevitable record was playing. He left the room for a moment to mix some drinks. During his absence, Judy Garland appeared, clutching a pile of records. She immediately replaced his record with one of hers. He reappeared as though he had heard a burglar. Then he laughed at his own reaction.

Since I was paid in England, we managed our journey by saving money from our expenses. Mexico whetted the appetite for future journeys, especially perhaps Yucatan, quite unlike the rest of the country. The ancient city of Merida nestles in the heart of a crew-cut jungle, an oasis of silence amid the catcalls of jaguars and the cackle of exotic birds. The only noise seemed to come from the groaning of windmills, which are everywhere. The kitchens, with their copper pots, are spotless, reminiscent of Dutch interiors, which go well with the windmills, and since the people, tiny, fragile and very soft-spoken, look like Indonesians, it is easy to feel that one is in some old colonial outpost in the East Indies.

The Mayan ruins in Chichen-Itza and Uxmal are quite as remarkable as those of the Aztecs and Toltecs.

Cuba was on the eve of elections, and Batista seemed to be the only candidate worthy of taking seriously. The city of Havana is lovely, but the atmosphere at the time was disturbing. The place felt as though it was irretrievably impregnated with American influence, which is not at all the same as saying that it was like the United States. Every advertisement was for an American product, and the cards we procured enabling us to swim in the Officers' Club also enabled us to swim and float among some of the most preposterous machos on record. It felt as though the changing-room would have a sword-rack and a spur-bin. I felt and said at the time that such a country could only explode in order to rediscover its identity. Cuban refugees, like Russian refugees, never tire of evoking the elegance of life in the past, which they refer to as free, and plaintively insist that they would have become modern states if only 'they had been left alone to develop in their own good time'.

Revolutions have never succeeded unless the establishment does three-quarters of the work. It was completing its contribution while we were in Cuba.

Haiti was different. Here there was a feeling of resistance to all outside influence, which is not difficult for a people so hypnotized by its own image and passionate history. The extraordinary figures of Toussaint-L'Ouverture, Dessalines, Petion, and Henri-Christophe dominated its early years, with Dessalines and Petion less known, but probably the most effective, whereas Henri-Christophe, crowning himself an Emperor in the image of

Napoleon and in hatred of the French, constituted an English type of Court, with the Grand Chamberlain, the Grand Duke of Don-Don, and the two masters of nobility, the Dukes of Limonade and Marmalade.

It would always be difficult for a people with such a colourful sense of both pomp and circumstance to find itself at home with the dry crackle of Marxist theory. Rather nervously avoiding a voodoo procession in the village of Leogane, which was far from being for tourists, we drifted into a ramshackle churchyard with simple crosses and mere sticks of wood. In the middle of it was a small and hideous mausoleum, its Grecian roof held up by weeping angels, dedicated to what must have been one of the great families of the Haitian Empire, for on it was inscribed the words 'Famille Actedoffrande-Milord'.

A little later, from one of the wooden houses dating from the Colonial period, we heard the strains of a Polish dance which must have been the rage at the time, a courtly Krakowiak hammered out on an old piano, full of crystalline runs with missing notes. Glancing through the windows, we caught sight briefly of a dignified rout in progress in an atmosphere reminiscent of the ante-bellum South, but with coffee-coloured beauties in huge and fanciful costumes, performing the steps accurately with their nimble gallants. It seemed as if the throbbing African nostalgia of voodoo was too vulgar for these stately ghosts.

On a walk, I ran into Peter Brook. It was a meeting of two Stanleys, both of us rather unhappy at not being alone in this strange world. Our disappointment was aggravated by the sudden emergence of Livingstone in the shape of Graham Greene. He seemed as horrified at seeing us as we had been at seeing each other. We had lunch together since there seemed nothing else to do. By the time we were ready for coffee, the atmosphere had warmed pleasantly. Instead of regaling each other with tales of distant Haiti in some London club, we were resigned to sitting in distant Haiti and regaling each other with tales of London.

We arrived back in England, which was slightly anticlimactic after our fill of exoticism. The house was beautiful, but hardly practical once there was a child. There were stairs and more stairs, up and down, and a never-ending series of redoubtable nannies, who never lasted longer than a week or two. The tensions in the house were often very difficult to take, and it was becoming abundantly clear that Suzanne had a dislike for many things English because of a particular prejudice which really had nothing to do with the English themselves, but with Canadians of English or Scottish origin. I had no means of judging the veracity of some of her accusations, but others I felt to be at least improbable. Imperceptibly I became a peacekeeper rather than an ally, and my only dignity was often my silence.

We went to France where I had been engaged to appear in Max Ophüls' film *Lola Montes*. We left in my car, taking a nanny wearing a uniform, which included a grey velvet collar, the dirtiest article of clothing I had ever seen except on a recluse. Reluctantly I carried Nanny's largest suitcase to the car, and noticed that its centre of gravity kept shifting as I walked. I placed it on the pavement and asked her what was inside it. She blushed and refused to say. I reminded her that we would have to go through customs, and she might be forced to open it there. She began to vacillate, and eventually allowed me to open it. It contained a collection of glass milk bottles, inadequately washed out, which now contained London tap water, rendered opaque by the remnants of milk. 'Well, I heard up in Edinburgh that the French water is undrinkable,' she pleaded. It was quite clear that yet another Nanny had outstayed her welcome.

The film of *Lola Montes* was destined to become a classic. There were precious few signs of this destiny during its making. Max Ophüls was a *rara avis* all right, a German giggler, who lived in his own particular stratosphere of subtlety, and who protected himself against the intrusion of philistines into his private world by a grotesque and wonderful perversity. When I had the sad honour of writing his obituary for *The Guardian*, I wrote that he had the gift of manufacturing the smallest wristwatch ever known, and could subsequently insist on suspending it from a cathedral so that passers-by could tell the time.

The new 'letter-box' format of Cinemascope was imposed on him for commercial reasons by the producers, but he whispered to me with the glee of a court jester that he had found a way of cheating them, and reverting to the beloved intimacy of the old small screen.

'How?' I asked, thinking he must have found some contractual loop-hole.

He held his hands up, far apart, and brought them slowly closer to one another.

'Two pieces of black velvet,' he whispered, and roared with uncontrollable laughter at the simplicity of his act of sabotage.

Max was the first great poet of bad taste, in that he was the first to exploit Art Nouveau as a thing of beauty and style, not merely as a curiosity, the visible cancer of a decadent and dying society, as my generation was brought up to believe it to be. He saw in its asymmetrical outbursts elements of controlled imagination which were eminently cinematic, and to borrow a phrase and even an idea from Calder, he made them mobiles with his camera, which never tired of laying pictorial ambushes for the human face.

In his endless search for subtlety, he would ask you to register hatred or brutality without changing the expression of your face, and then plunge you into shafts of darkness, or shoot you through a metal banister or a net curtain to obliterate every effect except your presence. He was a dictator in the image of a Prussian Junker, who found the most irresistible of all comic creations in this world, the Junkers of Prussia. His father had been a military tailor in Saarbrücken called Oppenheimer, who, like the Jewish tailor in Zuckmayer's *Der Hauptmann von Köpenick*, kept barking at his studious son to stand up, with his shoulders well back.

'*Halt dich gerade, halt dich gerade, sonst kommst du nie zu Militär!*' (Stand up, stand up, or you'll never make it in the army!)

The old man was shrewder politically than the majority of officers he fitted. He believed none of the military optimism of the time that the war would be a short one, and since some cavalry regiments wore black trousers, Max remembered him calling up to his assistants – 'Fix red stripes on all our tuxedo trousers, this war's going to go on a long time.'

Unfortunately he could not be expected to know that the cavalry would last a much shorter time than the war.

Max loved officers of the Belle Epoque, their utter uselessness, their obligations towards virility, their statutory quick temper over imagined slights, their generous ability to make room for younger men by eliminating each other on the field of honour. And yet his comments were never destructive, and he handled the objects of his attention like rare wines, as though the absurdity of years could be destroyed by an excessive movement of the bottle in which these rare essences were contained. He was a tender despot, more than a little in love with those things his intelligence most disliked.

A most Germanic idea occurred to him during the huge circus scene. The rhythm of Georges Auric's lilting score was taken up by a series of dwarfs and Lilliputians, moving up and down on ropes like pistons or like wooden horses on a gigantic roundabout. The dwarfs were fairly comfortable, unless any of them happened to suffer from vertigo, because their massive torsos were firmly implanted in the leather harnesses. The Lilliputians were less serene, however, since they were perfectly formed miniature people, and they had some difficulty remaining immobile in belts which had been patently designed for dwarfs. One Lilliputian began to slip dangerously, and the belt tried to become a collar, only his arms preventing him from either sliding right through, and dropping some thirty to forty feet, or else being strangled. The pathetic cries of his tiny voice could be barely heard over the caressing waltz. There was a general movement of consternation, nipped in the bud by Max's rasping imitation of a Prussian warlord.

'*Lass die Zwerge Hängen!*' (Let the Dwarfs hang!) I looked at him, appalled. He felt my presence, glanced at me with a guilty grin, and dissolved into his uncontrollable fit of silent laughter, taking the time to shout 'Cut!' The point was, he had his shot.

During another immensely complicated take lasting four and a half minutes, and involving horses, tumblers, and trapeze artists, and with the camera moving on an endless complicated track, spiralling and dipping, I, as the ring-master, sent a dwarf off for a glass of water, which was not part of the meticulous planning. Surprised, the dwarf ran off to fetch it. Since he didn't know where to find it, it took rather a long time, and my irritation increased, as did the hoarseness of my throat. At last he brought it, I drank it surreptitiously while shouting out my lines, like a head-waiter having a secret nip, and gave the empty glass to the dwarf, drying my mouth with a large silk handkerchief which was part of my costume. It was as relaxed as the rest was formal. At the end of the take, Max Ophüls expressed both the quality of his despotism and of his magnanimity. Taking me aside, for once rather sad, he said, 'Peter, the one thing I regret is that I didn't tell you to do that.'

I did one other film at that time, which was shot in Sicily, and its only remarkable feature was that the producers ran out of money after three days, a record even for Italy. But by then, I had already completed *Romanoff and Juliet*, a three-act play absolutely neo-classical in form. I had always remembered the joy of playing in *The Rivals* with Edith Evans, and I wanted to try my hand at something as direct and as undisguisedly theatrical, ignoring the famous 'fourth wall', and employing asides whenever expedient. I remembered that *The Rivals* had entertained troops, some of whom had never seen a play before, much more than the low farces specifically aimed at their intellect.

The theme was a variation on the tragic love of Romeo and Juliet, with Romeo as son of the Soviet Ambassador and Juliet the daughter of the American Ambassador. The intractable families, the Capulets and the Montagues, were replaced by the governments of the U.S.A. and the U.S.S.R., and the scene was a small neutral country, cringing in the centre of the political arena, its economy largely dependent on printing stamps with deliberate anomalies.

On its way to London, the night of our opening in the suburb of Golders Green, our son Igor was born. It was April 30th, 1956. I acted my part euphorically that night, and my father, by all reports, wept tears of quiet joy. Once again, I was grateful to hear, mother and child were doing well.

16

Romanoff and Juliet opened at the Piccadilly Theatre in London and was an immediate success. Even Harold Hobson devoted an unaccustomed amount of space to it, unaccustomed that is, by his standards when they were applied to me. In fairness to those standards, I must admit that there was more emphasis on the success of the evening than on any traces of quality which might have been thinly scattered over it. The hardened professionals of the gallery were still there, but interspersed with drama students and other young people. This time there was no trace of trouble, and I could at last bask in a glow of not just being a one-play man.

— May I say a word here? Before you go off along a straight chronological line, I believe there is room for an important tangent. Your imaginary country had no name.
— That is correct.
— Later on, when you made a film of it, you were compelled, by the realistic nature of the medium, to give your country a name. Concordia.
— Yes.
— Do you remember how this imaginary country began?
— Of course I do. As a small boy of eight or nine, I was walking along a country lane in Sussex – West Chiltington to be precise – when I passed by a farmyard in which a woman was in the process of wringing a chicken's neck. The sudden end of the bird's hysterical shrieking marked

a first rendezvous with death, and I returned home to the rented cottage sickened by what I had seen.

— It was not only your first rendezvous with death, but your first conscious confrontation with a certain aspect of nature.

— Of course, that whole terrifying process with which only madmen are ever entirely reconciled. Even the names are changed, out of deference to finer feelings. You don't eat cow, but beef. You don't eat calf, but veal. You don't eat pig, but ham, bacon, or pork. You don't eat deer, but venison. Cold-blooded fish are among the few living entities which retain their identity in death.

Certainly one of the inspirations of vegetarianism is a revulsion at this sinister cycle of survival by killing, the endless sacrifice of the weaker in order to make the strong stronger.

Nature is both magnificent and awful, both sublime in its equilibrium and horrifying in its detail, and a child must somehow reconcile itself to the necessity of refined table-manners while digging its teeth into fragments of a mild-mannered creature which had until recently been mooing peacefully in a field, and expressing a personality of its own.

There are those who renounce this process altogether, but who still brave the resentful gaze of salmon or the absurd squint of Dover sole. For the most squeamish, however, there is no escape from the ritual. Roald Dahl knew what he was doing to us when he vented his fantasy about salad screaming in anguish as it is eaten, and since no child starts its life with a hunger-strike, we are all irretrievably marked by the corruption of nature by the time our ideas of revulsion are awakened. Hunger has, quite simply, been a more compelling argument than dismay at the equation of existence.

By the time I saw my chicken garrotted, I had already suffered various excesses of imagination along these lines. I used to fight shy of drinking water when I was made to eat fish, because I fancied that fish, even masticated into a pulp, might miraculously come together if there was water in my stomach, and swim about in there as in a glass bowl. The chicken, however, was the hardest blow to this town-child, which had never before consciously associated the leg or wing on a bed of rice with the living nitwits that rushed in front of motor-cars like mad golfers in plus-fours.

There was, I found, only one escape from this nightmare, only one way in which I could keep a grip on myself in this vile world of grown-ups, and that was the establishment of an imaginary country, to which I owed total allegiance. The first article in the constitution of this land was that no chickens would have their necks wrung.

— Exactly. But with the passage of time, the country changed its character, did it not?

— Countries grow, as do humans. What had started as a childish revolt against the casual viciousness of adults became, with the passage of time, a growing reality, and even, I may say, a source of patriotism to me denied the usual racial sentiments by an excessive admixture of pre-natal ingredients.

— You mean, of course, that the country still exists.

— Yes. It is more real than ever, and eminently useful.

— Would you tell us about it?

— Certainly not. I will only reveal that it has a geographical position, an outlook of its own, and problems. Many problems. Just as an adult has many problems. It is no Utopia, no Erewhon. Those are countries whose secrets have been betrayed. Immediately you begin to share secrets of this kind, you begin to entertain, and then the utility of such a place, and its reality, are destroyed. All I can tell you is that the mineral wealth and transport are nationalized, whereas free enterprise is encouraged where human ingenuity and acumen are concerned.

— How about the fate of chicken?

— I am ashamed to say that I haven't given chicken a thought for many years now, and I have no doubt that their poor necks are wrung as they are elsewhere.

Interviewing
Alexandre Benois
for the BBC

Kokoschka by Ustinov

My parents

Their son
and grandson

Captain Vere in *Billy Budd*
(Allied Artists)

The Archbishop in
The Unknown Soldier and His Wife

The Marshal in *The Moment of Truth*
on American Television (Omnibus)

The cast of *Don Giovanni* before my backdrop,
Edinburgh Festival Opera, 1973

With Sir George Solti during rehearsals
of *The Magic Flute* in Hamburg

Nitchevo at Syros. Photograph by Henry Fonda

On board *Nitchevo* at Delos. Sketch by Henry Fonda

My daughters Andrea and Pavla

On the set of *The Last Remake of Beau Geste*
(Universal) with Andrea and Igor

With Sir Noël Coward

The Purple Taxi (Sofracima S A Rizzoli)

Irish extra, Fred Astaire, Jack Watson, Peter Ustinov

With my wife Hélène

— Disgraceful. Tell us what you can about your country, and tell us why all you cannot tell us must remain a secret.

— Our legal system is based on a form of medieval disposition, there being no counsel for the defence and the public prosecutor is given no voice in the proceedings, only being able to answer questions as a witness would. In other words, all drama is drained from the trial – drama which may be exciting, especially when idealized and concentrated in television playlets, but in which the shuttlecock so dramatically bandied hither and thither in this macabre game is nothing but the truth, and in which the score may militate against a human life or human career. This is acceptable on television, but not at all, I think, in life.

— So that all the judges, the advocates, and the jury are, at the outset, on the same side?

— On the side of truth. It is the evidence which may separate them, but never the roles in which they are cast initially. Their devotion to the truth must be absolute, and they can rebuke each other if any deviations from it are noticed, and accepted as such. All discussion is open, and everyone, including the prisoner, may make observations, according to a rigorous adherence to the rules of debate.

— Do you seriously think such a system would work?

— Do you seriously think the alternatives work? Apart from making good TV, that is?

— Well, we now know your country's relationship to chicken. How did you come by this idea?

— I developed it slowly, over the years – but it came to a head at my club, during the recess of a celebrated murder trial. In the gentlemen's toilet, a great lawyer stood relieving himself into one bowl. I recognized him as the Prosecuting Counsel. Next to him, engaged in the same relief work, was another distinguished counsel, defending an alleged murderess. They were discussing the morning's work in tones at once jocular and collusive. I was so shocked that I asked the one I knew better whether they always came to the urinal to discuss matters which were still *sub judice*. 'Where else can we do it?' he replied, and the other joined in the laughter as he adjusted his dress. Several weeks later the cause of all the levity was hanged.

— You actually used such a situation in a short story.

— It is wonderful when you reproduce a scandalous incident and yet have a perfect answer if some august authority seeks to refute your credibility. That is all that I care to say about my country, except that by now whenever a grave international situation develops, I react not as an Englishman, nor as a Russian, nor as one who is sometimes in America, France, Switzerland, or Germany, but as life-President of my own nation. I write protests, démarches, and am always willing to accept apologies, although, up to now, very few have been forthcoming.

— But you spoke before of the *utility* of such a country. Utility to whom?

— Utility to me. Its influence goes far beyond a mere pastime, a mere mental folly. When I began to work for UNICEF, and, at a later stage for UNESCO, both agencies of the United Nations which come in for more than their share of abuse from the ignorant, I realized that my addiction to my own point of view, or rather, that of my nation helped me beyond all measure to acquire the fully neutral stance necessary for such a job.

— By neutral, I presume you do not mean free from prejudice, because no man with an attitude can be entirely free from that.

— Of course not. I agree with you. The great heresies, however, come from precisely those who believe they *are* free from prejudice. 'UNESCO is at it again' read the leader headline in *The Herald-Tribune* of Paris, in many ways an admirable paper. The article blamed UNESCO for encouraging so-called Third World nations for wishing to escape from the informational hegemony of the American press agencies by creating press agencies of their own, and it was presumed that they wished this tendentious news of their own creation to supplant the truth. But it would of course not be the truth which they would be supplanting. All news is tendentious, depending on its source, its interpretation, and the temper of the times. And American news is as tendentious as any other. The fact that it faithfully reflects the tendencies of its readers does not mean that it is closer to the truth than any other, but merely that it is conscious of its obligations towards its readers' prejudices and therefore of its own commercial health.

— Well, naturally, opinion is, by definition, tendentious. That is quite true, but there are so many instances in the modern world in which there is no effort whatsoever to tell the truth that one can understand all too well a certain American impatience in the face of the kind of criticism you, or your government, level at them.

— Leave my government out of this. It is as sensitive as any other, and as childish in its reactions. Our only chance of being objective or indeed honest is by dealing with all subjects as an individual.

— Then why bother to have a country?

— Don't be ridiculous, everyone must have a country. The only difference between myself and the others is that they seem to be satisfied with what they have been given, whereas I was stranded with a cricket-ball, a caraway seed, a glass of wine and a copy of *Struwwelpeter*, to say nothing of the alloy spoon in my mouth. There has never been an anthem which sets my foot tapping, never an occasion which brings a lump to my throat. I can take no allegiance to a flag if I don't know who's holding it. My only allegiance is to my own conscience, and who is to tell me that that is not higher than any flag, or any mediocre tune written by a third-rate bandmaster to the words of a fourth-rate poet, to which men rise as a mass with a look of inane piety on their faces? Why have a country, you ask? How would I understand my fellow-men if I didn't place myself at the same disadvantage; if I didn't invent problems, how would I understand real ones? Especially today.

— Why especially today?

— You registered American impatience with criticism. My God, I spend my time in America trying to explain the Russians to them to the best of my ability and I spend my time in Russia trying to explain the Americans to them. Despite their fiscal and military collusion, they understand each other not at all. But since I am devoted to the concept of freedom, and consider the American concept to be insanely ambitious and absolutely wonderful, I am saddened by certain shortcomings in the realization of these ideals. Freedom of the individual is so sacrosanct that, ironically, it is not sufficiently protected. The individual too often becomes the victim of the pressure group, the protection racket, the little local law unto itself. We have already spoken of the dreaded McCarthy, and we know the folklore of the Ku Klux Klan and the fastest gun in the West, and Watergate, which I suppose might be characterized as the slowest wits in the East. After each is brought to heel, there are those superb optimists who maintain that each victory over malignancy is a proof that the system works. Yes, it works indeed, with an undeniable splendour, in a carnival atmosphere of wisecracks and intrigue and comic hats and streamers, but at what a cost to the very intimacy, the very solitude before beliefs, which it is sworn to maintain?

— This has always existed, everywhere, in some form or other. The British proudly believe that a man is innocent until proved guilty. You only have to look at the inside of a British law court to be convinced that a man has to be pretty guilty to be there at all. Not only ideals, but even ideas, have always been greater than men, greater even than the men who fathered them. You know that, You even told me you were an optimist, which proves you know that. Why now suddenly this pessimistic stricture, especially today?

— Why? Let me explain it by another cartoon, by the talented Mr Mauldin, also in the *Herald Tribune*. Two well-dressed men stare at the United Nations building. One says to the other: 'A First Class Idea, not given a Second Chance by the Third World.'

— Well?

— Just over two hundred years ago, the United States emerged like a phoenix from just such a third world. Has she forgotten so quickly what it was like to be poor, and pure, and young? Must she so soon filch the musty robes of power from the wardrobe, and behave as the British and others did when they were the flagellating fathers of the pupil world? Why this pharisaic impatience with those just fallen from the nest? Is it merely the impatience of the young with those still younger, or is it a trap laid by stealthy nature to try and lure America into a posture which was the cause of her own rebellion, her own birth?

— She is so much richer than all the rest of us, it is a miracle her people at least have remained as nice as they undoubtedly are. The British were never pleasant when a super-power, except as individuals. As colonists they were pretty awful.

— As colonists everyone was pretty awful, and the farther north you went, the worse they became. Come to that, the Americans weren't much good at it either. But you are quite right in saying that the Americans are far nicer than they have any right to be, and that in itself is a signal triumph, and it must be accounted as fall-out from the democratic system. To a certain extent they are bound to engender a degree of animosity, by virtue of their technical accomplishments and the extraordinary generosity of their soil, but it is sometimes true that they react according to the animosity they create instead of in spite of it, and they tend to shout the virtues of their system to the winds, although if we all adopted it, commercial intercourse would come to a full stop.

— How do you mean?

— If we could never take the responsibility for anything we said without referring it to the ratification of two national assemblies and a President, it would take years and years for any agreements to be signed. It is bad enough when one partner is compelled constitutionally to do so, and it does explain, paradoxically, why the United States prefers to do business with tawdry dictators. It is so much quicker, and you know where you stand. Equally paradoxically, the United States is directly responsible for the spread of Socialism, a movement she says she mistrusts and abhors, although she herself has digested many of its elements.

— How is she responsible?

— By the lack of restraint on huge supra-national corporations, who threaten the existence of many of the proudest companies in other parts of the world, which are eventually forced to seek protection behind the skirts of government. What America preaches and what she makes others practise are often as far apart as can be, and this, when applied to that developing world, towards which she owes an immense, a unique moral responsibility, is often very serious indeed.

— Was all this inherent in *Romanoff and Juliet*?

— For those who cared to look for it, yes. It all depended on the habits of the audience. To those who swallowed their pill whole, there was only the fleeting taste of sugar. To those who let it dissolve, the bitter tang of the medicine soon became apparent.

— Nevertheless, it did well in America.

— They usually swallow their pills instead of sucking them. They are in a hurry. But there were those who noticed. Harry Truman, for instance, who wrote me a most perspicacious letter, which I treasure to this day. He knew perfectly well that what you call criticism is engendered by respect and affection, not by any feelings of aversion.

— I was glad to be able to clear up that point, so often a cause of irresponsible comment, against which there is no defence, in the sacred name of freedom of the press.

During the run of *Romanoff and Juliet*, I accepted an invitation to play tennis in the Soviet Embassy in London from the Minister-Counsellor, Mr Romanov, who said he wanted his revenge for taking his name in vain, thereby demonstrating a rare grace and humour. My companion was a Conservative Member of Parliament. We were pitted against Romanov and his doubles partner, Comrade Korbut.

It was raining that day, a hopeless top to bottom rain, without inflection. I had the impression we were playing in a pointillistic picture.

'We can't play in this,' muttered the Member of Parliament.

'Isn't that what they're waiting to hear?' I asked, my upper lip stiff with cold.

'You're right, by Jove,' said the M.P., and bravely called across the net to suggest that play should begin.

'We cannot begin,' cried Mr Romanov, 'because the umpire has not yet arrived. He has been detained by the Ambassador.'

By the time the so-called umpire did arrive, we were ready to be wrung out like flannels. He turned out to be a steely-eyed man who stood at the net and quickly became as wet as we were.

'Play!' he barked, as though instructing a firing-squad to do its duty.

I was so enervated by his presence that I served a double fault.

'Love-fifteen!' he yelled.

By the time we arrived at deuce, my agitation had given way to a grim determination, and I served an ace.

'Advantage, Great Britain,' shouted the umpire.

And so it went on to an eventual victory in a thoroughly bad match.

We went into the shower, and Mr Romanov wagged a warning finger.

'Today,' he said, 'you won. But in a year . . .'

Stalin had, at this time, been denounced, but not yet entirely discredited, and there was some doubt as to what to do with him. I noticed, when we had first entered the Embassy, the shape of a large picture on the red brocade wall, a patch darker than the rest. This mystery was resolved in the shower, where we found Stalin in a huge gilt frame, smiling benignly at the naked athletes.

'Today,' he seemed to say, 'you won. But in a year . . .'

During the match I leapt for a high ball, and landed badly. Two days later I was hardly able to move, and had to spend eight weeks on a board with a slipped disc. I came out of *Romanoff and Juliet*, and was told by a celebrated doctor that I would have to wear a corset for life and that tennis was out of the question for the same length of time.

I was fitted for the corset by a gentleman in a morning-suit who presented me with a card claiming that his firm were 'Makers of Surgical Trusses to His Late Majesty King George the Fifth'. He made me lift my pyjama-top so that he could reach round me with a tape-measure, and the poor fellow, who was suffering from the early symptoms of Parkinson's disease, placed his ice-cold hands on my warm back, and soon I was shaking with uncontrolled laughter in what was one of the most embarrassing and macabre minor episodes of my life.

I still have the corset, which would find immediate favour in the wardrobe of a sado-masochistic transvestite, and which I declined to wear after one atrocious day. Luckily Suzanne had an acquaintance in Paris, a Romanian lady called Madame Codreanu, who had a great knowledge of things oriental, and who walked on my spine with all her weight, stubbing out imaginary cigarettes on every vertebra. I grew over an inch, which cost me a pretty penny in having all my trousers lengthened, but I am eternally grateful for the cure. Needless to say, I play tennis whenever I can.

Before performing *Romanoff and Juliet* in America, I shot a film in Paris with the redoubtable Henri-Georges Clouzot. He had a reputation for immense intelligence and for refined cruelty, neither of which I found entirely justified. He certainly betrayed ambitions to be cruel, but frankly lacked the equipment for it, and his intelligence was manifest mainly by his frequent changes of mind. Film, he used to say, was of no more value than paper.

In order to undermine my confidence, he told me that Gary Cooper would have been the ideal casting for the part I was playing. I answered him by saying that he could never have afforded Gary Cooper. We were all spies in the film, Curd Jürgens with dark glasses on, even then a tedious cliché for increasing tension, Sam Jaffé, speaking a French as extraordinarily American as Jürgens' was cosily Teutonic and mine sullenly Slavonic, and Martita Hunt, who had studied with Sarah Bernhardt, and who spoke a French far better than anyone, including Clouzot. Hers was not a French you expected to hear in a film, however, let alone a spy film. But then Clouzot's forte was his incongruity. It either came off, or it didn't. On this occasion, it didn't.

On one occasion, Clouzot eyed me icily and asked me, 'Why do we not get on better?'

'Let us say I am ill in some remote part of the world,' I replied, 'and I call for a doctor. You arrive and, without saying a word, you open your bag and extract the most sinister galaxy of surgical instruments imaginable – saws, needles, scalpels, and tubes. Meticulously you select the sharpest and thinnest of the needles and sterilize it in a flame. Then you approach my eye with professional resolve. You speak for the first time when I can already feel the heat of the needle.'

'By the way, what do you do in life?' you enquire.

'I'm a doctor,' I reply.

Clouzot turned and walked away. It was not the answer he desired.

I did an affectionate film after this neurotic fantasy, the story of a wicked lawyer in New York too avaricious to buy a dog, who barks through his door to rid himself of unwanted visitors. Inevitably, he turns into a dog himself for most of the film. This fable, called, if you please, *Un Angel Volo Sobre Brooklyn*, was shot in Madrid by the Hungarian expatriate director, Ladislao Vajda.

Then we went by ship to America, *en famille*, from Algeciras. On arrival we were met by the press, and by a duck-billed platypus, I cannot now think why, but it was a publicity stunt thought up by David Merrick. George Kaufman, then in his declining years, was going to redirect the play for American taste after Denis Carey's excellent job in London.

It was clear quite early on that George Kaufman, a towering figure in the American theatre, was by now beyond the chore he had accepted. There was an element of enormous sadness about the man, a pride which preferred a bitter silence to comment, and an inability to rehearse for more than three or four hours a day. He would arrive in an air-conditioned Cadillac and sit around listlessly in the auditorium looking like a deckchair which could never be folded up correctly. His contributions were minimal, because even at the best of times, our styles were very different, he being an inspired inventor of comic lines which were comic in their own right, whereas what I wrote could only generate laughter if said by a particular person in a particular situation. Poor George manfully went through the motions of helping until the dress-rehearsal, when he announced softly yet savagely that he would have given us notes if he hadn't lost them. It was the last time he spoke to us.

We opened to vaguely favourable notices, but like practically everything else on Broadway, it was touch and go until a veritable bombardment of the airwaves, engineered by David Merrick and carried out by me on every kind of television programme, had put the show over as though it had been a new and mildly controversial European car. We ran for a season, and then, after the holidays, we resumed on the road.

The holidays were spent in the South of France. During the course of them, I was invited to a cocktail party aboard a sailing-boat in Cannes harbour. It was an opportunity to see a business acquaintance, and I therefore accepted the invitation, although I had never met my host, a French North African carpet manufacturer resident in Mexico.

Before leaving the party, an hour after my arrival, I had bought the boat. It was, and is, a 58-foot ketch built of steel in Amsterdam in 1929 by De Vries Lentsch, as elegant and harmonious a craft as you could wish. Its past history was romantic. It had been ordered by Dr Boucard, of whom a portrait, test-tube in hand, was painted by Tamara de Lempicka; Dr Boucard had made a fortune with an emetic on a milk base called Lactéol, well known to French babies, and the first name of this svelte racing yacht was none other than *Lactéol*.

By the time I laid my hands on her, she was called *Christina*, which led to endless complications, since that was also the name of Onassis' floating palace. I received a few cryptic messages by mistake, such as: 'Time Not Ripe Baghdad Willing Suggest Twenty Repeat Twenty Million Adequate Karakristidis,' or 'Send Authorization Return Eighteen Tankers Cash on Delivery Monrovia Bestest Philemonopoulos.'

It was eventually immensely frustrating not to be able to react to some of these messages as I would have wished, and I resolved rather sadly to put an end to this flow of tantalizing information by changing the name of the yacht to *Nitchevo*. 'Nitchevo' means 'nothing' in Russian, but it is also redolent of Quien Sabe? and In shā'Allāh. If Allah didn't wish me to make my fortune in tankers by cracking codes, then I would be content with 'Nitchevo', and I have been ever since. My rash, thoughtless purchase has given me some of the happiest times of my life.

Had I been Getty or indeed, Onassis, I could imagine no luxury greater than arriving in Istanbul in my own good time, without the knowledge of Air France or T.W.A. or even of Türk Hava Yolari. To see the minarets floating on a sea-mist of pink, the setting sun caressing the golden globes for the last fleeting moments before being engulfed in the rich purple of late evening, while a crescent moon, fragile as a clipping from a baby's finger-nail, hangs palely overhead – that is beauty on the scale of personal achievement, in the sense that a runner bean from your garden tastes subtly different from one purchased in a shop.

I have faced high seas and even peril on old *Nitchevo*, with waves breaking on the roof of the deckhouse, arrows of icy water in flight as in medieval battle, little whirlpools scurrying round the calves and pushing at the ankles, seas angry and devious in their malice. All of it, even the moments of fear, was sheer exhilaration. Risk seems to be an intrinsic ingredient in a man's life, a means of sharpening his knowledge of himself, and I had missed its presence, even during the war, under impersonal bombs or lost in the sludge of administration.

The sea not only sharpens a sense of beauty and of alarm, but also a sense of history. You are confronted with precisely the sight which met Caesar's eyes, and Hannibal's, without having to strain the imagination by subtracting television aerials from the skyline and filling in the gaps in the Colosseum. And among the islands of Greece, or off the magical coast of Turkey, or yet again, in the sheltered splendour of Dalmatian waters, you rediscover what the world was like when it was empty, when time itself was the richness that oil is today, and when pleasures were as simple as getting up in the morning.

No fish tastes like fish you catch yourself, and every day is a journey of discovery. *Nitchevo* has been my inspiration in good times, my salvation in bad. The Captain who came with it, José Perez Jimenez, is an integral part of his craft. He was aboard when I bought it, and we have aged together. His wife Carmen, a blonde girl with a gentle Spanish beauty, a little doll-like in repose, tinged with both melancholy and humour in animation, sails with us, and cooks the fish we catch.

José himself has the aquiline gravity of the bullfighter, and would have inspired confidence in any of the navigators of the golden age. His passion for the sea is contained in an austere secrecy not unlike that of a monk for his God, and his controlled anarchy is utterly and uniquely Spanish. Salvador Dali's answer when asked whether he believed in God would suit this Spanish attitude to the ground, even to the sky.

'*Soy Praticante ma non Creyente,*' he said (I practise but I do not believe), a statement which was greeted with hosannas by the leading clergy of Spain.

Having read in his Baedeker that the island of Mikonos possessed something like three hundred churches and chapels for a population of 2,000, José turned to me like a grandee as an impenetrable fog swirled around us off the island, and said, 'three hundred churches, and so little light'.

He is a man to whom one can attribute valour, without it seeming overblown or eccentric. When dealing with the mundane obligations of earning a living, it is a marvellous consolation to know that in some distant harbour, white and peaceful, a venerable jewel of Dutch craftsmanship awaits my idle moments with a couple of dear friends aboard.

While on this first maritime vacation, I had completely forgotten another obligation which I had undertaken in New York prior to leaving. A certain Mr Weeks from a magazine called *The Atlantic Monthly* had contacted me asking for a playlet about the Russians and the Americans on the moon. I was none too enthusiastic, since I felt I had exhausted the subject of the Russians and the Americans in *Romanoff and Juliet*, and I also sensed that nothing that might happen on the moon could not happen more effectively and more comprehensibly here on earth.

I mentioned the offer to a few American friends, all of whom blanched visibly when I told them I was thinking of turning it down.

'Turn down *The Atlantic Monthly*!' they cried, of one voice. 'Why, there are those who struggle for a lifetime only to have a piece turned down by *The Atlantic Monthly*, and they consider *that* an achievement!'

I was made to feel like a kind of peacock, all feathers and no guts, and in a moment of weakness agreed to Mr Weeks's request. Then, of course, faced with the unsuspected joys of navigation, I forgot all about my holiday task. Back in New York, I suddenly remembered it with horror and then received a phone call from Mr Weeks asking when he could have it, and then forcing my response by telling me the deadline was in four days' time. I tried to get out of my obligation, but Mr Weeks was stern and avuncular. 'We have held the space, young man, there's no road back now,' or more trenchant words to that effect.

I sat down in my hotel room, and wrote a short story about the Swiss reaching the moon. I had never written a story before, and had a feeling of utter irresponsibility, which was not helped by extreme pangs of hunger. I knew I was back in New York, because every time I ordered a snack from room-service, the waiter, an out-of-work actor, sat on my bed to watch television and discuss the prospects of getting a job on a soap opera. I had no alternative but starvation if I was to meet the deadline.

At last I finished it, sent it off to Boston, and awaited the inevitable explosion. It came a few days later in the form of a request for seven more stories. I could not believe it. Mr Weeks became Edward, and shortly after that, Ted, and it was he who gave me the confidence to break out into the tantalizing world of non-dramatic authorship, where the terrible rigours of playwriting are no longer so stringent, where there is time to snatch a breath and turn a phrase only obliquely necessary to propel the action forward.

I wrote away on the road, in Columbus, Ohio, in St Louis, in Washington D.C. The most successful of these stories, which gave its title to the eventual book, 'Add a Dash of Pity', I wrote in the Plankinton House Hotel in Milwaukee.

Add a Dash of Pity dealt with the moral and material chaos created by generals who thoughtlessly write their memories long after the end of the war, stirring up the doubts, regrets, and sorrows of those who had either participated in actions or lost loved ones in them.

Years later, I heard from a distinguished publisher who had approached Admiral Chester Nimitz with a request for his memories. The admiral had refused to write them, claiming that he was influenced in his decision by my short story. It is an onerous responsibility for one of the war's least effective private soldiers to have so influenced one of its greatest admirals, and yet it is also an achievement in communications to have touched such a remote luminary on the simple plane of human sensibility.

The year of *Romanoff and Juliet* ended, and we went straight to Hollywood, where I was to act in an epic, by name *Spartacus*.

Spartacus went on for so long that our third child, a daughter, Andrea, who was born during the filming, was able to answer the questions of an inquisitive playmate before I had finished.

'What does your daddy do for a living?' asked the playmate.

'Spartacus,' replied Andrea.

17

Spartacus was a film with an extraordinarily rich mixture, and as full of intrigue as a Balkan government in the good old days. Kirk Douglas was the producer of this epic, as well as the incarnator of Spartacus, the leader of a slave uprising in ancient Rome. It was based on the celebrated book by Howard Fast, who had been regarded as left-wing by the hawks, and the script was being written by Dalton Trumbo, who had also been suspected of Communist sentiments by the same erratic authorities, but to complicate matters, he was no longer on speaking terms with Howard Fast. It was impossible to mention the fact that the author of the script, Sam Jackson, was actually Dalton Trumbo. I found out because Anthony Mann, the director, thought the whole masquerade too ludicrous for words, and took me to see Dalton Trumbo in exile up a side street in Pasadena, and from then on, I signed my various memoranda and rewrites, Stonewall Ustinov.

Before long Anthony Mann was fired with the peremptory harshness usual in those matters, and replaced by a young man with huge eyes who seemed at the time to have none of the vices, and few of the virtues, of youth, but who proved to be biding his time with brilliant political pragmatism, and shepherding his gifts through the minefields of concession towards a glorious future career. His name was Stanley Kubrick.

Laurence Olivier had been brought from England, I from God knows where, and Charles Laughton, John Gavin, Tony

Curtis, and Jean Simmons from up the road. We had all been sent scripts in order to tempt us, with subtle variations favouring our particular characters. No two scripts, we discovered, were the same. Since Larry Olivier had arrived a week prior to the majority of us, he had already inspired a yet newer version of the script in which his role had somewhat grown in importance. He has played sufficient Shakespearean villains superbly well to have a great confidence in his own powers of persuasion, and it was always amusing to watch him at work in the wings, in the process of getting his own way. When discovered, he would give you a mischievous wink, and what had begun as an artifice ended as a performance, simply because he was being watched.

Laughton, whom I had not seen for more than a passing moment since being forced to sit through *The Sign of the Cross* for the second time, was a very different sort of person, almost aggressively vulnerable, and sometimes petulant. In this company, he seemed to sit around, waiting to have his feelings hurt, and there was no great love lost between him and Larry, the result of an animosity much older than my career, of which I understood nothing and about which I was singularly uninquisitive.

Knowing that Laughton was shortly to attempt the role of King Lear at Stratford, rather late in life, Larry gave him some hints as to where the dead spots were to be found on the stage as far as acoustics were concerned, a solicitude which Laughton interpreted as veiled hostility in the guise of ostentatious comradeship. Their whole careers had been eminently different, Laughton was the man of concessions, who regarded acting as part art and part whoring. He had sold his soul to Hollywood, in a way, but had kept a grip on his impenetrable integrity through thick and thin, playing roles as improbable as American admirals in 'B' pictures, but, when the occasion demanded it, able to hold an audience spellbound by readings from the Bible with no props apart from the hypnotic calm of his personality, his eye flicking like the ignition light on a car, an indication that the engine was still running and would spring into action at any moment.

He had a house, and a pool, in which he floated like a topsy-turvy iceberg, only the tip visible beneath the surface. On one occasion the toilet flushed, and he opened an octopus eye to call, 'You do that deliberately to annoy me when I'm trying to think.'

Yes, he had signed his soul away for comfort, and yet, within his sanctum there were his collection of Renoirs and of Pre-Columbian art. He was surrounded with things of beauty, which were part of his soul translated.

Larry Olivier meanwhile had set up in a rented house with Roger Furse, the designer, a delightful bearded figure. Like an odd couple they would make laundry lists and shopping lists, determined to survive within the limits of their living allowance, walking advertisements for Britain's financial embarrassment.

Larry had confided to friends long ago that his ambition was to be Britain's first theatrical peer, and his dexterity in handling a career unique in its unswerving distinction is above praise. He was the vestal virgin to Laughton's whore, and yet whereas Laughton feasted his eyes on the work of great painters as he emerged dripping from his pool of contemplation, Larry fretted at arithmetic and tried to pick holes in the bills of the supermarket. Their ambitions were utterly different, and each had but scant consideration for the viewpoint of the other.

For some reason, perhaps availability, I was picked as confidant for both. Charles was very sensitive to the influence Larry was supposed rightly or wrongly to be exerting on Kirk Douglas, and since he felt he could no longer carry sufficient weight to counteract this nefarious plotting, he decided to sulk, an activity at which he was particularly adept. He refused to act the scenes given him, and I was solicited by the management to try and bridge the gap by finding out what he wanted.

The result of this was that I rewrote all the scenes I had with Laughton, we rehearsed at his home or mine, often slogging away into the middle of the night. The next day, we rearranged the studio furniture to conform with what we had engineered at home, and presented the company with a *fait accompli*: Kubrick accepted what we had done more or less without modification, and the scenes were shot in half a day each. Laughton was easy to work with, in that he overflowed with an almost carnal glee at the process of acting.

One of my first scenes with Larry Olivier consisted in my rushing up to his horse as it cavorted among a huge mass of prisoners-of-war, grabbing its bridle, and gazing up at its immaculate rider: 'If I identify Spartacus for you, Divinity, will you give me the women and the children?' I said, in the character of the sleazy slave dealer.

There followed the most enormous pause while Larry let his eyes disappear upwards under his half-open lids, licked his lips, pushing at his cheeks from within with his tongue, let his head drop with a kind of comic irony at the quirks of destiny, hardened once again into the mould of mortal divinity, looked away into the unknown as his profile softened from brutal nobility into subtlety. 'Spartacus!' he suddenly cried, as though slashing the sky with a razor, and then hissed, 'You have found him?'

I was so absolutely staggered at the extent of the pause that I expressed precisely the surprise I felt. Now I gazed over the prisoners with a closed expression, giving nothing away. Then I let a furtive smile play on my lips for a moment at some private thought, chasing it away, and seemed about to say something, but changed my mind. I ran the gamut of impertinence, of servility, and of insincerity as he had of vanity, power, and menace. At long last, when he least expected it, I let a practically inaudible 'Yes' slip from my mouth.

'Dear boy,' said Larry, in a business-like voice which ill-concealed a dawning annoyance, 'd'you think you could come in a little quicker with your Yes?'

'No,' I said politely.

We both looked at each other straight in the eye, and smiled at the same moment.

Larry is, as everyone knows, a magnificent actor, unparalleled in certain roles. His Richard III had a hypnotic power, an evil elegance and wit the like of which I had never seen before, and have not seen since, and in certain comic parts his imaginative brio is quite superlative. For my taste, his Hamlet, prefixed as the story of a man 'who could not make up his mind', was rather less suited to him, since of all actors he is the most difficult to imagine as one who has not made up his mind.

Everything about him is so superbly stage-managed, so utterly controlled, so immaculately rehearsed that there is very little room for surprise, for the casual or negligent. He can be, and is, a delightful companion. When he was avoiding the press at the time of the break-up of his marriage to Vivien Leigh, I met him at Rome airport, and, with the agreement of the Italian authorities, whisked him off to my rented house in my car directly from the tarmac. In New York, he and Joan Plowright dined with us before their relationship was suspected, and now, after the harrowing experience of illness, he seems to have found a peace of mind and to have taken the time to bask in his most merited glory, surrounded by very young children and a wife brilliantly talented in her own right.

At that time, however, I must admit that, in spite of enjoying his confidence and trust, and being at pains to merit it, I was never absolutely at ease in his presence, either on or off the stage. He seemed to know so utterly what he was doing at all times, in arrogance or in modesty, in gentleness or in strength, that a mental guard just refused to come down in my defences. Whereas the scenes with Laughton had some elements of abandon in them, of folly even, those with Larry were more in the spirit of a fencing match.

When I won the Oscar for the best supporting performance in *Spartacus*, Larry sent me a cable thanking me for having supported him so well. It was a joke, of course.

Later, when we were both up for an Emmy award, he for *The Moon and Sixpence*, I for *Barefoot in Athens*, I was informed by the Academy of Television Arts and Sciences that he had sent a message that he could not be present, and that if he were to win he would like me to accept it for him. Being a little superstitious on such occasions, I prepared a speech of acceptance for him. A few hours later I had won the award, and had only to give the acceptance speech I had thought of for him, with certain improvised emendations. I was compelled to reveal the reasons for my hesitations, and the laughter made of this a joke as well.

There is no possible doubt of his preponderent place in theatrical history, more especially since his great contemporaries could only have been what they are, whereas Larry could have been a notable ambassador, a considerable minister, a redoubtable cleric. At his worst, he would have acted the parts more ably than they are usually lived.

Our English accountant thought we were gone for a year, and I must say, so did I at first, but Suzanne had other ideas. The recurring theme was Switzerland, and whereas I did not much care for the stigma attached by the press to the so-called tax refugees, I was sufficiently irritated by the greed of the British tax authorities when it came to those engaged in the liberal professions not to turn an absolutely hostile ear to the idea of emigration. I felt that, if successful, we were treated as little factories, and I thought then as I think now that the attitude was disastrously short-sighted and damaging.

As always, there were many ingenious loopholes for those engaged in commerce – the South of France abounded with luxury cars with British registration and immense yachts at the times of the most draconian travel restrictions – and, since I spent less and less time in Britain anyway, it began to be a form of masochism to expose myself to the endless and ruinous inconvenience of acting as custodian for monies which would be confiscated, apart from the tip.

Naturally attention was already focused on Noël Coward and

Richard Burton, brain-drain pioneers, today accorded the same grudging admiration as conscientious objectors. I was in Canada when I received a call from the *Daily Express*. A supercilious voice said: 'Ah, Mr Ustinov, there's a rumour going around town that you're about to do a Noël Coward. Is there any truth in this?'

'You mean that I'm going to appear at Las Vegas?' I asked.

There was an appreciative snigger, and then: 'No. That you are actually going to set up house abroad.'

'Oh,' I cried, as though my dull head had seen daylight for the first time, 'you don't mean doing a Noël Coward, you mean doing a Beaverbrook!'

His tone was hardened at the mention of his boss. 'What exactly are you suggesting?' he enquired.

'There's a rumour going round here in Canada that he's left to go to England. Is there any truth in this?'

There was a pause. 'Fair enough,' he said, and hung up.

Naturally the great drawback for a writer is a feeling of being out of touch, but then, if one is a certain kind of writer, one has to ask, out of touch with what? Graham Greene is not out of touch in Antibes with his tortured gentlemen in foreign parts, nor was I out of touch with my secret country, and Noël Coward's great charm was being constantly and defiantly out of touch. Unless you are a writer who, like a weathercock, feeds on every little burp of local wind, there is no compelling reason to be in touch here more than elsewhere. The great resurgence of regional writing in England, accompanied by regional acting, gave sudden impetus to this kind of quasi-journalistic expression, often coarse in texture and therefore seemingly accurate to the ignorant, but since I could at the best of times play no part in this intimist revival, I reflected that it was none of my business.

We began our exile in a rented châlet in Villars-sur-Ollon, which was rather too high for my comfort. Instead of working, I spent most of my time falling down on the ice, hip-deep in snow, and distinctly drowsy. It was wonderful that the children took to ski-ing as I had taken to water long ago, and it was a compensation that I was able to offer them amenities and outdoor pleasures which I had never had, but I felt uncomfortable at this altitude.

Eventually we took a permanent suite in a hotel in Montreux, living an appalling existence, like exiled royalty patiently awaiting assassination out of fatalism and force of habit. The lake created its own kind of mildewed background to the wrought-iron of the balconies and the screeching of the ravens that landed like wet face-flannels on the grass.

It was a place of empty bandstands and old ladies in groups and marmalade with people's names on it; shops selling cuckoo-clocks and lace. And above us, surprisingly, Vladimir Nabokov, living like us, and drawing strength and inspiration from the surrounding deadness.

Now it was no longer Sinatra and his endless songs; it was Nabokov and his perfumed English, so dense and intense you can hardly read it without taking deep breaths. '*He* can work here. *He* doesn't complain.'

Into this stifling atmosphere, Suzanne now introduced our parents, hers and mine, in a great festival of reconciliation which was to bury bygones and institute an era of good-will. This was no more successful than the many lakeside disarmament conferences had been in the past. Klop could not understand a word Suzanne's father said, whereas Nadia and Suzanne's mother just smiled at one another in permanent anticipation that something might happen to break the ice. Her father had been King's Printer in Canada, and was a garrulous old gentleman, very confident in his own powers of persuasion, gesturing away, a twinkle in his eye, with no trace of the Indian ancestry which had been attributed to him. Her mother, on the other hand, had a long-suffering look, not entirely without justification, and a vocational smile which faithfully reflected the goodness of her heart and the simplicity of her soul. Far from being a refugee from the Nazis, as I had been told, she came from pious stock, many of her relatives being nuns or priests, and the rest regretting not having been.

Out of desperation I bought a plot of land in a place called Les Diablerets. It is so rare to have a village named after the Devil, or rather minor devils, that it was probably a spirit of revolt against the pervasive holiness of my surroundings which engendered this purchase. Here we began the construction of a châlet, since, unlike Nabokov, I found the faded fragrances of Montreux stultifying, especially when the mournful halls of the hotel echoed to the shouts of healthy and frustrated children.

Like all good French-Canadians, Suzanne was drawn like a moth to the city of lights, and we acquired a furnished flat in Paris, which we used intermittently. De Gaulle's 'Vive Québec Libre' was already in the offing, and a great many Frenchmen, fighting a rearguard action on behalf of 'Francophonie' before the incursions of the language of the Anglo-Saxons (whoever they may be), were ready to be excited by tales of battles fought by the linguistic underground on the heights of Abraham. Whatever the subject at dinner, it sooner or later veered round to this stale topic, enlivened only by the ever-increasing fancy of its illustrations. I sat through this in calculated silence, having no contribution to make, and finding it impossible to generate a sense of outrage at second hand and without proof more convincing than that which seemed to excite the other diners.

Secretaries now came and went with the same dizzy rapidity that nannies had come and gone before. There were always apparent incompatibilities, and I began to pay too highly in negligence for my peace of mind. Once, returning from a brief journey, I found the secretary had been replaced, which was no great surprise in itself, except that the new girl, a colossus of over six foot, could neither type nor take shorthand. Running into a journalist friend in the street, I discovered rather late what *le tout-Paris* evidently knew already, that my new secretary was a French-Canadian activist who had been apprehended while trying to blow up the Statue of Liberty. It would, of course, be unreasonable to expect such a person to be able to type.

I put my foot down on this occasion, since I didn't think that anyone with an idea as monstrously silly as blowing up a statue would be capable of understanding any thought expressed more quietly. Overnight I became a reactionary and a capitalist hyena, I must say, with some relief.

It was quite a relief to be called away again, this time to Australia, by Fred Zinnemann. It was, alas, always quite a relief to be called away by just anyone, which the children resented, but of course, I only found this out later. One always imagines, fool that one is, that marriages must be kept going for the sake of the children, and in doing so, one merely reflects the inexperience of the celibate priests who are so ready with their advice in territories where their moral guesswork is of no practical use. Children are the first to sniff insincerity and the makeshift harmony of moribund unions. They crave a higher standard of honesty than adults are prepared or able to offer.

I fondly imagined that by removing myself, I was removing the cause of discord, but this proved to be untrue. I merely buried my head in distant sand instead of being content with the pile on my own front porch.

Australia was about as far as one could go from the frictions of family life, and the intense rural existence to which we were subjected in the film *The Sundowners* had something about it reminiscent of a stint with the Foreign Legion. Fred Zinnemann, the director, is a character of the most disarming purity of vision, a man without compromises, endlessly listening for some inner echo to the calls of his observation, and unwilling to make a move until absolutely satisfied that he is not betraying his creative juices by hasty judgements. He is, therefore, slow as a conscientious magistrate to arrive at his conclusions. There are fallow days in which nothing works because he will not allow it to, and other days more felicitous when everything is on a propitious wavelength, without static.

He imposes an authority rare among directors by subjecting himself as well as you to the scruples of the oracle hidden at the heart of his consciousness. Working with him is a permanent lesson in integrity, the process one of painful elimination rather than by erratic flashes of genius. A genius Freddie may be, but he mistrusts the word, denying its existence. He used to play the violin; the only composer he never tired of was Bach. Crossword puzzles are too unconstructive for such a mind. Battles exist so that they can be won, and they are no use winning unless they are difficult.

He is Austrian and Jewish, but his approach is German in the highest sense of the word. He lacks all traces of Austrian grace or the occasional extremism of Jewish intellectuals, nor has he any visible feelings of superiority, but is timid, and open-minded, and tight-lipped. No wonder that he made of *The Nun's Story* one of the sexiest films ever, in which abstinence became an erotic barometer and the unrequited longings of the protagonists kept hovering on the brink of obscenity. When Edith Evans, a benign and practical mother superior, casually handed Audrey Hepburn a scourge wrapped in a velvet container, it was one of the truly probing moments of cinema, enervating as no piece of mechanical pornography can ever hope to be.

Freddie made a beautiful film of *The Sundowners*, unfashionable in manner and matter, a Western without gunfire, but with human problems unsugared and devoid of artificial colouring. Robert Mitchum was superb in the role of an Australian, his usual distant look matched by an accent authentic beyond belief, while Deborah Kerr displayed her vibrant femininity, more exquisite even in what was left unsaid than in what was said.

One day, in rehearsal, I went through my part with a cigarette stuck to my lips. I still smoked then. Suddenly Freddie grabbed the cigarette and wrenched it out of my mouth, drawing blood.

'You can't concentrate with that,' he cried angrily, throwing it away.

I picked it up, dusted it down, and replaced it in my mouth.

'That's not true,' I said. '*You* can't concentrate with that. Then why not ask me to put it out?'

He flushed. I let a moment of silence pass, and said 'Certainly, Freddie,' and stubbed it out.

That was the only contretemps we had, and it was not very serious, but very typical of the level of earnestness in which his talent flourished. There was a scholastic element in working with him, an element of homework well or badly done, an element of good or bad marks at the end of term.

All this time, I had slaved away at a novel, my first, inspired as ever in my desire to break new ground by the untiring efforts of Ted Weeks, an author-baiter if ever there was one. I was, and still am, largely ignorant about the world of publishing, and he calmed my fears and stimulated curiosity.

The Loser appeared in 1961 and excited no great eulogies or aversions. It was a picaresque investigation into the Nazi spirit, based on many of my own experiences with those unfortunate people, and one or two excellent notices in England proved to me that it was liable to be better understood in Europe than in America, although on its appearance in Germany itself, it was categorized as '*Sehr Bitter*', which surprised me, although perhaps it should not have.

Universal Pictures, who had been the producers of *Spartacus*, were very hospitable after my Oscar, and the fact that my diplomacy had smoothed over the difficulties with Laughton. They said they would be interested in a film version of my play *Romanoff and Juliet*, so long as it cost no more than $750,000. Those were the days.

I have always found it difficult to digest the same meal twice, and perhaps I was too eager to keep those moments which had really worked in the play intact, even if it was part free-wheeling fantasy and part photographed play. The leads, Sandra Dee and John Gavin, were then Universal contract stars, and they were given me for a small consideration, but although they tried manfully, neither of them was ideally suited to the style of the text, and the film suffered from an intrinsic incongruity, although it had many elements I was satisfied with.

After a long absence, I was preparing my return to the theatre with a play, *Photo-Finish*, which was subtitled an 'Adventure in Biography'. I wrote it quickly, as I often do, but after much mature consideration and considerable daydreaming.

The sets were doggedly and depressingly realistic in order to give freer reign to the experimental nature of the work. An old man sits in bed in his library, while his old wife, hostile and sarcastic, potters about, enjoying her freedom of motion and his immobility with the same nagging glee. She talks exhaustingly as she tidies up.

'Books,' she says, 'I don't know what you see in them ... I can understand a person reading them, but I can't for the life of me see why people have to write them.'

It is clear that he is at work on his autobiography. She prattles on in a monologue at times lachrymose, at times vicious, at all times wounding, for a full three minutes. He controls any desire to participate in the scene. At length she fusses over his blankets, straightening them, worrying them into some form of tidiness germane to her.

'You are, without doubt, the silliest, most stubborn, most childish old man the world has ever known ... and it's just impossible to keep up a conversation with you. If you need anything, ring the bell like an ordinary person, don't start shouting. Goodnight, Sam, and sleep well, or whatever it is you do down here.'

With that, she kisses him on the forehead, and goes out. It is only when he is gone that he speaks for the first time.

'I enjoyed that chat, Stella ... thank you very much.'

As he prepares to sleep, the door opens, and a man enters, opening the secret drawer in his desk with a key only he owns. It is himself at sixty, preparing to seduce a showgirl with the undignified aid of a £7,000 necklace from Cartier. Sam at eighty knows that the girl will be the cause of a near fatal heart attack, but that knowledge only makes him at sixty more dogged in his pursuit. Eventually Sam forty puts in an appearance, and Sam twenty with a very young and lovely Stella, and, in the Second Act, even Sam's father, who died relatively young, confronts his very old son in a scene which is one of the best I have ever written.

'In my day,' concedes the father, who was a full-bodied vintage Victorian hypocrite, 'there were things that were done, and things that were not done, and there was even a way of doing things that were not done.'

It is a play which takes place in four different epochs simultaneously, with none of them predominating except at the very end. It is not a flashback or a flashforward but both, and neither. It is a play about forgiveness, about understanding, and finally about courage. And if the portrait of the woman is unflattering, it was perhaps a small symptom of my own personal sadness at the time.

When we played it in Boston, I noticed that at all four matinées the front rows were occupied by rather odd-looking people whose mouths tended to hang open and whose heads tilted at surprising angles. Then a distinguished psychiatrist came round and told me he was using the play as therapy with patients who had never come to terms with their parents, a fact I found both intriguing and disturbing.

In London the play was a considerable success at the Savile Theatre. Thank goodness it also held an appeal for those with no parental problems. In New York we fell foul of a newspaper strike. For once that I had a rave review in the *New York Times*, it had to be passed from hand to hand like a Samizdat in Moscow!

What gave me renewed satisfaction were the play's success in Paris, with Bernard Blier superbly crotchety as old Sam and Philippe Noiret divinely opulent as the reprehensible father, and the triumph in Germany, with that remarkable actor Martin Held, and subsequently with Heinz Rühmann.

The play appeared at exactly the same time as my best film, *Billy Budd*. Based on Herman Melville's long story and a fine dramatization by two American authors, I leaned heavily on that consistently extraordinary battalion of British character actors which are the real backbone of our theatre. Robert Ryan, a massive and wicked presence on the screen, agreed to play the part of Claggart, the embodiment of evil, while I gave the part of Billy Budd, the embodiment of good, to an unknown, a hesitant, uncertain young actor called Terence Stamp. Captain Vere, the Pontius Pilate of this Passion, I played myself, not because I thought I was particularly suited to the role, but because I could find no one else at the price, and the old Dansker, the Recording Angel, I confided to Melvyn Douglas, who had practically retired, and who was by chance holidaying in Spain.

As sometimes happens, every stroke of luck militated in our favour, and we felt ourselves blessed from the outset. Behind the leaders stood that cohort of wonderful talent, actors like Paul Rogers, John Neville, John McCallum, Lee Montagu, Niall McGinnis, others too numerous to mention. Don Ashton designed the scenery, Antony Hopkins wrote the music, Tony Mendelson did the costumes, Bob Krasker was the cameraman, as he had been in *Romanoff and Juliet*.

It was only when we had finished shooting that my troubles began. Allied Artists, who had financed the film, began looking for a happy ending. I remonstrated with them.

'Would it have helped *Ben Hur* if Christ had not been crucified?' I asked.

Two of their faces lit up with enthusiasm until convinced of the absurdity of the idea by the head of the company. Their British distributor, A.B.P.C., refused to put the film out, suggesting it should be livened up by stock footage from various pirate films. The parent company sent me a cutter from Hollywood to show me how to make the movie more commercial. The ideas put forward were too awful to contemplate.

I called the Film Censor, John Trevelyan, a remarkable man, who sat in an office under a picture of the Queen, as in a Consulate.

'Tell me about the film,' he said. 'There are I suppose no scenes of violence in it, nothing to justify an X certificate?'

'There's a flogging,' I said shyly.

'A flogging?' His eyebrows raised. 'Do you really need that flogging?' His head shook negatively in anticipation of a reasonable reply.

'Yes I do, John,' I insisted, and explained how Billy Budd is impressed for service aboard his merchantman, and he arrives on the man-of-war just at the moment a flogging is taking place. His eyes meet those of the victim ...

'Of course,' said John Trevelyan, 'everything is said in that look, and for that look to retain its eloquence, that flogging is absolutely *vital*. Right. Now there's no second flogging, I trust.'

'Yes there is,' I practically whispered.

'*Two* floggings in one family film? Oh come, come, Peter, you are rather stretching my credulity!' And then, with a weary sigh, he added, 'All right, suppose you tell me about the second flogging.'

I explained how Billy had prevented the murder of Claggart, and that now, because of his intervention, the would-be killer was being flogged, an event for which Billy felt some responsibility.

'Well, there is absolutely no similarity between the two floggings,' conceded John Trevelyan. 'Both are admirably motivated, and entirely different in character despite the rather similar visual quality which, in the nature of things, they both share. Very well, we'll let them both go. Now, I hope you're not going to tell me there's a *third* flogging!'

'No,' I said, but added, 'there's a hanging.'

'A hanging!' gasped Trevelyan in a grave voice, and recovering from his surprise, went on – 'However, I presume you have the good taste not to actually show the noose around the neck.'

'Oh yes,' I said. 'His last words, "God bless you, Captain Vere", are known to all with the remotest culture. How can you dramatize the greatest of Christian virtues, that of forgiveness, unless the noose is actually around Billy's neck?'

'You can't,' he conceded in hushed tones, and then added magnanimously, 'Very well, you can have your hanging.'

It was after this discussion that he saw the film together with a friend he had invited, Fred Thomas from the Rank Organization. Mr Thomas confessed himself most impressed with the film, and stated that Rank would distribute it in England on condition that it could be prized away from A.B.P.C. without too much ugliness.

John Trevelyan's black eyes glistened. 'This,' he said, 'is where I come in. I am going to give the film an X-rating.'

Both Thomas and I began remonstrating. John held up a hand, and we fell silent.

'A.B.P.C. will drop the film like a hot brick.'

'What then?' we both asked.

'Then you will make the terrible but necessary concession of cutting a single blow from either one of the floggings, I don't care which, and it will be suitable fare for the family.'

Billy Budd opened at the Leicester Square Theatre under the aegis of J. Arthur Rank, and was a great critical success. The reception in New York was no less cordial. But the morons had not had their last word yet. When I took the splendid review of that most difficult and influential of magazines, *Time*, in to the director of publicity, he withdrew the cigar from his mouth, and lisped in his gritty worldly-wise voice: 'Oh Jesus, don't say we got a good notice in *Time Magazine*. That's the kiss of death.'

– 18 –

In giving my impressions of some of the great actors with whom I have been privileged to work, I would be churlish if I left out Paul Rogers, since he is the prototype of that extraordinary tradition of British character actors who have made a contribution to the reputation of the drama and cinema in Britain out of all proportion to their fame. To him and to his kind a sense of responsibility towards the work in hand is primordial. Even if blessed by stardom, he remains first and foremost an actor, for it is only as an actor that he feels safe.

In rehearsal, he will always volunteer to hear your lines, to discuss an artistic matter with you in moments of perplexity, or to give younger members of the cast the benefit of his experience, without for a moment being doctrinaire or officious. He is always learning, which is his greatest strength apart from the sterling solidity of his character.

I remember meeting Paul in New York while he was playing in a work of Harold Pinter's, and it was wonderful to see how exhilarated he was at entering the secret world of this important playwright. A man who had every right to be blasé as an undoubted master of his craft was, on the contrary, bubbling with youthful enthusiasm as he submitted himself to new sensations and new techniques.

I was privileged to work with Paul in both *Photo-Finish* and *Billy Budd*, and he enriched my consciousness of my profession as no one else has done, before or since.

311

The danger of autobiographies is not so much what is written as what is not written. I would be ungrateful not to acknowledge the enormous confidence given me by Noël Coward early in my career, and the subsequent help I received from two very remarkable men of the theatre, Sir Peter Daubeny, with whom I shared not only many happy working hours, but also a birthday – we were born on precisely the same day – and Alexander Cohen, who actually seems to find the financial climate of Broadway bracing. Both these men have done extraordinary work in the propagation of good theatre, and both have benefited from wives who rose without effort to the height of their visions, Lady Molly and Hildy, part and parcel of these two very different men's success.

It was during my work on *Photo-Finish* that I was asked by Sir George Solti to direct my first opera, or rather operas, since he and Sir David Webster envisioned a most curious triple bill, consisting of Puccini's *Gianni Schicchi*, Ravel's *L'Heure Espagnole* and Schoenberg's *Erwartung*. We had five weeks to do them in, each with a different designer, and each with different singers. Since I could not work on matinée days, this cut our rehearsal period down even further.

The Italian designer Clerici, a pale man with glacier-mint rimmed glasses, soft-spoken as some power behind the Vatican throne, devised a shallow set on which the singers climbed up and down like insects on a chest of drawers. Sir Geraint Evans gave one of his characteristic performances, in that whatever I did to integrate him into any concept I might have, he seemed to do what he had done successfully many times before and would do many times again elsewhere.

The French designer, Ponnelle, today a celebrated director of operas and musicals in his own right, did a wayward sketch of the set with no indications of the height of doors or the mechanical details of clocks, with the result that I spent one Sunday in the empty Covent Garden working out the dimensions of clocks within which singers had to conceal themselves. I sat there with a ruler, a pencil, and a thermos of café-au-lait, reflecting on the unpredictability of life. Ponnelle meanwhile had a dress-rehearsal of *Kiss Me Kate* at Düsseldorf. If that isn't Show Business, at least that's Opera.

Erwartung, whatever its musical qualities, is a piece of bilious inanity conceived in a Vienna sickening for World War I, in which a woman searches for a real or imagined lover in a forest, and finds a real or imagined corpse in the course of nineteen minutes of fretful music. Amy Shuard had a voice of extraordinary magnitude, but she was happier singing than acting, so that Herr Schneider-Siemssen and I conceived a set which moved more than she did, a process which included projections by means of slides. Schneider-Siemssen hand-painted the slides, but neglected to use unbreakable glass, with the result that they all cracked when inserted into the lanterna magica. He was in tears of rage until I pointed out that sticking plaster gave them an even more abstract quality than before, and seemed to add to the agony of the meandering soprano a hint of clinical foreboding. He was well satisfied, and even enthusiastic about my defence of sticking plaster as a new texture in theatrical design, as were the press, who found that works such as *Erwartung* were exactly what Covent Garden should be doing.

My next operatic venture, some five years later, was once again thanks to Sir George Solti, under the aegis of Professor Rolf Liebermann, in Hamburg. The work was *The Magic Flute*. To my mind, Mozart, the divine Mozart, remains to be rediscovered, and perhaps needs to be rediscovered by each succeeding generation. It is typical that there should be a prejudice against Schickeneder and a belief that in some way he was unworthy of Mozart, and that therefore, whereas the music is sacrosanct, the text is not. Klemperer even went as far as to record the opera leaving out all dialogue.

My view is entirely opposed to this heresy. Admittedly Schickeneder was a journeyman dramatist, a gag man, a play doctor, an improviser, but if he was good enough for Mozart, he's certainly good enough for me – more especially since *The Magic Flute* is a kind of pantomime, with something of a popular farce and something of *The Tempest*, its grave moments sublimely elevated by Mozart on to a celestial plane, its reassuring moments of contact with a vulgar funny-bone entrusted to Schickeneder. The moral of the tale is disarming in its simplicity, masonic or just human. Why then mystify the clear and limpid line by making of the rituals cloistered and foetid mysteries when they are open to the sky, unregimented, free and democratic? There is nothing more at stake than the eternal struggle between day and night, the sunburst and the moonglow, good and evil, with tiny mortals torn apart and brought together by those elemental forces.

On another level, it is not without dramatic sophistication, which the demands of nineteenth-century taste have eliminated, as is so often the case.

When the rose-bushes part, revealing the Queen of the Night in all her evil glitter, Monostatos scampers to the footlights and says, dramatically, 'That is the Queen of the Night!'

Well, he doesn't, as I was at pains to point out to some learned musicologists who accused me of tampering with the original. Monostatos scampers to the footlights and says, 'That, if I am not mistaken, is the Queen of the Night!'

This is one of many such bowdlerisms, where the wit and colour of Schickaneder has been eliminated by the erosion of time and its servers.

The sets of Jean-Denis Malclès were fresh and lovely, and I regard the production as a success.

When it went to the Maggio Musicale in Florence, William Weaver wrote in the *Herald-Tribune* 'It was superbly realized, beautifully paced . . . When it was new, some time ago, this Peter Ustinov staging of *The Magic Flute* came in for some criticism. It is hard now to see why; it is surely respectful of the text and faithful to the music, and yet inventive.'

This led to an offer to do *Don Giovanni* at the Edinburgh Festival, with Daniel Barenboim. Peter Diamond suggested I do the sets and the costumes, an offer I somewhat rashly accepted. The theatre in Edinburgh is more or less of the dimensions of the theatre in Prague where *Don Giovanni* received its original production, and its intimacy imposes a certain simplification in both means and methods which should be all to the good. As with *The Magic Flute*, I insisted on an absolutely continuous action, without those ponderous silences punctuated by the clatter and rumble of scene-changes, and the sight of scurrying feet with every undulation of the curtain.

Don Giovanni, described by Mozart and Da Ponte as a *Dramma Giocosa*, has been brainwashed even more thoroughly than *The Magic Flute* by the intervening generations of those who loved their opera unwisely, but too well. Nowadays it is treated as a psychological tragedy, in which the advent of Freud and his buddies has added condiment upon condiment until the origin of the meal is practically undistinguishable.

First of all, indiscriminate copulation is not the stuff of tragedy, and all the unjustified theories about Don Giovanni's impotence do nothing to elevate in that direction. They are merely the miserable result of modern psychological research on the story of a joyously inconsiderate cad. The result of all this pretentious nonsense is that the sets are usually as black as ink, that the statue of the Commendatore is left to the imagination, and that even the Don's comeuppance is in the form of a self-inflicted death by the bursting of his overcharged conscience. It is one of the baser trials of the human intelligence that it enlarges the field of stupidity; the stupidity of a stupid man is mercifully intimate and reticent, while the stupidity of an intellectual is cried from the rooftops.

We have already been made to stare at empty canvases and listen with reverence to immobile pianists sitting at silent pianos. What we gain or lose from such experiences are our business, but when the mentality of smartness, of vogue, grips an authentic masterpiece, then we have a right to rebel. To perform *Don Giovanni* as I saw it on the French television, designed with the utmost elegance, as though they all, peasants and landlords, had been to their fittings at some sixteenth-century Dior boutique, and now glittered as virtually the only sources of light in a mine-shaft, is indicative of the confusion of our times. It was highly praised by members of the French government eager to help their ailing opera, and the pundits universally lauded this stylish travesty, in which there was not the smallest trace of '*giocosa*'. To make my evening complete, there was Sir Geraint Evans, his cheeks glowing in the dark, giving the identical performance to the one in my very different production.

His great qualities are a permanent commentary on all that makes opera inviting, and finally impossible, to someone trained in the theatre. With his fine eighteenth-century face, looking like many of the actors' portraits in the Garrick club, dark eyes, bulbous nose and chubby cheeks, on the small side, bristling with invention, ferociously energetic, helpful, greedy, understanding, and unscrupulous, he knows from the outset what he intends to do, usually because he has already done it successfully, and rehearsals are spent getting his own way by running the whole gamut of techniques, from charm to bluster and back again. His strength is that he is not of this century. Surrounded by singers who can sing but can't act, who can sing and can act, or who cannot do both at the same time, he impregnates himself against these inconsistencies by doing his own thing, and doing it brilliantly, alone. I believe *Don Giovanni* is what it is supposed to be, a *Dramma Giocosa*, a morality in which the graver moments are dark shadows in the sunlight, not an added intensity to the pervading gloom. The seriousness with which everything is taken is deliciously Spanish, redolent of *prie-dieu* and crucifix rather than psychiatrist's couch.

So determined were the contemporaries of Meyerbeer to make this unyielding material tragic that they chopped the end off, bringing the curtain down on Don Giovanni's disappearance into hell, an awful warning to fornicators. This concept has lasted till now, the excuse being that musically the facile coda is not up to the marvellous confrontation between Don, Commendatore and Leporello. And yet it is the coda which brings us back to the spirit of the opera.

Oh, you should have heard the outcry from the purists when I brought two policemen on at the end, late as ever, to measure the hole through which Don Giovanni had disappeared in preparation for a long-winded report to Madrid! What was the justification for such a facetious conceit? Quite simply, *signori miei*, that they are in the text if you only bother to look. Don Ottavio, frustrated in his attempt to rid the world of Don Giovanni (largely owing to the influence of the women, who can't bear to see their tormentor dispatched), has recourse to Madrid with a formal charge which he waves about as he swears revenge, and he returns finally, when it is too late to matter, with '*due ufficiali*'.

It all makes sense if you treat the work as it was written. If, however, you load the fragile vehicle with all the baggage of contemporary psycho-analytical claptrap, then you get what you deserve, a resounding success, and congratulations for having made something halfway valid out of a work now deemed unplayable.

My next essay in this weird world of compromise was at the behest of Rolf Liebermann, for the Paris Opera. Massenet is no Mozart, and his *Don Quixote* was an attempt to supply Chaliapine with a role worthy of a great Boris Godounov. Now Nicolai Ghiaurov wished to revive this curiosity, a piece of fustian in which Dulcinea becomes a demi-mondaine, devoid of all peasant force, doing a few Iberian gestures on a balcony to the delight of the villagers, who shout, 'Anda, Anda!' in unison, and in which Don Quixote passes among the crowds like Christ among the lepers, dispensing thoughts as profound as those on a calendar.

The trouble began very early on, when I received letters from angry old baritones in retirement and other ornaments of the French musical establishment, denouncing me for thinking I could do justice to an authentic *French* masterpiece, while Duval, Dupont, and Duroc were still alive, to say nothing of Dulac,

Dupré, and Duchamps, who although dead, would have done it better than me alive, and probably better than Duval, Dupont, and Duroc. Rehearsals were like trying to find a porter in an airport, a milling crowd of choristers obliterating the leading singers under the swinging arms of a chorus-master who walked backwards through anything that barred his way.

Everybody talked at once, even if everybody sang at different times, and nothing was ready when it should have been.

A lady of great and evidently bitter experience in this house, who had taken me under her capacious wing, kept prompting me in the usages of the place. *'Maintenant il faut gueuler! Mais menacez, Maître, menacez! Un peu de colère, Maître, voyons!'*

I was incapable by nature of following her instructions since anger is such a rare commodity in my armoury that I can never afford to use it tactically to futile ends.

I had to design some windmills, the smallest of which worked well with men inside them, but the largest one had an electric motor placed on top, which propelled the blades at a snail's pace, and consistently broke when any weight was placed on them. Since Don Quixote, or rather, a stunt-double, had to be taken up into the flies on one of the blades, the prospect became distinctly depressing after the fourth breakdown, on the eve of the première.

I have never worked in such an atmosphere of utter confusion, and they could find nothing better to do than to blame that confusion on me, because some of my designs had been handed in late, months before for the most part, and because I failed to shout as loud as the others. There are more ghosts in that building than in the whole of England and Scotland put together, and all of them are ill-natured, discourteous, and malevolent.

All this may sound like sour grapes for the disaster that awaited my production. I swear there is not a sour grape in the whole tiny harvest. My hat is raised higher then ever to Rolf Liebermann for the wonders he managed to achieve with such unpromising material, and I surprised even myself after the gale of booing which broke out at my appearance at the curtain by turning my back on the audience, a gesture which produced a great roar of dismay, and then going out for a very good meal in the highest of spirits. The fever had broken, and I was once again in the best of health.

For the record I must add that on the last night the big windmill worked, although its blades rotated in the opposite direction from its brethren. I asked why they bothered with such a detail once the harm was done, and they replied that under the financial structure of the house, they wouldn't touch the credits for the next opera if they didn't account for every franc in the pre-production projection of this one. I had, indeed, worked in the last block-house of the Ligne Maginot.

Ghiaurov and the singers were wonderfully loyal, and as a final error of this whole nonsensical episode I cherish the headline in the Milan evening paper, which said, with a bitchiness in the highest tradition, 'At last something worth seeing in the Paris Opera House.' It was La Scala galloping to the rescue, but it wasn't true. By some miracle there have been many wonderful productions at the Paris Opera as well as a few indifferent ones.

The miracle is, of course, Rolf Liebermann. Berated by an interrogating critic five years after the event, he defended his choice of me as the director of *Don Quixote* by saying that he loved it but that perhaps the two of us had been ignorant at the time of the unwritten traditions of French opera, and further declared that his decision to invite me to undertake this production had been prompted by the fact that my *Magic Flute* in Hamburg had been the best he had ever seen. I hope that his critical sense is as acute as his exemplary loyalty and ethical serenity.

This brings me to an artistic confession. I am used to criticism in that I expect it, and by now I feel I am almost sure enough of my taste to be able to make light of it, even if it rankles. No performer can please consistently. There are times when he must swim against the tide in order to progress, in order to grow. That is normal.

So that it is not attacks on my work or even on my person which I find perplexing so much as praise poured on the works of others which I dislike or which I consider unworthy of serious consideration. This, more than anything, makes me aware of changing times and changing climates, forces me as an old fighter to roll with the punch. Books are different. They keep their secrets better than plays. They do not require interpretation, and, most important, make their appeal to one person at a time, in secret, in isolation.

Perhaps it is an illusion typical of one who has worked for a certain length of time in a chosen profession, but I began to feel that standards were no longer as high, that critics were no longer the austere customs officers who asked you what you had to declare and judged you by your appearance, but rather young officers who leapt on to the parapet, encouraging the playwright to charge in the direction of this or that faction or trend. The very word trendy never existed when I was young –

— I can't let you go on. You suddenly write as though you are ninety, a toothless, gutless old dodderer.

— That's what comes from trying to be sincere.

— Look at the facts!

— No need to shout.

— Look at the facts. You merely changed gears, as it were. Things happened to force you to look deeper into yourself. You began to wonder whether you were really doing what you wished to do, what you were meant to do. It is very exciting when this happens in the middle of life instead of at the beginning. It happens often at the beginning.

— What happened, apart from the fact that my marriage was drifting inexorably on to the rocks?

— Your father died.

— Oh. I had not forgotten.

— He, who had sworn that he would not reach the age of seventy,

320

died on December 1st, 1962, at eight o'clock in the evening, four hours before his seventieth birthday. He had been in a virtual coma for three days before the end, except for a sip of champagne now and then, and an extraordinary moment of lucidity when he looked you straight in the eye with a slightly puzzled expression and said, in French, '*Tiens, je te reconnais de mes rêves.*'

— Yes, I recognize you from my dreams. That must go high on the list of famous last words – and I was the only one to hear them. So vanished a man I never really knew, and whom I, like all sons everywhere, needed to know better. There is no fault attached to this. The need and the awkwardness lie somewhere deep in human nature. The cross-currents of jealousy, of ambition, of protectiveness, of authority try and work under the level of consciousness however well they are controlled by breeding and usage.

Our true natures are perhaps best illustrated by the behaviour of dogs, ferociously protective of their young for a while, and suddenly, overnight, bitter rivals for bone or bitch. They seem to forget their family obligations, and indeed, their family, whereas we are not permitted to do so by our social and religious habits. Our behaviour in this area has no precedent in the animal world from which we have raised ourselves so laboriously. It has therefore no prolonged basis in instinct. It is because we know who our parents are that we treat them as such. If we didn't, we wouldn't. This means that the intellect guides the instincts, with all the confusion that such an awkward compromise automatically entails. Add to this gruel the spices of hypocrisy, filial piety, parental example, duty, *amour propre*, and the rest, and you have a cuisine ready for the culinary magic of great novelists and playwrights.

— Did your father's death bring you closer to your mother?

— No. Curiously enough, it brought her closer to him. She who had chided him for his drift into incapacity and death; she who sought to interest him in the life around him; she who did all she could to stimulate and invigorate him, now became slowly as apathetic as he had been, playing scrabble with her sister Olga, who had settled down with her.

The two sisters were entirely different in character, Olga, who always had a weight problem, wandered round the tiny cottage like a dreadnought. Because she had no abiding interest in life apart from the manufacture of patchwork quilts, which she turned out in vast quantities like a cottage industry, she was also inclined to be insensitive towards the qualms or phobias of lesser folk. She was seventeen years older than Nadia. One day Olga complained to me that my mother had been a most obstinate baby – that on one occasion, she, Olga, had grasped her sister's minute foot, held it aloft, and asked a rhetorical nursery question, 'Who does this little foot belong to?'

The baby had apparently withdrawn its foot with some annoyance. Nadia flared up at the memory of the incident.

'What the hell did you always want with my foot?' she growled.

Olga looked resentful, and after a moment of silence, she limped out of the room, offended.

When a television crew arrived to talk to Nadia about the publication of her book on my father, Olga insisted on being in the picture, if only to outstare the viewers with her round pebble eyes. She seemed to believe she was being snapped by some Victorian family photographer.

Suddenly, with the cameras running, she interrupted Nadia, who was struggling to give a little coherence to her ideas.

'Your nose is dripping,' she announced.

'Let it drip,' Nadia snapped, and continued with her hesitant narrative.

Once again Olga looked offended, and made no secret of her feelings.

Olga was a redoubtable presence in the house, and a source of comfort in a way, even if, when she died at the age of ninety-one, Nadia made no secret either of her sorrow, or of her relief to be alone once again. But by then, of course, she was very rarely alone. There was a whole team of gallant ladies taking it in turns to look after her, among them her golden-hearted neighbours, Mrs Tovey, and Miss Sorrel-Taylour.

— Meanwhile the children were growing. They knew her, of course.

— Yes, and they took great delight in each other's company. Except for the *idée-fixe* of my mother's that it was quite natural that the cycle of love within a family should not be reciprocal, but should gravitate towards the future. In other words, she was resigned to the fact that my interest in my children should be greater than my interest in her, just as her interest in me had been greater than her interest in her own parents. Because of this theory of hers, she was extremely undemanding and, while very warm by nature, rather undemonstrative.

— But where did you spend most of your time?

— That is difficult to say. I did the film of *Topkapi* in Turkey and Greece, with a little of it in France. It was directed by Jules Dassin, a fine, meticulous director with a great sense of humour, who dedicated his career to his wife, Melina Mercouri. It is no reflection on her to suggest that perhaps he could have had a rather more remarkable career if he had not dedicated himself so devotedly to her service. It is, I believe, ever so with husband and wife teams, with the undoubted exception of the Lunts, who possessed an uncannily integrated style in which neither seemed to be making concessions to the other.

Having worked with the Burtons, as they have been inter-mittently called, Elizabeth Taylor and Richard Burton, on two different occasions, once in Peter Grenville's version of Graham Greene's *The Comedians*, and again in a strange film I directed called *Hammersmith Is Out*, I can only confirm my opinion that the chemistry of having them both in a film, regarded as a rare 'coup' by financiers, in fact lacked mystery. Love scenes, and even worse, lust scenes between people who presumably have them anyway in the privacy of their home are inevitably somewhat flat on the screen, and if they happen to be passing through a momentary crisis, such scenes are worse than flat, merely a tribute to their professionalism, and there are few things worse than that.

Richard is a fine actor with a wayward quality women find hard to resist, but the waywardness is somehow stunted by the image of off-screen propriety in opulent wealth. Elizabeth too, a person of tremendous instinct and surprising intelligence, requires a latitude which the outward appurtenances of the super-star somehow blunt. Now that they are on their own again, it may be a blow for romantics, or merely for those of us who like them both, but it may well be a salutary liberation for their careers.

— You received an Oscar for *Topkapi*.

— Oh yes, I was reaching the age of compensation. I had, on my desk, two emasculated gentlemen, and two emasculated ladies as well. These were the Emmy awards, which I received for playing Dr Johnson and Socrates, and the four of them made for a fine mixed-doubles match. Then I won a third Emmy playing an aged Jewish delicatessen-store-owner on Long Island, at grips with racial prejudice in the shape of a proud black boy, in a fine if rather sentimental script by Rod Serling. We now had an Umpire as well.

— And in spite of all this, you were subject to feelings of mournfulness, of decrescendo?

— Well, I also performed an Arab potentate in a film starring Shirley MacLaine, with whom I dearly wanted to work, and will always dearly want to work. I knew the script was overblown, over-farcical, and I began to feel, in reading many new scripts and seeing many new films, that we were in a transitional period, and that comedy as I conceived it was losing its way. It was all overstated, and mannered, and weird, as though laughter away from the laugh-machine was unreliable. Nudity made its appearance, first in shadows, then boldly, then explicitly. After millions of years of life

324

on this planet, human beings were told there had been a breakthrough in that their eyes might now rest on pubic hair for the first time. Just as music was being confused with sound, and painting with decoration, so organization was surrendering to happening, order to chaos. Novelty became as ephemeral as a mayfly. Styles were being revived even before they were obsolete. So desperate were we for the lost disciplines that the seventies began reviving not only the twenties, the thirties, the forties, the fifties, but even the sixties. Eventually the seventies will revive the seventies, until December revives January!

— You *are* getting old.

— Now it's my turn to upbraid you. There's no need to say that with a sigh. In 1968 I was elected as Rector of Dundee University, remember?

— Will I ever forget! Half a bottle of whisky you had to drink out of a silver goblet as you were dragged round the city in a landau, pulled by the university football team in lieu of horses.

— Those were just the light-hearted japes of high-spirited medics, and they were fun. Perhaps more fun for them than for me, but that was half the point. The six years that followed were the real test. The cool machinations of the social sciences' Marxists, young fellows gazing at you resentfully through the odd gaps in the hair which cascaded down their faces, already well versed in all the low tricks of political chicanery. There was never any trouble from the dental students, the medical students, or the engineers, those who had tremendously difficult disciplines to master, and therefore had no time for university politics, but the social sciences were the overflow for all those who had not yet decided what to do with their lives, and for all those whose premature frustrations led them into the sterile alleys of confrontation. They called wildcat meetings among themselves, informing no one else, and in secret passed a vote calling on me to resign. 'Forty in favour of your resignation; six against' read the telegram.

That was the time to be tough.

— Why did they wish you to resign? I can't remember.

— I refused to support them in an illegal strike which took the form of refusing to pay for their lodgings. What they wanted was a higher government grant for students. I wanted this too, but I didn't approve of this slipshod and silly way of going about it, in which the University had the last word if it wished to utter it. No tactical advance is worth it if it entails strategic retreat. No, that's not Clausewitz, that's me.

I asked for a new vote of confidence by secret ballot, sending the forms to the entire student body of the University. There were by now about forty-five in favour of my resignation, but instead of six against, the figure had risen to almost 2,000. There were howls and bleats of unconstitutional behaviour on my part. I ignored them, wrote an article for a leading newspaper, and met the lads in a head-on collision on television. They protested to me in private at having gone to such lengths to defeat them. I informed them that what they wanted above all was publicity, and that, as a good Rector, I had acceded to their request.

— Now what has all this got to do with growing old?

— Everything. There is a tendency in men of my age, and in my profession, to pretend to be younger than they are. In Hollywood I recognize only half my acquaintances. The bald ones have neatly sewn hair; the hirsute ones have their ears covered in cosy mobcaps of russet locks. And they all wear faded jeans with lumps of gold on chains round their necks. There are no old men any more. *Playboy* and *Penthouse* have between them made an ideal of eternal adolescence, sunburnt and saunaed, with the gray dorianed out of them.

— Gracious.

— Yes. Well, the young need old men. They need men who are not ashamed of age, not pathetic imitations of themselves.

I have said elsewhere that parents are the bones on which children sharpen their teeth. It is true of rectors too, and teachers. And of what use are those bones if they are soft, if they expose their marrow to the searching tongue, if they are not hard, and why not, unbreakable? I became, at last, what they needed me to be.

— But why this intensity, when you take your plays and films, your failures and even your successes, for granted?

— Oh, I still had *Hot Millions* to come, with the splendid Maggie Smith, the most sensitive actress of all that I have worked with; I had three films with Disney, *Blackbeard's Ghost, One of Our Dinosaurs is Missing, The Treasure of Matacumbe*; I had *Viva Max*, in which I played a Mexican general, and which was banned in Mexico; I had *Logan's Run*, in which I played a man of ninety. Among my plays I still had *Halfway up the Tree* to come, a lightweight piece which ran a year in London with Robert Morley in the lead, and *The Unknown Soldier and his Wife*, the most ambitious of my works for the theatre, brilliantly directed by John Dexter at Lincoln Center in New York, and played by me at Chichester and then in London. In this last production I had the pleasure of working with my eldest daughter Tamara, now a delicious girl I was beginning to know again after a false start to both our lives as regards our relationship. She married a most talented young director, Christopher Parr, and they spend much of their time in Edinburgh.

I must not forget my second book of short stories, *The Frontiers of the Sea* and my second novel, *Krumnagel*, which is certainly one of my better works.

— Is that all you are going to say about them?

— They can, and must speak for themselves if they are capable of speaking at all. I know, for instance, that *The Unknown Soldier and his Wife* is a difficult play, but that does not mean it needs translation by the author of all people. All I have done in my life must stand or fall by its own merits or lack

of them. There is nothing I can add, except perhaps to cast
a little light on the secret person whom I am discovering with
your help. That is why childhood and extreme youth are so
much easier as a personal archaeological site than maturity
and middle age. I have no wish to defend myself again at ages
when I was already capable of defending myself. My hope was
to analyse myself at an age when I could only submit, or stand
aside, or pretend the opposite of the truth was true.

— And this explains your ardour as the Rector of a small
Scottish University. You prefer to talk about that than about
your plays?

— Infinitely. It was a renewal. I did it for six years. Twice elected
for periods of three years each. They may have thought of it
as a joke, but they did not realize that for me it was a vital
moment in my life, when I bent my mind to new problems,
to real problems, compared to the mere careers of plays
or films.

— I always thought that the Rectors of Scottish Universities
were sinecures.

— So did everyone. It so happened, however, that at one and
the same time all the Rectors decided it was time for this
to stop, and that ombudsmen in the modern world were a
very sound and a good idea, even if this function had been
conceived as long ago as the very beginning of the fifteenth
century. The Rectors began to meet, and compare notes, Jo
Grimond, Kenneth Allsop, John Cleese and others, to the
extent that our activities created the same alarm as secret
meetings between regimental mascots might occasion among
colonels. The Vice-Chancellors always wanted to know what
we were up to, and sooner or later, they found out.

My time of office was made a pleasure by the many interesting
people I met, people I would never have met in a more normal
course of events. And I shall always cherish the resilient grace
of the Queen Mother during my inauguration, when we were
pelted with toilet rolls by the students, which she picked up as

though someone had mailed them to the wrong address. She also went beetroot-red when the janitor opened a door with a key, and said to me in a fine Scottish brogue, 'Rector, there's no' a way around it, you'll have to share this room with the Queen Mither.' She giggled furtively just as she was about to open the fine new dental centre, when I pointed out to her on the plan that three contiguous departments were designed in the highest body-snatching 'traditions' of Burke and Hare in nearby Edinburgh, the departments being Emergency, Post-Mortem, and Experimental.

And of all the memories I took away from there which gave me a personal glow of satisfaction, the most disarming came from a distressed parent appealing for consideration for his wayward child. The envelope was addressed to 'The Lord Rectum of Dundee University', and that is how I have seen myself ever since in moments of self-doubt.

19

— You are so reticent about some of the events that interest me
  most, that I feel I will have to stay with you practically till the
  end of the book.
— You are most welcome, Dear Me, I assure you. After all, we
  are coming to the most difficult of all parts.
— Why?
— Oh, you know. People have their image. Hateful word! I once
  reluctantly appeared on a television talk show in order to
  propagate a play, to counter-attack some critical carping, and
  it became a habit – in the United States, that is. I discovered,
  and they discovered, that I have a certain gift of the gab which
  happens to coincide with a time when television has imposed
  special demands on the orator, that he destroy his projection,
  that he become natural, that he act with the same propriety
  as he would in people's homes.
— Explain yourself.
— TV may well be the medium in which to address the nation,
  but it may no longer be treated as such. You are talking to
  units of one, or two – to lonely old ladies to whom television
  is the only comfort. Such people are easily frightened. They
  don't wish a rude fellow pinning them to the wall with his
  insistence. As a medium, it is basically bland and insidious,
  and yet it is also a kind of lie detector, which ferrets out
  insincerity with unparalleled efficiency. It was television
  which destroyed the bad McCarthy. Occasionally it showed

him when he was not speaking, but whispering into the ears of his aides, or being whispered at. We saw a man whose mask of sincerity was down, a man relaxing and showing his real self in his corner, between the rounds. Nixon was no more successful when he told bedtime stories to the nation. One was invariably more conscious of the intention than of the achievement.

— Do you consider that television has a function of which nobody is apparently aware – as a kind of arbiter of sincerity?

— Yes. I believe it has affected priorities more than any other profession; its influence on us all has been enormous. When before was a runner accompanied on his attempt at a record by a stopwatch visible to all, and when could the results of a close race be judged by everyone? And when before has time, its chance gestures, its gratuitous orchestration, been captured in the form of instant replay? And this instant replay can be used not only for sport but for assassinations, bank robberies, and other daily occurrences.

These are new and wonderful techniques, and yet to my mind, there is nothing more extraordinary than television's ability to outstare a politician, and say to him, 'convince me'.

To the experienced eye, every reticence, every avoidance, every joke helps to build a pattern of the man's true state of mind. How lucky were the great men of the past! They could disappear for a while to let dust settle, to let things blow over when they had gone wrong. Today there is no respite. The camera lies in wait in the most unexpected places. We know all our candidates far too well for their own comfort, their own peace of mind. Popularities fluctuate as hysterically as values on the Stock Exchange as we notice some detail which displeases us, or a casual *faux-pas* is blown into a national calamity by the media.

— It seems to me you don't quite know whether to admire television or to condemn it.
— Neither, and both. It is an instrument, like the telephone. If asked whether you like the telephone, you are liable to reply that that depends entirely who is on it. As the harbinger of news that you have just inherited a million, it is probably appreciated. With a crashing bore on the end of the line, it tends to be cursed. But even at the worst of times, there is not much point in condemning it. It is here to stay, in ever-improving form, and personally, I have a great deal to thank it for.
— Tell me, before we plunge into the present, and glimpse the future. Who were the men, and women who have most impressed you in your life? I am not changing the subject, incidentally, since it is really an extension of your concern with politicians, who, in your mature life, seem to have taken the place of the military as your favourite targets.
— The military are décodé. It's a far cry from ceremonial parades to the indescribable nightmare of nuclear conflict. In spite of this, there are still romantic toughs about, acting out their pathetic fantasies as mercenaries in developing countries, or as heroes of anonymous resistance, placing bombs in suitcases in public places, and reaping casual harvests in the destruction of innocents. These madmen are to be pitied. They belong to the rabid wing of Miss Lonely-hearts, and they find their consummation in the company of other crackpots.

By now the difference between the possibilities of total and immediate destruction for all, which is a matter for technicians, not for soldiers, and the small part of the spectrum reserved for what are demonstrations rather than wars with conventional weapons, which are still a matter for soldiers, is so great that it is difficult to see what they have to attract a young person to what used to be known as the call to arms.

Politicians are still realities, even if they have become attached to show business because of their compulsive addiction to television. I do not for a moment subscribe to the Communist heresy that political figures are superior to men of other professions; that they have an obligation to oversee the activities of the arts and sciences with a severe pedagogic eye in the interest of political orthodoxy. That is to stultify the liberal arts and other professions and to stifle necessary sources of criticism.

What is interesting about politicians in a democratic society is that, whereas they are motivated by power as they are in all societies, everything is done constitutionally to make that power an obligation instead of a source of enjoyment. One cannot help noticing how often a removal from power in a dictatorship entails disgrace, the end of a career, or even the end of life, whereas in a removal from power in a democracy the initial disappointment is often mitigated by a huge sigh of relief. This is as it should be. When power is enjoyed, it is abused.

Starting with politicians, then, I have been impressed by Edward Heath, the only European who can match Jimmy Carter smile for smile. I admire him not for his politics, with which I have always been in some disagreement (except for his championship of Europe, with which I am in absolute accord), but for his passions. A man who loves music as he does, not merely as a stealthy purchaser of records, but as a Walter Mitty who dares to cross the frontier of the imagination into unfriendly reality, and conduct an orchestra with precision and verve, is bound to be a person with an extraordinary courage and grip of abstractions. If you add to that his accomplishment as a sailor, you realize that he is as good a conductor on a moving platform as on a still one. Alas, he has been a consistent victim of that miserable prejudice which believes that a Prime Minister should be a person without visible talent; that talent in high places is tantamount to a lapse of taste.

That excellent violinist, Jeremy Thorpe, fell victim to a hypocrisy which one would have hoped Britain to have grown out of; but no, the bittersweet piety of the Victorian moralist has survived the scorn of the emancipated, and still succeeds in doing its damage by erosion on those who admit that life has changed beyond recognition for the multitude, but who insist that a minority, because of the office they hold, must continue to pretend to live as no one ever could.

One could see the rot propagated in the sad case of Profumo, when it was seriously maintained that a celebrated model could have passed military secrets to a Soviet naval attaché. Such a preposterous idea might have held water in 1914, when a French general, rendered forgetful by the delights of orgasm, could have moaned, 'Ten divisions, two of them mounted,' into the attentive ear of Mata Hari, but in today's world of science what kind of military secret is it that a model, or practically anyone attentive for that matter, could glean as a result of Mr Profumo's inattention, and thus pass on, some time later, to a Russian lieutenant, in the form of idle pillow-talk? Absurdity has a place of honour in contemporary civilization, so long as it does not grow irksome, and affect the careers and, indeed, the lives of men.

Ernest Bevin was certainly the most remarkable of the British politicians I knew. I once referred to him as Britain's only peasant, in that he had a wonderful rural quality, and an ability to reduce the complexities of foreign affairs to the scale of the farmyard, thereby creating an Orwellian world which was, however, neither frightening nor full of foreboding, but merely understandable.

'I mind me,' he used to say, 'when we was institutin' trade talks with the Russians, they sent over a young man called Denakosov or maybe Dekanosov, and I put one of my best young men with 'im . . .' He hesitated, and he consulted his wife, Florence, as always when in doubt. ''Oo was it, Floss? Was it Harold Ramsay?'

'No,' she piped, 'you sent him to the Argentine for the meat, remember?'

'Oh, yes,' he grumbled. ''Oo was it then?'

'I think his name begun with a P,' Florence suggested.

'You're right!' he called, triumphant. 'George Gibbons, that's 'oo it was!'

His tone of gravity returned.

'They was gettin' on like the proverbial 'ouse on fire,' he continued, 'and just as they was gettin' ready to relegate their findin's to a 'igher level, Dena . . . Kanosov disappears . . . never 'eard of again.'

His jaw set grimly as he remembered the event. Then he became casual again.

'Well, next time I saw Molotov, in Lake Succ-ess, over in . . . in . . .'

His memory failed again for a moment.

'America?' suggested Florence.

''Merica,' echoed Ernie, 'I said to 'im, look 'ere, Molotov, I don't know where your young man's gone, and I admit it's none of my business. But nevertheless, in the interests of common courtesy, next time we 'ave trade talks, will you please do me the kindness of tellin' me in advance if your young man is going to disappear before the end – then I won't put one of my best young men with 'im.'

Bevin came under tremendous and bitter attack from Zionists because of his reluctance to end the British mandate in Palestine prematurely. He was determined to a point of stubbornness that when the State of Israel did become a reality, it should do so on a firm and equitable basis with its neighbours, and who is to say today that he was entirely wrong? The impatient excesses of the Haganah and Irgun and Stern Gang only strengthened his resolve, and incidentally provided a model for the P.L.O. to follow in later years. To level accusations of anti-Semitism at such a man is to indulge in the facility of extremism, and to be about as grossly unfair as it is possible to be. He was a noble person and probably a great Foreign Minister.

Among his other favourite tales, in which he foresaw some of his country's future troubles, was a fable he told with cosy relish.

'There was three men in a boat, see, a Communist, a Fascist, and a good Union man. All of a sudden, the boat sinks, and the

335

three men are thrown in the water. There's people on the river bank. The Fascist does his salute at them, but finds it impossible to swim with one arm, and 'e drowns. The Communist begins shouting slogans at them, exhausts 'imself, and 'e drowns. This leaves only the Union man, swimmin' towards the bank with strong easy strokes. He's almost within 'is depth, when the factory siren goes, and 'e drowns.'

An artist in somewhat the same mould as Ernest Bevin is J. B. Priestley, a no-nonsense Northerner who shared with Bevin, the West-Countryman, an extraordinary memory for ancient music-hall routines. Whenever Bevin felt the atmosphere sagging, be it in Bristol or in a private home in London, in the White House or the Kremlin, he began singing old popular songs, long forgotten, for which Floss and he had an infallible memory. These abrupt outbursts must have puzzled Stalin.

Jack Priestley too, with all his appearance of intolerance for the mediocre, the second-rate, has an immense compassion for the lives and problems of uninspired entertainers. He is a proud man, with a magnificent instinctive intelligence tempered occasionally by a deliberate reversion to small-town hard-headedness.

Invited to his lovely apartment in the Albany, I set eyes on a painting by Sickert hanging over the mantelpiece, depicting the audience in a theatre gallery.

'My God,' I said, 'that's a wonderful Sickert!' He gazed at it through the self-generated blue coils of pipe smoke.

'That is the second finest theatrical Sickert in existence, and I have the other one.'

At that time, we tried to form an English Playwrights' Company, in emulation of the celebrated American producing organization, run by the playwrights themselves, Elmer Rice, Maxwell Anderson, Sidney Kingsley, Robert Sherwood, and Marc Connelly. The British team was to be Priestley, Terence Rattigan, James Bridie, Benn Levy, and myself, and we had two meetings in Priestley's flat, under the chairmanship of Benn Levy, the bearded

Socialist parliamentarian and dramatist husband of Constance Cummings.

We arrived at a purely financial consideration in the course of the agenda. Benn Levy said, 'I think this is a matter which only applies to highly successful dramatists, but, since we all live and write in hopes, I suppose we should have a ruling.' At this point he addressed himself to Rattigan. 'Terry, perhaps you would tell us in confidence your solution to this problem?'

Terence Rattigan never had time to answer, for Jack Priestley interrupted, his hackles halfway risen. 'I think I ought to remind you, gentlemen, that I too have had my share of success . . .'

The second meeting was no more fruitful; it was, in fact, the last.

'I hope it is understood,' said Jack Priestley, puffing away at his pipe, 'that as a result of this free association of dramatists, we all from now on write plays expressing the right ideas.'

I noticed the angular Dr Mavor Wince. He wrote highly personal and capricious plays under the nom-de-plume of James Bridie. His eyes grew in size and his nose pointed at Jack, while his Scottish voice caressed his words.

'I owe what little success I have known by expressing the wrong ideas, Mr Priestley, and I think it is really too late in life for me to change now – for any reason, however specious.'

That was the end of that, and a very good thing too.

On another occasion, I was chairman of some meeting of the League of Dramatists at Claridge's. I am a very poor chairman at the best of time, most especially in England, where I consistently forget that usage forbids guests to smoke before the Queen's health has been drunk. The evening in question was no exception, and I suddenly became aware of Jack Priestley, doubled up as he dodged in and out of the tables, holding his dead pipe like a revolver, resembling an officer involved in some heroic action in 1914.

Eventually he arrived by my side, convinced that his approach had been inconspicuous.

'I'm as good a republican as the next man,' he whispered, fiddling agitatedly with his pipe, 'but don't you think it's time for the Loyal Toast?'

Finally, there is one story so apocryphal that it has to be true.

'Mr Priestley,' said the gushing interviewer, 'we are conducting an enquiry for the magazine. What would you do if you had a million?'

'I've got a million,' replied Jack, and walked away.

He is a man opulent in his contradictions, and sometimes absolutely outrageous in his remarks, but one is always delighted to see him. His robust self-confidence and his gruff rejection of sentimentality are a permanent vote of confidence in human nature.

— I notice that your examples are all English, or at least British.
— That is quite normal, since I lived there most of my life, and the men and women I met during my formative years were almost exclusively British. Later, in New York, however, I was privileged to spend some time with that extraordinary triumvirate which guided the destinies of the United Nations during a particularly dangerous period, Dag Hammarskjöld, Andy Cordier, and Ralph Bunche.

I dined and lunched with them on occasion, and it is horrifying to think that they are all gone. Hammarskjöld, shy rather than cold, showed me photographs of Khrushchev beating his shoe on his desk during that famous incident in the General Assembly. If you looked carefully, you could see that he was wearing both his shoes, which meant that he either borrowed the shoe from a hapless aide, or else that he smuggled the shoe in to the General Assembly in a paper bag, disguised as a sandwich.

There is no doubt that Hammarskjöld's northern sense of propriety was deeply shaken by the roughness of the outburst, and ironically, since the Russian code of what is socially permissible comes largely across the Baltic from Sweden, it was precisely this rowdy behaviour of Khrushchev's, dubbed ne-kulturny

(Uncultured), which eventually proved his undoing at home. Had he lived to know this, Hammarskjöld would have been unexpectedly reassured.

Ralph Bunche was as quiet, as reserved as Andy Cordier was outspoken. One had to strain at times to hear what Ralph Bunche was saying, whereas Andy's foghorn voice left nothing to the imagination, not even the dynamic force of his character. Of course, the mystery of Ralph's quality of reticence was not far to seek, and yet, what always came as a surprise was the extraordinary toughness which his mildness of manner concealed. Apparently he had been the protégé of a wonderful old teacher of another generation. He worked hard to bring out all his unique pupil's brilliance, and it was when Ralph was leaving to go to the University, into which he had passed with every manner of commendation, that the old teacher produced the unkindest cut of all, in guise of the greatest compliment he could pay.

'Bunche,' he said, with a tear in his eye, 'congratulations. And, Bunche . . . I want you to know, I never considered you as a Negro.'

Adlai Stevenson was frequently a member of this civilized and glorious team. Accessible and chipper, he was the type of American who is unfortunately no longer called to the greatest heights, as indeed I am convinced that neither Harry Truman, nor either of the Roosevelts would be if they had the opportunity of running today. Such manifest intelligence is somehow suspect, as is any outward demonstration of character. It seems to be the habit to elect presidents for their lack of evident vices instead of for their possession of evident virtues. The existence of vices is allowed to become apparent during the incumbency. In such computerized calculations, in which those seeking to be everything to all men end up being precious little to any, there was no possible place for someone as twinkling with minor malice as Adlai Stevenson.

'The work of the Catholic missions in New Guinea,' he declared at one of our dinners at the Brussels Restaurant in New

339

York, his voice portentous, 'is beginning to pay dividends. Statistics have shown that on Fridays the staple meal is fishermen.'

During the enervating days of the Cuban crisis, it was clear that he was left completely in the dark by the Kennedy administration. There were no doubt very good reasons for this embarrassing oversight, in that enough was going on in Washington not to have to bother about New York and the U.N. as well, but it did point to one increasingly obvious discrepancy, and that is whereas small and new countries send their best men to the United Nations, large countries only send those they can spare, since the fountainhead of their policies are not there. In that sense, Adlai Stevenson was far too fine a mind to entrust with the window-dressing of an American presence among the meek.

His isolation led to embarrassment for him and for anybody of the remotest sensitivity. On the second Sunday of the crisis, we were invited to brunch at John Gunther's. Early in the morning, the television announced that the Russians had protested about a new overflight of their territory by a U-2. There was enough tension in the air without that.

Adlai Stevenson arrived at Gunther's saying how he was looking forward to brunch, the first civilized meal he was going to enjoy for a week. He looked very tired, but the twinkle was there.

'Things seem calmer at last,' he said.

'Despite the U-2 flight over Russia?' I asked.

He laughed, but then reined in his reflex.

'You're joking, of course,' he replied, with a distinct feeling that, if it was a joke, it wasn't all that amusing.

'No,' I said, 'I heard it on the TV at about nine o'clock.'

'I heard it at ten,' said Lord Caradon, who was present.

When Adlai was sure it was 'on the level', he asked to use the phone. After a moment he returned and said regretfully that he could not stay for brunch.

It was the last time I saw him.

The Sunday before I had a date to play tennis with Max

Blouët, the then manager of the Drake Hotel. We had to wait to begin because our fourth player had not yet turned up. He was none other than Monsieur Kosciusko-Morizet, then French Ambassador to the U.N., since Ambassador to Washington. Our third player was the Ambassador from Cambodia, who waited patiently with us.

When M. Kosciusko-Morizet eventually turned up, he was both apologetic and deeply annoyed about something far beyond tennis. Eventually, as he smashed the third easy ball into the netting surrounding the court, he exploded.

'It is just impossible to be a French Ambassador these days. The Americans tell us nothing. Nothing! Why am I late? Just as I was leaving I had yet another telephone call with disagreeable revelations – and on a Sunday!'

Needless to say we lost, the Cambodian's patient lobbing and drop shots being a subtle foretaste of the style of future hostilities. Later that day I had to go to Washington. The British Ambassador, Sir David Ormsby-Gore, now Lord Harlech, a personal friend of John Kennedy's, asked me in for a drink.

'Well, it's a grim situation,' he said, his fine medieval face reposed and earnest, 'but there is one element of consolation, the Americans are keeping us informed of every move.'

This was too much for me.

'Oh,' I said, 'that's curious. I've just been playing tennis with Kosciusko-Morizet – '

The British Ambassador's eyes lit with pleasure.

'How is he?' he enquired.

'Perhaps not as well as he should be,' I suggested. 'He told me the French are being informed of nothing at all. Nothing, he emphasized.'

The life drained from the British Ambassador's eye once again.

'He actually *said* that, did he?' he enquired.

'He actually *said* that,' I echoed.

The Ambassador took a deep breath, and then said casually,

'Well, it's quite true, of course, but we do have to put up *some* kind of appearance.'

The incident was a succinct explanation of the relationship between the three countries at the time.

— You met de Gaulle, remember?

— How could I forget? But I must say that my purpose here is not name-dropping or an acquisition of illusory self-importance, and so I only mention those with whom a contact, however brief, had some meaning which is worth sharing with others. After all, thousands of people knew de Gaulle far better than I, if anyone knew him at all.

Every great man, upon departure, leaves the most unconscionable mess behind him, a confusion of unfinished business, of regrets, of recrimination, of love, of awe, all the ingredients for social and political chaos. Georges Pompidou had the unenviable task of making order out of the loose ends, and of imposing a period of quiet growth on his country still enervated by the absence of its secular pontiff, and all the unpredictable excitements of his reign. Pompidou came out of this trial bluff and blunt, but never dull. He somehow exemplified a quiet courage, a discreet yet trenchant wit, very different from the 'superbe' of de Gaulle, but quite as French. Like Truman after Roosevelt, he began as a disaster, born out of disaster, and ended mourned by all, with a suspicion that he might, at the final stocktaking, run his haughty predecessor very close indeed as a President.

As a man he was certainly most engaging, preserving his initial simplicity with no effort whatsoever. In fact, he was the only person in his position who consistently and plaintively bemoaned the fact that his high office kept him segregated both from his friends and those he would have liked to have known better.

He had an absolute passion for the arts, and was determined to understand and savour even the most obscure of abstractions, turning certain rooms in the Élysée into exhibitions of unashamedly forward-looking furniture. He believed that France was a haven of the creative senses, and that it behoved her chief executive to be as up-to-the-minute as its most advanced pioneer.

I was fortunate to be present at the farewell lunch M. Pompidou gave Christopher Soames, then at the point of relinquishing his post as British Ambassador to Paris in order to take up his new appointment as Commissioner to the E.E.C. in Brussels. There were a mere sixteen people seated at table on this moving occasion. Suddenly the President claimed our attention by tapping his glass. He then, soberly and quietly, proposed the health of Christopher Soames, adding that his sincere hope was to live long enough to see Christopher fill a place to which he would be admirably suited, that of first President of Europe.

The toast came as a quiet bombshell, and bereft Christopher of any suitable answer. In fact, there was no answer suitable for such a patently sincere and magnanimous wish. A year later, at a function in London, Christopher asked me if his memory of the incident was accurate. Had Pompidou actually proposed such a toast or was it all a dream? I was able to confirm that I had heard it too, although until the question was put I too had had vague doubts that I had heard it aright.

M. Pompidou's successor, Valéry Giscard d'Estaing, began his Presidential career as demurely as Georges Pompidou, but soon noticed that the French, a nation of hero-worshippers, demand men they can look up to, and so he consciously toughened his attitude to become a kind of national examiner, judge and advocate at one and the same time. Like many Frenchmen, tired of the ever-changing governments of the past, under the aegis of Presidents who were sinecures, he became fascinated with American 'presidentialism', and the idea of an all-powerful President, only limited in his authority by the time-span of his incumbency, guiding the destinies of a government whose Prime Minister is an emasculated figure. The perils of such an arrangement seemed lost on the French for reasons of novelty and modernity, and they chose the year of Watergate to make their greatest progress in the direction of a transatlantic style. De Gaulle was a convenient precedent, which seemed to give credence to an arrangement quite new in French parliamentary history, although it was de Gaulle's personality rather than any constitutional prerogative which created such a possibility in the first place.

Whereas de Gaulle was a military figure, Giscard is a lay figure from the world of the 'Grandes Écoles', answering questions with a finicky clarity of syntax and often categorizing his replies to questions in several numbered sections. It is he who seems to correct France's exam papers, and every session of the cabinet has the odd appearance of a reunion on the first day of term, the ministers refreshed and eager to do well under the temperate yet unforgiving eye of the professor.

One begins to realize the greatness and the accuracy of Molière as France's national playwright *par excellence* when we discover echoes of his creations in the living. De Gaulle could have been a superb creation of Molière's if he hadn't been a superb creation of his own, and Giscard too, with his conquered timidity, the modulated style of his utterances, his patience with those presumed slightly slow of wit, his prissiness, and his gracious nod in the direction of destiny, could have stepped out of a Molière play, his sidelong glances contradicted by the austerity of his habit.

Pompidou would have found less favour with Molière, since he had less to hide, and hid it not at all.

— I notice, as I am sure others will notice, that there is not a woman among the gallery of those who have left an impression on you.

— Women have left great impressions on me, but hardly in a manner I can communicate. They have been remarkable for their constancy, their charm, their courage. I am talking about friends now, mark you, nothing else. Leaving out those I have already mentioned, like Edith Evans, or those who deserve to be mentioned again and again, like Sybil Thorndike, there is one woman in particular whom I do wish to talk about. Moura Budberg took her name from one of her marriages. She had also been married to a Count Benckendorf. And she had been the mistress and muse of Maxim Gorki, of H. G. Wells, and of Robert Bruce Lockhart, author of *Memoirs of a British Agent*. A large woman, bearing a striking resemblance to Peter the Great, and born strangely enough at Poltava, scene of his greatest victory over the Swedes, she lived a long life on the fringe of literature, translating, advising, lending her knowledge to the movie industry, but above all she was a great intangible influence on all who came in contact with her.

She was strikingly original. Staying with us in Rome, she said at breakfast, as an afterthought, 'You must be careful of burglars in this house.'

'Why?' we asked nervously.

We had to wait for the toast and marmalade to be masticated and swallowed before a reply was forthcoming.

'Because I saw a hand reach for my handbag through the window in the early hours of the morning.'

'What did you do?' we asked, now thoroughly alarmed.

Once again, the toast and marmalade had precedence.

'The hand was within range of my walking-stick. I hope I didn't break the poor man's wrist.'

During the war, owing to a circumstance as eccentric as herself, she found herself locked out of her London apartment naked. Instead of doing what most women would have done, which is to call for help while attempting to conceal their modesty, Moura placed a fire-bucket over her head, and went down into the street to solicit assistance.

In Moscow I saw her ask a policeman for a taxi. He pointed out that he was a policeman, not a commissionaire. She said that in her day a policeman would not have needed to point out that he was not a commissionaire in order to hail a taxi for an old lady. Eventually the poor man was blowing his whistle

345

desperately and waving aimlessly at all moving vehicles in order to rid himself of this majestic presence.

Despite her long liaison with Maxim Gorki, she was a great friend of Gorki's widow, and they sat in rocking chairs reminiscing about the object of their adoration on the verandah of a dacha near Moscow.

She represented for me an indomitable side to the Russian character, one which, despite the creation of my own nation, consoles and comforts me.

I may have been brought up to accept British thought patterns, and to have been exposed to the style of the French, the casualness of the Americans, and the atmospheres of many other peoples, but when I was in Moura's presence, I felt deeply and serenely Russian. It was, and still is, a sentiment which I could not do without from time to time.

— Who supplies it now that Moura has left us?

— Her memory is as alive as ever. But I am conscious of my Russianness when I am with Russians, even if my knowledge of the language is far from adequate. Nabokov comforts me too, despite his professorial affectations and a spoken English quite other than his highly personal written English and giving every evidence of having been learned at the knee of some Scottish nanny in St Petersburg. He has a merry laugh, and he is willing to use it. At the same time, his prejudices are sometimes so curious that they are difficult to share even when the imperative is mere politeness. An old hiker with staring eyes turned up in Montreux, revealing himself to be the son of the Russian liberal Prime Minister Stolypin, assassinated in 1911 in Kiev, and of whom Lenin had said that if he were allowed to continue his reforms, revolution would become unnecessary. Stolypin junior was longing to meet Nabokov.

Respectful as ever of the privacy of creative artists, I said he was very busy, but I would nevertheless try. The great man answered the phone himself. I explained the nature of my call.

'Stolypin?' said Nabokov, 'no, I do not think I wish to meet him.'

'Oh, come on,' I urged, 'you have something in common at least.'

'Oh?'

'His father and your uncle were both assassinated.'

'Yes, admittedly, but for different reasons. Tell him I regret, and when he has gone, come up for a drink.'

He too has something indomitable about him.

— And Solzhenitsyn?

— I don't know Solzhenitsyn, but I have the gravest misgivings about everything except his courage and his sincerity.

— I only brought him up because, once we're on the subject of the indomitable –

— I understand. No one can fail to be impressed, even over-awed by his extraordinary singleness of purpose and his almost superhuman self-discipline, and yet, whereas he is an undoubted authority on horror in the camps and of official obtuseness out of them, once he came to the West he was under an overriding obligation to speak. Why? Because he was confronted with that most terrible of all temptations, that of being listened to. He revealed himself quickly to possess a new version of an old cosmic vision, and to be a Russian mystic in an ancient tradition, in which acuity and intolerance mingle with the fumes of incense and of woodsmoke. I fear that the Russians were as shrewd in letting him go as he was in accepting their offer.

— What makes you say that?

— An offer from an American magnate in the South to fly thousands of miles for a handsome wad of dollars, in order to read aloud Solzhenitsyn's Warning to America at a socio-political function. My soul too has been open to temptation, but I never thought to recognize Solzhenitsyn

347

among the tempters, but there he was, large as life among the Southern aristocracy.

— You refused?

— There are certain things I cannot bring myself to do, even if I am starving. To lend myself to a viewpoint I find unreal and undiscriminating is one.

— And yet you lent your name to a wine commercial?

— Ah, cruel. I will explain in the next and final chapter.

— Do you remember, at the poolside of the Beverly Hills Hotel, an elderly gentleman in a flowered cabana-suit gripping your wrist, and saying, in one breath, 'I want you to know I admire everything you do and I own Manischewitz'?

— I do. I was flattered both as a person and as a wine salesman.

— I suppose you know that many people assume that you are Jewish?

— Sometimes I wish I was. It would save so much trouble.

— Trouble?

— Yes. Earlier on I spoke about UNESCO and the Press Agencies, remember?

— Yes.

— Well, by means of a reckless canard, the Jewish newsagency reported me to have slandered the state of Israel in a highly reputable Dutch newspaper. The item was as incredible in its inaccuracy as it was in its spitefulness, and it ended with the statement, 'Mr Ustinov is of Jewish origin,' whatever that may mean by way of nuance. The result was the cancellation of theatre parties to a play of mine which was then on the road, and other regrettable consequences. I was, quite clearly, a traitor to a sacred cause.

— Did they do nothing to check the truth of your origins or your statement?

— Nothing. Whereas the investigators of Watergate went to immense pains to check every detail of their serious allega- tions, these anonymous creatures did absolutely nothing to substantiate their claims or to enable me to raise my voice in my own defence at such outrageous calumnies.

— What is your opinion? Answer now.

— I believe that the Jews have made a contribution to the human condition out of all proportion to their numbers: I believe them to be an immense people. Not only have they supplied the world with two leaders of the stature of Jesus Christ and Karl Marx, but they have even indulged in the luxury of following neither one nor the other. If I were Jewish, I would be as proud of my origins as Jews so naturally are. The fact that I am not Jewish means merely that I have an equal right to be proud of whatever it is I am, and this has taken me over half a century to find out and even now I am far from sure.

Obviously no one can afford to believe in the intrinsic superiority of one people over another. It should be our pride that we are members of the human race rather than of one of its innumerable sub-divisions, but I fear we are not ready for this and doubtless never will be. The dog will always be a better friend to man than are other men. But even here the thoroughbred is often more highly prized than the mongrel, which is as tactful an outlet for racialism as any.

— Didn't they ask you, in Israel, why you thought the Russians had an aversion to them?

— Yes, I replied that the Russians probably found it impossible to forgive the Jews for the Revolution. Lenin and Stalin were two of the very few of the original Bolsheviks who were not Jewish intellectuals; Kamenev, Zinoviev, Trotsky, Joffé, Litvinov, Radek, the list is endless, and I doubt if the Russians would ever have been capable of putting such ideas to the test unassisted by the permanent Jewish fermentation in the world of thought.

— What is your connection with Israel then?

— My connection is with Palestine. This is not a provocation, merely an historical accuracy. All my family had left by 1917,

349

with the exception of my Aunt Tabitha who had married a Palestinian Arab, Anis Jamal, and who lived in Jerusalem until forced to flee at the time of the creation of the state of Israel. Israeli friends protest that no one was forced to flee, and that all residents could have stayed on and become useful subjects of the new republic. Opinions have varied about such cases in other countries, including Russia and Algeria, and probably they will occur again in the cases of Rhodesia and of South Africa, but it is difficult to see how a country described as a 'National Home,' a theocracy as well as a democracy, can extend full equality to all its citizens, without regard to race or religion. In any case, with the bullets of hot-headed patriots flying around, it was not the moment to stop and argue. My aunt, now a widow, lives in a small flat in Beirut. Her house in Jerusalem is, I was told there, under the jurisdiction of the Custodian of Enemy Property.

In the words of an enlightened Jewish friend, a noted sociologist and humanitarian with whom I have been honoured to serve on many committees, 'The Palestinians are the last victims of Hitler.'

I will not reveal his name lest he too should become the target of hasty judgement and misrepresentation.

The allegation that some of one's best friends are Jewish is always a cue for a gale of ironic laughter. When an allegation that some of one's best friends are Palestinians produces the same sarcastic guffaw in lieu of the stunned silence of today, we will know that the problems of that tortured corner of our globe are well on their way towards a pacific solution.

20

— Your mother died in 1975?

— In February. My father had been cremated. My mother had always had a horror of such a process. At her death, she left a letter asking to be cremated too. Their ashes are buried in a village churchyard, at Eastleach, in Gloucestershire.

— Your father murmured in French in his coma, your mother in Russian.

— The mysteries of the subconscious. She had never really liked things Russian. Having been born there of foreign heritage, she always hankered for Western ways and means of expression, and yet now, in her last hours she spoke almost exclusively in Russian. She reacted to Mozart on a small transistor radio, changing her expression according to the subtle sounds of the music, and sipped water whereas Klop had sipped champagne. There was no hint of sadness. It was part of a functional process almost as old as life itself, and there was a kind of serene complicity between us.

— She was happy?

— As happy as the awful discomfort of dying would allow.

— She had spent so much time and energy worrying about you with her usual discretion. As usual, you only heard about it through other people.

— Yes, a diary I discovered was searing evidence of the moral injury she had suffered as the results of events which I have briefly hinted at, and her anxiety for my well-being was both selfless and discreet. Luckily I had time to reassure her as to my spiritual serenity before she died.

— In what way?

— That is a leading question, and I am not sure I am ready to talk about it yet.

— You had better hurry. There are not many pages left.

— I will, I promise you. In any case, the book would not be complete without its coda, its bridge to the unrecorded future. Meanwhile, is there anything of more general interest you wish to ask?

— Your mother followed your life from a self-imposed distance?

— She was the opposite of the demanding pervasive parent. Even if she treated me as being somewhat younger than I ever was at a given time, she wanted a man as a son, not a boy. She followed my career with alternating approval, annoyance and relief. She could be damning in her criticism, but her expression of it was always polite and gentle. She knew too well the difficulties of creation to be negligent in her condemnation or unstinting in her praise. If she had a fault, it was to laugh too loudly at my jokes, and to laugh even louder at her own.

— She knew about your extracurricular activities, at the University and with UNICEF.

— Oh yes. She regarded them with a sort of quizzical interest, as though they might deflect me from more suitable work. When she understood that they were good for my soul, however, she wanted to know all about them.

— When did you first begin to devote a little time to UNICEF?

— I received a telegram back in the late sixties asking me to act as Master of Ceremonies at a UNICEF concert at the Théâtre Nationale de l'Odéon, in Paris. At that time I knew nothing about UNICEF, the United Nations International Children's Emergency Fund, and was merely tempted by the extraordinary quality of the participants, the like of which no commercial enterprise could possibly muster for a single performance. I accepted, and during the course of rehearsals met Leon Davičo, a Yugoslav journalist from Politika in Belgrade, seconded to UNICEF.

It was this forthright and winning man who first contaminated me with the happy virus of enthusiasm for this vital cause. Even if I hate galas, which seem to me an incongruous way of raising money, I did help to put together quite a few of these on behalf of UNICEF, in Italy, France, Switzerland, Germany, and Japan. On television, they brought a handsome revenue, even if it was only a drop in the ocean of children's needs.

This is no place for propaganda, even if the burden on private charity is rendered practically unbearable by the scandalous negligence of governments, but I was impressed from the beginning by the selfless work of those often maligned international civil servants who have a passionate interest in their work and who are content with the knowledge of its constructive nature as a moral recompense. It is so easy, as I have suggested elsewhere, to attack the United Nations as a fertile field for undemocratic or anti-democratic ideas, but such critics conveniently overlook the fact that it was constituted as a democratic forum, and that the ideas of the majority cannot be roughly pushed aside just because they happen to be temporarily out of favour in some influential places. Orthodox Communism is under quite as much pressure as is Western Capitalist Democracy. Everywhere new countries, conceived in rebellion, growing up in poverty, are seeking their own way and their own interdependence in a confusing and often brutal world. The prerequisite for maintaining a clear head in such a world is, of course, a certain modicum of faith in the possibilities of human nature, and it is not the excesses of this African warlord or of that dapper South American general who can sway such a necessary faith any more than those brave outriders of the Western bandwagon, the arms manufacturers whose pockets are loaded with grease for eager palms, or their Eastern counterparts, who still move divisions to silence the voices of legitimate complaint. The General Assembly and the Security Council are but the shop window, in which views are presented and opposed, and in which we can be elated or depressed according to our convictions. Within the shop, however, all is different. Nationalities and creed are largely forgotten. Confronted with problems, Christian and Communist, Moslem and Socialist, Buddhist and Conservative do their best within the means at their disposal to solve them. This is a source of confidence even to the most jaded cynic.

— Are you sure this is not an idealized picture of what goes on?

— Perhaps it is, but it is an idealized picture shared by many of those involved. The *esprit de corps* of these international organizations never ceases to surprise me, as well as the quality of those in charge.

— Who, for instance?

— Harry Labouisse is an astonishing American, a career diplomat who keeps his own counsel, and has an experience in human affairs on which he continually and mildly draws in order to be tough and outspoken where it matters. As sometimes happens with men of quality, age only reinforces his qualities and makes his vision more acute. He is the head of UNICEF at the time of writing. His wife is the daughter of Pierre and Marie Curie.

The director-general of UNESCO, whose task is, if anything, more controversial, is M. M'Bow, a Senegalese educationalist with a splendid and necessary disdain for difficulties and a cool head, utterly negligent of pressures and confident in the irrefutable logic of his neutral but never reticent position.

— Why do you say his task is more controversial?

— It is easier to raise a tear over babies, even among the hard of

354

heart, than it is to beg for sympathy for students or to appeal to philistines for help in saving ancient monuments.

— I see your point.

— UNICEF was the only agency of the United Nations to be allowed into Nigeria after the Biafra war, because of its apolitical nature. UNICEF was also the only agency to have an office in Hanoi throughout the hostilities and, in the last days of the war, all shades of opinion in Vietnam made urgent appeals to UNICEF to help save the lives and guarantee the well-being of children caught in the tidal wave of battle. This could not be said at the time because of some ruling of Congress that the United States could not support an organization having contact with an enemy. Is it to be believed?

— But tell me, honestly, did this sudden interest in the fate of children not coincide with some dramatic events in your private life?

— No. I am grateful that my interest grew out of a dissatisfaction with a life of merely amusing, of merely diverting. It managed to predate the climax of my personal problems, except of course that these had been growing inexorably over almost twenty years. It may well be, however, that my consciousness of children's needs was fired by my own observation of a growing family. As I intimated, it was only by watching my own family that I grew aware of many basic relationships between human beings. I became conscious of the need to give affection without an immediate ability to do so. I was too far gone, as it were, in the ways of solitude, to break through the barrier without difficulty. And yet it had to be done. I recognized the necessity.

— You have always, if I understand you, mistrusted those who, because of some personal tragedy, suddenly join the crusade against that which has afflicted them or their families?

— Mistrust is hardly a word I would use in this context. Tragedy is never foreseeable, only sometimes premonitory. When the

355

wind is in our sails, we never think as deeply as when the wind is contrary, and who is to blame us? Nevertheless, I believe that the time for thanksgiving is when all is going well. Better early than late, even if better late than never. Most of us are negligent creatures. Things, even those under our noses, have to be brought to our attention.

— I'm glad you said that.

— Why?

— Because sooner or later you'll have to talk about yourself again, instead of pontificating about generalities.

— That is the square Russian in me.

— I recognize it, but you can't put off talking about the end of your second marriage forever, like a visit to the dentist. The book is nearly over. Be brave.

— You know perfectly well that my second marriage is the theme for another book, a book which will never be written. At least, not by me. If one of the children should take it into his or her head to be as crisp and objective as their grandmother was about their grandfather, or as I hope their father is with their grandparents, that is a legitimate prerogative of a later generation. They may have at their disposal by then psychological insights which were denied me, and which could explain the irrational with greater assurance than I can, and which could analyse with serenity and precision the sources of my despair.

— Is that all you are going to say?

— Yes.

— Are there not revenges you feel bound to take?

— No.

— Well, that's that.

— Not quite. Whereas I have scruples about imposing my version of the truth on the living and even on the dead, I have absolutely no compunction whatsoever in talking about the divorce itself, because it drifts away from the private and dramatic into the field of light entertainment. It also shows how far we have moved along the path to a just society in the intervening twenty years.

You will remember that my first divorce took place in London, under the aegis of the Lion and Unicorn rampant, in an aura of sanctity. The décor, in other words, was the same as the one in which men had been sentenced to death for stealing wallets a hundred and fifty years ago. Poor Isolde, so eager to marry again, had to sit in a sordid hotel room and play cards with a rented gentleman, waiting patiently for a detective to break in at an appointed hour and discover them. After such a compromising incident, there was a six weeks' delay before the issuing of the Decree Nisi and the subsequent hearing, so that the King's Proctor might assure himself that there had been no hint of collusion. Ah, divine hypocrisy! With what style was dirty linen laundered in public in those days!

Nowadays, all that is laundered is money. My second divorce proved it. At the risk of pontificating again, I must slip in a few generalities in order to place the particular in its context.

In this terrifying world of computers and headlong progress, groups of people demonstrate on behalf of the enfeebled environment, and against the installation of nuclear power plants. These are, ironically, the true conservatives of today, although they prefer the term conservationists. In Switzerland, an admirable country in many ways, the banks take the place of the nuclear power plants for the time being. The fall-out from the overheated economy seeps out across the green valleys in an imperceptible haze, destiny's secret weapon against the lofty Calvinist conscience. It was never, as Bernard Shaw suggests, a country organized deliberately along the lines of a large hotel, nor is its only title to glory the cuckoo-clock, as alleged by Orson Welles.

It produced the toughest mercenaries in Europe in the not too distant past. Why else would the Pope employ Swiss guards if not to feel adequately protected against the Italian princes? There came a point, however, in which the Swiss found themselves

357

consistently killing each other, albeit for high salaries, and decided to put their instincts for banking to a more constructive use. Their neutrality attracted vast sums of money, unexplained and anonymous, legitimate and corrupt, cold and hot, clean and filthy. They claim, perhaps a little nervously, that money has no personality once it is in a vault. One suspects that the bankers are the victims of this contagion, and that while the slumbering money retains its personality the bankers lose theirs in their determination to appear mere custodians of the unknown.

I might have foreseen the disasters which would follow once a group of Swiss lawyers suggested what is known as a 'Divorce à l'Aimable' which is merely a private contract between the parties, so that the judge is relieved of the necessity of attributing blame. He has little else to do but register the existence of such an agreement and, after a while, proclaim the divorce to be effective.

It would seem, on the face of it, to be an ideal manner in which to allow two civilized people in discord to go their ways.

I was to pay half a million dollars for my freedom. I was given three years in which to accomplish this task, which I thought impossible at the then rate of 4.20 Swiss francs to the dollar.

My lawyers pointed out to me that I owned a tract of land which would fetch very nearly the requisite sum if sold to some derelict Chief of State in exile or to some Arabian knight with an eye to the unsteady future. I would consequently scarcely feel the divorce at all. It had been generally conceded that I was to have custody of the children, so that I was not merely suing for my freedom but for a continuation of a joyous and vital responsibility. I signed the agreement.

The next event was a new Swiss law temporarily preventing the sale of any land to foreigners. In view of the size of the country and the extent of foreign investment I could understand this law very well, but I hardly expected to become one of its first victims. I suddenly found myself burdened with my broad acres, which for a while threatened to be designated as a 'Green Zone' or parkland, and my huge debt undiminished.

To render the situation even more unpleasant, the dollar slipped from 4.20 to 2.40. My debt began to approach a million dollars. And you ask me why I did a commercial for Californian wines?

My dear fellow, we live in a world which fondly believes every man but a fool to have his price. Heads of state are on trial for having accepted bribes in order to push an aircraft at the expense of others. One noble public figure even expressed irritation at the end of a lunch that he was to receive one million dollars instead of the expected six millions as a recompense. He deemed his lunch a failure. Such a lunch would have solved all my problems, but then, thank goodness, I am not in a position to push weapons for my well-being.

I stuck to wine, and a line of cameras which none other than Lord Olivier had already advertised in America but had declined to show himself in the light of a salesman to his peers, so I followed meekly in the steps of the master, stifling my approval of his scruples.

Next, the Union of Swiss Cheese tempted me with a substantial financial reward to be seen guzzling Emmenthaler while dressed as a mountaineer before the background of the Matterhorn, this choice thirty seconds to be seen on all the screens of Western Europe. I declined the offer, feeling that my divorce had already caused me as much humiliation as I could bear although I do often fancy a piece of Emmenthaler in private.

When I did the wine commercial, I was not to know that my employer was in contention with a trades union of field workers, who were busy boycotting grapes and lettuce, a luxury which only a very rich country can afford, even though European viticulturists have been busy recently dumping grapes on freeways in order to attract attention to their grievances.

The result of all this opulent absurdity was that while I opened in a new play in Newhaven, Connecticut, there were pickets outside the theatre blaming me for underwriting blackleg lettuce and pirate grapes by doing a commercial, and all this because of the unadulterated amiability of a Swiss court! Now do you understand why I call this divorce light entertainment?

— That was the same play that was already suffering cancellations from Zionists who had swallowed unquestioningly what you were supposed to have said about Israel?

— Indeed. But I can't really blame the lawyers for that. Suffice it to say that I did many things I had no taste for during this period, simply in order to make ends meet, and to contrive to give my children an adolescence as serene as their childhood had been tormented.

— Was it not a high price to pay?

— No price is too high to pay. And, after all, if the children turn out well, is that not an achievement their mother can be proud of too? I would have signed that document if it had cost me twice as much, which indeed it has, since I have over the last six years paid the interest on the money as though it had been delivered, and a little extra to conform with the rising cost of living.

— Your nonchalance in the light of this crushing burden is really scarcely credible. I know the facts, but are you seriously asking our readers to believe that you consider all this water off a duck's back?

— Sufficient water will sink the duck. Of course, I know, as you know, that my particular sensitivity takes refuge in laughter as others may take refuge in tears, or in murder, or in suicide. All I do have is an inherent toughness, a refusal to submit, a quality really no more admirable than obstinacy. The more my marriages gravitated towards the rocks, the more insanely idealistic did I become about the limitless possibilities of love, simply expressed and deeply felt. As things went wrong, I saw more and more clearly how things should be. And, of course, there is no element in this existence which gives you a clearer sense of responsibility than children, and mine

360

have already given me immense joy of a kind I can never consciously repay.

Tamara is now married. I well remember my first encounter with her husband, a talented young director called Christopher Parr. Had I written the scene in a play, I would, no doubt, have fallen into the trap of tradition, and made the young man nervous, and the prospective father-in-law a model of compassionate understanding. The truth was, needless to say, quite other. Young Master Parr was the model of composure, studying me through huge horn-rimmed glasses, whereas I was a bundle of nerves, determined not to let my beloved daughter down at this vital moment in her life.

I cracked a few jokes, to which the young man failed to respond. I became earnest and he smiled wanly. Every now and then I would glance at Tammy, and fancied I could read anxiety behind her usual limpid composure. I ended the encounter utterly demoralized, quite convinced that I had failed an examination, and had lost the job, not only for myself, but for those who depended on me.

A few weeks later, by means of the faithful press-cutting agency, I received a cutting from some paper in the north of England. It was an interview with Chris, in which he was asked if he were not a little nervous of becoming the son-in-law of someone vaguely notorious. He was quoted as answering, 'No, why should I? He's a rattling good sort.' This unexpected piece of archaic flattery made me shudder with incredulous relief, as though I had been elected after all, after a recount.

The other children have not, at this time, put my maturity to a similar test, but they no doubt will. I have eyed various aspirants as they drifted into my eyeline, some of them with pleasure, some with a relative indifference, some with frank alarm. Pavla has a classic, yet very individual beauty, although I say so myself. She is a bit of a *femme fatale*, gifted, surprisingly with an acute sense of the comic, of the absurd.

I have now worked with both Tammy and Pavla, and know

them to be very differently, yet very distinctly, endowed with the instinct for our particular profession, which gives me great satisfaction. Andrea is the soubrette of the family, with a robust sense of fun and a piercing kind of intelligence which consistently baffles me by its almost surgical capacity for analysis. Igor is more of a dreamer, at home in his own abstractions, and a fellow of considerable natural charm, which he has learned to use with the discretion it deserves.

These are, of course, cursory assessments, and therefore highly unreliable. Igor, who is studying sculpture, biology and mathematics, may easily take me by surprise tomorrow by sharpening the focus of his vision, while Andrea could quite as easily discover the expressive possibilities of the nuance, the hint. It is while youth is making its choice that it is at its most fascinating and rewarding, even if parents tend to sigh with relief when that choice is made.

Naturally I dwell mainly on their qualities, not only because I am a very conventional proud father, but also because their virtues seem to be more than a little miraculous, whereas I recognize their shortcomings as old enemies of mine which I have tried to hide in myself by education, manners, and *savoir-faire*, all to no avail.

— That's all very well, but are you asking me to believe that you recovered your buoyancy after a particularly long and difficult chapter of your life simply by a ferocious and almost possessive attachment to your children's destinies?

— No, of course not. That would be most unhealthy, and even unpleasant. I am not, and never have been, possessive. I consider possessiveness to be the most dangerous and underrated of all human vices.

— Curiously enough, I agree with you. Once the human animal must face the terrifying fact of his solitude, it is unnatural to deny him the few advantages attached to being alone.

— Such as freedom of choice?

— All the freedoms possible.

— There aren't that many. Look at America. That must be the

greatest and noblest experiment in collective freedom known to man, and yet when such advantages are officially and traditionally encouraged, individuals seem to acquire cold feet, and to spend their time imitating a collective image of averageness, and their one ambition seems to be to disappear inconspicuously into a human mass as typical and as free as themselves.

— It's like growing up. There's nothing like restrictions to give freedom its true flavour, the unattainable perfection, always inches out of reach. The truth is that if we ever could be entirely free, we wouldn't know what to do. In a panic, we would reconstruct our prisons. We need the prison of our minds, we need its limits. We could no longer measure distance without a scale; the only real freedom is in order, in an acceptance of boundaries.

— Did you not write that once we are destined to live out our lives in the prison of our mind, our one duty is to furnish it well?

— Yes, I believe I did.

— Have you furnished yours well, in your opinion?

— Ah, you have led me to my final confession with all the diabolical refinement a torero employs to lure the bull towards the picador!

— I hope with happier results.

— Well, I have made many mistakes, and been guilty of many errors of judgement, sometimes while trying too hard to do what I thought was right. And then, when the weight of my cumulative stupidities seemed for a moment to be overwhelming, I rediscovered, quite by chance, the tennis partner who had deflected my attention from my game so many years ago. A great deal had happened to us both, and neither of us had been extravagantly happy in the intervening years. My friendship with Hélène du Lau d'Allemans matured gradually to a point where we became inseparable. Our mutual attraction has grown with time, and

363

this extended springtime has surprised us both. I would no longer know what to do without her.

— Can you say that she is the love of your life?

— Comparisons are odious. When I was young I was capable of being lovesick. I could burst into tears for reasons which seem frivolous in retrospect, but which were not so at the time. It is for that reason that I try never to patronize the youthful. I may have gained some experience with the passage of time, but at a price. I have half-forgotten what it was like to be young. I do remember, however, that being young is difficult enough to deserve the greatest respect. I loved my wives with the means at my disposal, only I am older now, and I love Hélène, my third wife, in a manner which seems to have matured like wine.

— An example, perhaps, of your vintage loving?

— For instance, if you wake up in the night, and as your eyes become used to the dark you begin to make out your favourite features creased with the kind of concentration babies devote to sleep, and you catch yourself smiling at the sight with an unaccustomed warmth, you can be pretty sure you are looking at the woman you love. It gives me an enormous pleasure to watch her when she does not know she is being watched, when she is being publicly engaging, or privately thoughtful, buried in a book, before the make-up mirror, or just asleep. And she has the kind of sense of humour which invests trouble with proportion and happiness with grace.

— She sounds like the perfect woman.

— A perfect woman could have no personality. Hélène is a harmony of delightful imperfections, which is the most flattering thing I could say about anyone. I only hope my imperfections seem half as delightful to her. It is so easy to give if there is someone willing to take; it is so easy to take if there is someone with so much to give. She has made me into something approaching the man I once hoped to be, privately and secretly. She came to my

364

rescue at a turning-point during that exhausting, terrifying and magnificent journey of self-discovery we call life. And for that, I am endlessly grateful.

— That seems to bring us to the end.

— The end? We have gone through so much together, Dear Me, and yet it suddenly occurs to me we don't know each other at all.

— We discover each other in retrospect, with the passage of time, and it is then that we also discover that we don't know each other very well, which is perhaps a good thing.

— Perhaps. For the moment, all that interests me, with a greedy, inquisitive fever, is the future.

— I'll be there when you need me. In a few minutes' time, if necessary.

— Thank you, remorseless spirit.

— Don't mention it, all too solid flesh.

– INDEX –